A Brooklyn Rose

Suzanna Lonchar

Printed in the United States of America

I would like to dedicate this book in memory of Rose Finazzo. Throughout the years my mother, Rose, talked of writing a book, a book that eventually she and I were striving to write but never accomplished because of her deteriorating health and early death. She wanted to tell the world about lost family traditions and her extraordinary childhood in Brooklyn, New York. So in all respects I feel she is the true author of this book. I would also like to dedicate this book to my Aunt Phyllis (Finazzo) Lonchar, and Uncles Frank Finazzo and Salvatore Finazzo, who made this book possible with their true stories, adventures and endless patience in providing all the various details and family history to complete Rose's story. Also a special thanks to my cousin Geriloma (Finazzo) Ireson who helped with the editing of this book.

A Brooklyn Rose

Table of Contents

A Brooklyn Rose

Top row left to right: Mary, Rocco, Marian, Louie, Frankie

Bottom row left to right: Sally, Luiji, Fannie, Giroloma, Rosie

A Brooklyn Rose

Top row left to right: Marian, Mary, Frankie

Bottom row, left to right: Giroloma, Fannie, Rosie, Sally

A Brooklyn Rose

Preface

Rose Finazzo started reading the book *Honor Thy Father,* and when she got to a certain page, she was astonished to discover that the characters were people she and her family had known in Brooklyn, New York. Even more astonishing was the fact she was reading about the very neighborhood, North Fifth and Roebling Street, where she grew up. As she continued reading, she was to discover that even the town where her parents had originated from in Sicily, Castellammare Del Golfo, was the same town featured in the book.

Ever since I can remember, my mother Rose had told me stories of her childhood in Brooklyn, and I always felt she had a story to tell the world. It is story about a little girl who faced enormous, even unbearable hardships. A story about a little boy who grew up to become famous by receiving the title of "Light-weight Champion of the Pacific Fleet of the Navy" and then go on to live an adventurous and fascinating life, his world travels and appearances in movies, making him a celebrity. Also about another little boy who grew up to win the "Golden Gloves" championship in boxing. This is a story about an immigrant family who traveled to America in search of fabled "American Dream," only to find hardships, tragedies, death and murder. It is a story of a bonding together of a family who, only through each other's strength, was able to face their hardships and accomplish their survival.

It is a true story of the era of prohibition, speakeasies, and a little later the Great Depression, Gangsters, Racketeers and the Mafia. It was an era in history with few surviving voices now who say they lived through it. So now it is the year 2011; a new millennium has begun, and I feel more compelled than ever to tell Rose's story as she told it to me, word for word, so we all can remember a place, a time in history, of lost family traditions. This story is based on the Finazzo family, though some incidents have been improvised, some names and places have been changed to protect their privacy and are purely coincidental to anyone sharing the same name.

No material in this true story is meant to offend anyone from any particular ethnic group or race, but rather is used to show the prejudices of the era, which the immigrants who wished to live among their own particular ethnic group had developed through the segregation of the neighborhoods.

Rose was not a famous person, but she was an extraordinary person with an extraordinary life. Her magnetic personality, generosity and zest for life will be remembered by all those who knew her and loved her.

The Rose saith in the dewy morn, I am most fair; yet all my loveliness is born upon a thorn.

_**Christina Rossetti,**
"Consider the Lillies of the Field."

A Brooklyn Rose

Chapter 1—A MOTHER'S TEARS

Giroloma stood at the window in her second story tenement house watching her beloved husband, Francisco, walk across the street. He seemed to be in a hurry to meet some men he was aquainted with from the Italian club where he attended meetings. Her five children crowded around her as they waved to him, anticipating the ice cream that was promised them on his return. *'He's still a handsome man, even after all these years of marriage,'* she thought. She remembered his bright blue eyes against his dark tan and how especially handsome he looked last night in his gray pinstriped suit. She watched his easy stride as he crossed the street. Sensing that they were still watching him, he turned and gave them a wave. She waved back and started to shut the window.

Suddenly three men appeared, walking toward him. Without a warning she heard the horrifying sound of loud staccato shots coming from the machine guns they carried. To her horror, she saw her beloved husband as he was repeatedly shot. She saw his body jerk and jolt as each bullet hit its target. Then, like a rag doll, he slowly crumpled to the ground, and the three men fled as quickly as they appeared. She stood transfixed, unable to breathe. Then there was a quiet serenity, no movement, no sound. It seemed an eternity...it was too still...time had stopped...the world had stopped. Giroloma opened her mouth to scream, but nothing came out. Then she knew that somehow she had died that day, too. Suddenly, as if in protest to the dead, her stomach turned and the little life inside her gave a large thrusting kick.

Luigi stood staring at the marble headstone studying the clear engraving *which read: 'Beloved Husband, Father and Brother Francesco Finazzo, 1883-1911.'*

"Why did this have to happen to you? We should have stayed in Castellammare! Maybe back in our home in Sicily you would've still been alive. Now you are in the ground, leaving behind a widow with five children and another on the way." Luigi's tears tasted like salt, and the fresh smell of earth and flowers seemed to fill the air. The aroma brought fresh memories of his homeland. Luigi thought of all the killings over there with the Mafioso, vendettas, and even the neighboring farms that were feuding with the people in the city. He then remembered the letter his older brother Francesco had a relative write for him:

Come to America and stay with me and my family in Brooklyn, New York. Here you can have a new life where there is more opportunity for the ambitious, not poverty, fear and hatred. I am afraid either you'll go to prison like most of our young men or be killed by the vendettas wars between families or the Mafioso. I still grieve for our brother Emanuel who was killed by the police.

Luigi sobbed: "Dear brother, you said those words to me and now I am standing at your grave because you were killed by Mafioso." Just then he felt the grasp of a small hand.

"Uncle Luigi, let's go home now," said the small voice of a child.

As Luigi walked he thought, *'Destiny sure played a cruel joke. Yeah, come to America watch me be killed and give up your life to take care of my family.'* Luigi's unique style of walking was more like a march. He led all the children on the long walk of four blocks to visit Giroloma's brother John Coppola.

As he entered the grocery store that John owned, he heard the friendly greeting: "How isa everything?

Giroloma's getting mucha better now," Luigi replied. "I comea to ask you what we should do about Giroloma and the *beechadeedas* (babies)," Luigi continued. Feeling suddenly dizzy, he took out his handkerchief and wiped his brow.

"I don't know…it's a problem," answered John in ancient Sicilian mixed with broken English.

"I been thinking, she needa someone to takea care of her and the *beechadeedas*. Maybe we should makea matrimony."

"No, I don't think that's a good idea. You are a younga man, and Giroloma's too old for you," John replied, shaking his head. "The marriage woulda be a bigga mistake.

But there is nobody else. She was my brother's wife and it's my responsibility now," replied Luigi in Sicilian.

No, that's the way it was in the old country, but here you have no obligation, justa be a good brother-in-law.

Well, something has to be done pretty soon or they will be deported, and people are starting to gossip about me living ina the same house," Luigi added.

"I write a letter to the old country to see what everybody thinks," said John. "That letter writing isa what started the whole trouble with my brother," Luigi sadly replied.

"No, what started the trouble wasa Francesco getting in the middle of the war between the Valanti family and the Bizzocchi family. Justa because your sister Rosa married into the Bizzocchi family, he should've stayed out of it. Hisa concern should've been for his own family, hisa wife and children. He crossa the lake to come to a different country to get away from all the trouble and he still couldn't escape!" John angrily added, using his hands in a gesture to apply the full impact of his meaning.

"He wasa sorry for the people ofa his family over there, ana he thought he could help by having letters wrote informing them about the Valanti relatives over here," Luigi explained. "Hisa bigga mistake wasa having the letter read by an informer to the Valanti family."

"It seems like sucha pity that a man who couldn't read or write could get killed over a letter," John sobbed. "I cry for him every day; I know he wasa a good-hearted man who only tried to help. I have word they will be paid back for what they did vengeance is on the way," sobbed John, wiping his eyes.

Luigi couldn't control his anguish; tears were rolling down his cheeks. He wiped his eyes with his handkerchief and sobbed, "All these killings can't bring my brother back."

John handed Luigi a bag of vegetables and said, "Take this home for Giroloma, and don't worry, we worka something out."

Luigi took the groceries and called the children, who were playing outside, then said to John, "I'll stop by ana see you tomorrow."

Giroloma stood at the sink preparing supper. She was still weak from the illness that had overtaken her shortly after her husband died. Luigi had taken charge, cooking, cleaning and taking care of the children while she lay in bed. She knew her illness was much more than the grief she felt over losing her husband. In a strange way she welcomed it. Those first few weeks after Francesco died were the hardest for her. She would lie in bed and cry, asking God, "Why did you take my beloved husband from me? Wasn't it enough when you took Mary, my firstborn baby girl? Even then, in my grief, I had Francesco to turn to for comfort."

As far back as she could remember, Francesco had been in her life. She had lived over a high hill that separated her family's homestead from Francesco's. As a child she could remember when the families visited each other. Francesco was her playmate and later he was her sweetheart. Her three brothers would chaperone them wherever they went. It was Sicilian tradition that a young unmarried girl was always chaperoned. She was even more overly protected because she was the prettiest daughter. She remembered the long walks they shared, up and down the high hill, to and from each family's homestead, and her three brothers only a few steps behind.

Then she remembered another walk a few years after her marriage to Francesco; this time they were walking alone to the small village to purchase some merchandise and groceries. Giroloma and Francesco were entering a desolate area that was covered with trees and brush on both sides of the road, when they spotted a small group of people walking toward them. As the group of people neared, Francesco recognized his sister Rosa and her inlaws among them. Before Francesco could gesture a greeting, shots rang out from the bushes. Francesco's quick reaction saved Giroloma's life, by grabbing her hand and running into the roadside bushes.

The horrible scene unfolded before them as they watched the small groups of people get massacred. The angry assassins had no mercy as they savagely shot at the unfortunate victims. They watched in shock as a small boy was shot, the impact throwing his small body several feet into the air and causing him to land with a sickening thud. Then a baby that a woman was carrying was shot, along with its mother, the impact sending them rolling across the dirt road. When the evil deed was done, the dead bodies were scattered along the roadside in ugly unnatural poses.

Francesco saw the face of one of the assassins as he neared the bodies to inspect their evil deed. The man looked in his direction, spotting Francesco, and was about to fire his rifle when he was interrupted by another man yelling for him to run. The man fired his rifle at Francesco, but, to his misfortune, he was out of ammunition. He then gave Francesco a dangerous look of warning before he ran into the woods, disappearing amid the high bushes and trees.

Giroloma remembered how her heart pounded with fear as she lay on the dirt ground, afraid to move. She could taste the bitter soil as she pushed her face into the earth, as if to hide from the horrible scene. Then she could feel Francesco's touch on her as he gently lifted her from the ground. She was sobbing as he tried to calm her down with his soothing words of comfort, repeating, "It's all right, it's all over now, and they are gone." When she started to regain her control she heard him say, "You stay here…I must check to see if anyone is alive."

"No, I must go with you to try to help," she said in a shaky voice.

The scene that met them was etched in her memory forever. A small boy was lying in the road, his body angled in an unnatural position next to what was left of a tiny baby, whose little body was blown apart, exposing a large gaping wound in his skull. Among the dead twisted bodies covered with blood they heard a whimper. It was Rosa and she was badly hurt, but alive. Francesco gently picked her up and carried her the long distance back to his family's homestead.

A few weeks after the disastrous assassination, Francesco stood patiently while his uncle screamed at him: "You have got to go away from here! You and your entire family are in great danger! You were recognized by the Valantis and they will come after you because you witnessed their crime. The only safe place for you is in America, and you must leave at once before something happens to you. I will make the arrangements for you to stay with Giroloma's brother John."

"But it's much too hard to leave now; our baby, Emmanuel, is only one month old and Giroloma is still recuperating from his birth. This trip might be hard for them," Francesco argued. "It was a heartbreaking thing to lose our first baby, Mary. I see the fear on Giroloma's face. I hear the ship is full of disease and many people have caught dipheria. I won't endanger the health of my family by the long journey."

"It is better to take your chances now than wait for sure death," the elderly uncle warned. "Your family will be safer on the boat then here. Both Giroloma and the baby are strong and healthy; they will survive. There is nothing here anymore except killings, so you must go and pave the way for our relatives. The war between the city people and the farmers is getting more dangerous every day."

Giroloma's mind skipped ahead, remembering the huge ship that was to take them to America. She could almost smell the fresh, cool aroma of the ocean as she remembered her excitement over the adventure of the long journey, a journey that was to take them to the strange country of America, where she and her husband would share the American Dream.

The year was Nineteen Hundred and Six when she boarded the ship with her handsome husband, and they were ready to face the future in a land where they could be safe, away from all the senseless killings that overtook the small village where they lived. She remembered her clumsy steps as she descended to the lower deck. When she reached her destination she was nauseated by the stench of human body odor, the result of too many people pressed into the overly crowded area. The people were mainly poor immigrants who were anticipating the journey that would take them into a new land. Their friendly faces were filled with hope and excitement over the adventure. It wasn't long before the large ship started sailing, sending them to their unknown future.

They passed the long days sitting on the bottom deck, enjoying the cool breeze from the ocean and socializing with the other passengers. A man had an accordion, on which he played Italian folk tunes, changing the atmosphere into a pleasant gala occasion. Some people sang along with the happy tunes while some danced and others laughed or simply enjoyed watching the scene. Children ran and played while the more serious sat and played cards. Giroloma enjoyed the diversion, which took her mind off the sickness she felt from the rocking ship.

One day, as she was sitting on the deck, she noticed how black the sky appeared, so she clutched her small baby closer to her as she sensed danger.

"It looks as though we are headed for a bad storm," she said to the lady sitting next to her. Her words were lost to the sudden gust of wind. She felt the ship sway dangerously as she almost lost her balance. Suddenly Francesco was at her side, taking the baby from her arms.

"We better go below where it is much safer!" he yelled against the crashing sound of thunder. Once back in the lower deck, the heat from the closed-in airless room was unbearable from the packed in bodies that suddenly seeked shelter. Giroloma lay on the small cot holding the baby. Francesco looked worriedly out of the port hole window, but all he could see was the splashing of waves as they crashed against the window. Suddenly the ship lurched, tilting almost on its side. The cot that Giroloma was lying on slid half-way across the room, and she couldn't remember when she had been more terrified in her life.

"Oh, God, we are all going to drown, and we are never going to see America!" she cried.

Francesco held her and quieted her fears. After a while the storm calmed down. "See, I told you that nothing is going to stand in our way of going to America," he said as he comforted her.

After the storm, the days seemed to pass slowly and were uneventful, with the majority of their time spent sitting on the deck, listening to the happy sounds of the accordion player and making plans for their future.

Finally the day arrived when they entered New York. Giroloma and Francesco couldn't hide their excitement at the magnificent sight of the Statue of

Liberty as they entered the harbor. They hugged and laughed along with all the other passengers as they all shouted, "We are in America!"

Giroloma's present illness lasted for weeks, her grief making her illness linger on longer. She had lost her reason for living during her illness, and would lie in bed and reminisce about her life with Francesco, remembering every detail, refusing to face the reality that he was gone.

She lay remembering how their lives had changed after they arrived in America. At first they stayed with some relatives for a few months, then Francesco got a job at a factory. When they saved enough money, they rented the tenement house. She remembered how happy she was to move into their first home in America. Soon she gave birth to another boy they named Vincenzo. Very soon after he was born she had another boy, Luigi, and then came a daughter, Marianna, and then Mary. Now she sadly thought, '*I am having another child, but my Francesco will never see this poor baby.*'

Then one night she had a strange dream in which Francesco was looking at her with tears in his eyes.

"Please don't grieve for me anymore; you must be with the living and take care of our children. We will be be together again, soon."

Giroloma woke up with a start. She lifted her head to look around the room. She felt light-headed, then she heard noises coming from the kitchen. It was chatter of little children's voices talking to Luigi. Then she heard the soft laughter from the game Luigi was playing with them. Giroloma was overcome with guilt. How could she want to die when there was so much life around her? Her stomach gave a lurch as the baby moved inside her. She was reminded of another life soon to be born. They were all part of Francesco, a reminder of their love. Suddenly she wanted to live again for her children's sake. She heard Luigi's hardy laughter while playing with the children. He was Francesco's younger brother and he was so kind. She realized what a burden this must be on him. Besides working he had to come home and take care of her and the children.

Giroloma gradually regained her strength. She knew Luigi was relieved that she made an effort to resume life again.

Giroloma had drained the pasta and was stirring the sauce when she heard Luigi arrive home with the children. The sudden noise startled her out of her day dream. Luigi looked pale and shaken as he sat down at the table. On the way home he had been worrying about how to approach the subject. He lapsed into the ancient Italian dialect of their language as he spoke.

"Giroloma, come sit down, we have to talk. I'm worried about you and the children. You know Francesco didn't have any papers. That's a problem because you and the children could be deported. We have to do something? You need somebody to take care of you. Now, today I heard people are starting to gossip about me living here." Giroloma stared vacantly, unable to think of a solution. Her grief, still fresh in her mind, gave her no time to consider her circumstances. She knew she had to go on living for the children's sake, but she had no inclination of how to survive. Luigi stared at her grief-stricken face, where her once bright gray-hazel eyes now seemed so lifeless and desolate.

"Giroloma, you know how much I respect you, and I know how much you loved my brother. I loved my brother, too. You are alone in a strange country. You can't even speak the English language. You must understand you need someone to care of you and the children. I think we should get married. It is the only way."

"Oh no, I can't do that to you. Luigi, you are only nineteen years old, and I am ten years older then you. You are young and good-looking, and you have your whole life ahead of you. You should start fresh and marry a young woman who knew no other man and has no children. I only want the best for you. We will think of something. There has got to be another way," Giroloma said with firmness. Luigi started to say something more, but instead broke into a fit of coughing. Giroloma put her hand over his forehead and said, "You're burning up with fever. Come, you better get in bed." Luigi didn't argue; he suddenly felt very dizzy. The room was spinning, and his legs felt weak as she helped him get into bed.

Luigi didn't know how many days he had been sick; he simply lost track of time as he slipped in and out of consciousness. He wasn't sure what was real, as everything was in a dreamlike state. His mother was there wiping his brow, and they were in Sicily. She was outside sitting in a chair by their stone summer home. He could see the sun's reflection on her platinum white hair, bringing out the few golden strands that remained. She was crying into her handkerchief, "Luigi, I'll never see you again."

The scene slowly changed, and everything was hazy then, turning colors, purple colors. He was in the grape vines tasting the sweet thick juice of the grapes. His brothers were laughing at him. The purple juice was covering his hands.

Slowly, everything was whirling around him again and bright colors were spinning until they focused on the decorations of his donkey. He was a small boy again, preparing to ride the animal to the village, but the stubborn donkey just sat, refusing to get up. Then his mother took the jug and tucked it under his behind while he pulled the rope tied around his neck. At last the donkey was on his feet. He climbed on him and was riding him, making him go faster and faster, when suddenly the donkey came to a fast stop, causing him to fall. He was falling down, rolling down a hill. When he finally landed, he was at the ocean. He could feel the soft sand beneath his feet. He stared at the blue rippling water, so inviting. With a large splash he dove into the ocean, feeling the cool wetness soak his body. He was under water, swimming and totally at peace with the clear cool world. An unknown force caused the water to suddenly swirl, resembling a whirlpool. The force pulled him up until he surfaced on the ocean. The cool air smelled crisp and clean, mingling with a slight scent of fresh fish. Soft musical laughter filled the air, and he turned around to see a girl standing there. The soft rays of sunlight behind her caught the glimmering golden long wavy hair. It was Carmellia, his childhood friend. He put his arms around her tiny waist and lifted her up.

"I'm going to bring you to America to be my wife," he said.

"No, you can't. It is Sicilian tradition you must marry your brother's widow."

Everything was spinning again and the scene changed. Now he was at his brother's grave. His brother was sitting on top of his tombstone, pointing a finger at him.

"You must give up your life. You must marry my wife; you must raise my children; you must show me respect."

Luigi was screaming, "I'm young! I want my life!"

Luigi felt himself spinning again. Soft pastel lights were billowing, then focusing in on a bride. It was Giroloma. She was young again and dressed in the same egg-shell white satin dress she wore at her wedding. She was tall and willowy with her waist-length honey brown hair blowing in the soft whirling wind. She looked like an empress with her head held high, and he heard a stern voice say: "Do you, Luigi Finazzo, take this woman for your wife?" He smelled a sweet honey aroma of the flowers she held. But when he looked into her beautiful gray-hazel eyes they had tears.

"Luigi, Luigi, wake up, wake up!" Everything was still spinning. Bright lights were hurting his eyes. He looked up to see those same gray-hazel eyes, now filled with concern.

"Luigi, are you all right? We were so worried about you," Giroloma said, as she held a bowl of honey mixture to feed him. "You have been delirious for days. The doctor has been here everyday. We almost lost you. The doctor said you have meningitis. I couldn't stand it if something happened to you, too," she cried, wiping her eyes.

Months then went by since Luigi's illness, as his recuperation was very gradual. Giroloma was at his side for all his needs, nursing him back to health. She fed him, washed him and faithfully sat by his bed ready to attend his every need. Finally the day came when he could get out of bed, and his improvement was rapid after that. It wasn't long before he was completely recovered and back to work.

Luigi was a handsome man with coal black wavy hair so thick that the several dark layers of waves stood high at the crown of his head. His dark olive complexion enhanced his beautiful white teeth (a feature that had been bestowed on all the Finazzo men). Although his soft brown eyes were his most captivating feature, Luigi's shyness and soft-spoken voice attributed to his overall charm. Giroloma tried in vain to arrange meetings between him and nice women, but to no avail. He would say, "Now what woman would want to marry me, knowing that I have another family to support?"

One day while Luigi was at work Giroloma felt her first labor pain, and called out to her oldest daughter, "Marianna, go get the midwife—the baby's coming."

Upon arriving home from work, as Luigi walked up the steps, he was greeted by the children.

"Mama had the baby, it's a boy!" the little girl happily announced as she continued to skip up the steps. Luigi rushed into the tenement house and was met by the midwife.

"She had a hard time, and the baby is a very tiny boy. It is going to take a long time for her health to come back. You can go in the room, but don't stay to long," she cautioned.

When Luigi entered the room, Giroloma was lying in bed, holding a little bundle. Luigi walked over to the bed and stooped over to examine the new baby. It was a small baby with thick black hair. Giroloma looked very tired, but strangely content.

"I'm going to name this one Francesco after his father," she said.

It took several months for Giroloma to regain her health—this baby had taken a lot from her body—so Luigi took over the household chores again.

Giroloma was so weak she couldn't nurse the baby, as she had no milk in her ample breasts to feed this little one. Luigi solved this problem by improvising. He used an eye-dropper to feed the hungry infant. After awhile the baby gained weight and Giroloma also was back to normal.

One day Luigi arrived home to find Giroloma sitting up in the overstuffed chair holding the infant. He noticed that Giroloma looked happier than he had seen her in along time. Her eyes almost looked bright again, bringing a radiant beauty back that he forgot she had.

"You know, you and I have been through a lot together these past few months. We've had our share of sickness and we couldn't have made it without each other's help," Luigi said thoughtfully.

Giroloma nodded and replied, "Luigi, I don't know what I would have done without you."

Luigi's soft brown eyes then took on a serious expression as he said, "You know we have to marry."

The only sound that could be heard in the room was the ticking of the clock as he waited for her reply. Finally, after an uncomfortable pause, she nodded in acceptance. She was resigned to the fact there was no other way. Luigi was so kind to her after her husband was killed; they had become very close. He was her best friend and they respected each other. She knew he was tens years younger than her and the only reason she had not wanted this marriage was because she felt he deserved better. She knew this was not a marriage of love but a union of two people who respected each other enough to keep a family together.

The wedding day soon approached, and Luigi was dressed in his finest gray suit. Giroloma was dressed in a black silk dress. Today she was a bride, but she still considered herself a widow. It was not the happy occasion she had experienced with her first husband. That memorable day was the happiest day of her life. She remembered the egg-shell white satin elegant wedding gown with rows of pearls and embroidery of tiny white roses around the high neckline. There was such a gala atmosphere of the reception party afterwards, with little Luigi being only ten years old. She laughed bittersweet tears, remembering how he ended up in bed with them on their wedding night. He had drank too much wine and wandered in their bedroom. The very next day he was teased, good-naturedly. In Luigi's childhood innocence he hadn't realized he did anything wrong; he always had slept with his big brother,

Giroloma looked at her groom, his face grim and serious. She wished more than anything in this world that he could be standing next to someone who could make his heart sing. She was overcome with guilt, so in that moment she vowed to be a good wife to him and make his life as pleasant as possible.

Luigi's eyes stared at Giroloma when he heard the priest pronounce them man and wife. The tragic expression was still on Giroloma's face. He wondered if he could ever erase the sorrow in her eyes, then he sadly thought of Carmellia, the girl he was betrothed to back in Sicily.

"I must say good-bye forever," he whispered to himself. He stared at the bride in black and vowed to put the light back into her gray-hazel eyes and the beautiful smile back on her grief-stricken face.

The wind howled outside, escaping into the window sills of the tenement house, making a cold draft where Luigi sat in the overstuffed lumpy chair. The stormy windy day was November twenty-second, Nineteen Twenty-Two. Luigi could hear the moans coming from the bedroom door where his wife

Giroloma was giving birth. He had sent all the children over to stay with relatives until the new baby would arrive. The midwife was an old Sicilian lady who did all the deliveries in the neighborhood. She was a very agile for her advancing years, which seemed unusual because her pronounced limp. The only other sounds Luigi could hear were the scuffling of the cat as she played by his feet with a ball of yarn. Luigi looked down at her and thought, '*You have got to earn your keep around here kitty; I've got enough problems without worrying about you. I hope you caught a mouse today.*'

Luigi took out his pocket watch to check the time. Only two hours had gone by. Time sure was going very slow. He started getting nervous about Giroloma. '*I hope she will be alright,*' he worried. Then he scolded himself for such thoughts. '*I have been though this two times before and everything went alright.*' The thought brought happy memories of little Frankie's birth and how special little Frankie was to him. He remembered how he had to feed him with an eyedropper and how strong he grew every day through his care. Luigi felt the bond stronger with him because, although the other children called him "Papa," Frankie knew no other papa. Soon after Frankie's birth another son was born, Luigi's first biological son. He was named Salvatore, after Luigi's brother who still lived in Sicily. Luigi analyzed his feelings toward Frankie and Salvatore. He could not favor one over the other. He loved them both, as if they both were his natural born sons. Now Giroloma was having another *beechadeeda* (baby), but this birth was not a welcomed birth, and Luigi didn't know how they could afford to feed another hungry mouth. His job at the factory barely could pay the rent.

Luigi heard the noises that were still coming from the birthing room. The soft moans and the thumping noises, brought on by the midwife moving around. He looked down at the cat; she had curled up and fallen into a contented sleep. He looked out the window, and it had begun to snow. Homesickness overwhelmed him as he thought of missing the autumn in Castellammare, Sicily. It would be one of the most beautiful seasons of the year. In the autumn everything would be green. The heavy rains made everything more like spring where, vegetation would flourish. Wherever one looked one would see the color green and the wild green grass would sprout up everywhere. Green grew in the olive gardens, in the vineyards, and just about everywhere he looked. He remembered when autumn came, how hard he and his brothers had to work. This was the time of the year that the grounds would be soft from the heavy rain, time for the plowing of the vegetables that would be saved for the coming winter. Most importantly was the olive harvest when everyone would join in the back-breaking work. Olive oil was very precious to them and besides using it in their cooking, pasta and salads, it was also used for many home remedies. Luigi's favorite use of the oil was spreading it over fresh baked bread. Luigi could also remember spreading it on his skin, mixed with lemon to prevent chapping.

Luigi could remember *I Morti*, meaning *The Dead*, which took place in November. This day would mean All Saints Day. This day was dedicated to the dead and was considered one of the biggest holidays of the year. The excitement was felt by everyone as the eve of this holiday approached. The children were especially excited because they knew they would receive gifts from their dead relatives in the morning. This was accomplished by their beliefs that the dead relatives would come out of their graves on the eve of this holiday and walk around the small village. It was a festive time of the year. Luigi could remember going to the graves and saying prayers for all his dead relatives because the gifts would be received by the children who remembered the dead. It was custom that all the girls of the family would clean the graves and place fresh flowers upon them. All the pastry shops would try to produce the best pastries because competition was tough on this day. Their specialty was the sugar statues and marzipan, a cornucopia of fruit and vegetables molded out of almond paste. Strange this day was not frightening to the children. It was a time to rejoice with all the relatives. He could still smell the fragrance from the flowers and hear the laughter as the family gathered together.

Luigi was the youngest child of five children. He had lived in the village in the winter and moved to the families little white summer home in the summer, remembering always the scent of honey perfume of the blossoms on the almond trees there.

Everything had such a distinct aroma: the lemons, orange blossoms, and the fresh crisp air of the ocean. He could remember looking in one direction and viewing the mountains, then looking in the opposite direction and seeing the ocean. The memory of the centuries-old stone castle which stood along the bottom of a mountain, by the sea, would forever be in his mind. It was said the town took its name after it: *Castellammare del Golfo.* Many times he and his friends would spend hours playing near it, imagining that they were protecting their town from invading ships that came to conquer their island of paradise.

Luigi's summer home was a small stone cottage with a grapevine nestling on top of the entrance door. He thought he had had a wonderful childhood, filled with the love of his parents and family. He could remember all the laughter on the lazy hot summer days, which were spent swimming and fishing. It was a beautiful land, a paradise.

Suddenly Luigi heard the wailing of the infant, which immediately startled him out of his daydream. After a few minutes the midwife hobbled into the front room. She tiredly wiped her brow and said, "Mother and baby girl are fine…you can see them now."

When Luigi entered the room his gaze fell upon Giroloma who was lying in the bed holding a small bundle. She had a sad expression on her tired face.

"It's a girl, but she is so tiny I don't think she'll live. The midwife said that she weighs only four pounds." Giroloma started sobbing, more out of guilt than concern for this child. She didn't want this baby. She was tired…she had had too many babies, too fast. Her body was worn out. '*This is just another child too worry about, another child too suffer the hardship, the agony and pain of poverty,*' she thought.

Suddenly the tiny little infant gave a loud piercing cry and it was a shock to Giroloma, because she thought, '*How could this piercing noise come from such a wee tiny bundle?*' She unfolded the blankets to see the large round piercing dark eyes staring at her as if in a trance. The baby's eyes were the largest she had ever seen, but it wasn't just their size that held her hypnotized, it was their bold expression of fierce determination. Suddenly a tear that had remained on Giroloma's face somehow splashed on the infant's small cheek, and the baby puckered and squinted her little face as if she were offended, then let out another loud wail. In doing so she threw up her little fists almost comically like a pint-sized boxer, it was as if to say, "Here I am…I'm going to live and you're going to love me." Giroloma then felt a great rush of overwhelming love. She instinctively knew this child would survive. This child was different…this child had something special.

Luigi gazed admiringly at his wife, then at this little creature, his daughter.

"We will name her Roseria after my sister. She reminds me of her spunk. Well, I had better get busy and gather some bricks to heat to keep her warm," he said with a twinkle in his eye.

Giroloma was smiling, wiping away her former meaningless tears.

Chapter 2—ROEBLING STREET

"It's your turn to trow out the garbage tonight, Rosie," Sally remarked. This was one chore that all the kids took turns doing. Rosie didn't mind helping with the chores; she even enjoyed doing some of them. Whenever Mama needed something from the store, she was most anxious to go, but this was the one chore she absolutely dreaded.

"Are yuh sure it's my turn?" she asked. This was her one last attempt at procrastinating the dreaded chore until she heard Luigi's angry voice say, "You been putting thisa off for almost an hour now ana it's getting dark. I no like you outa side so late. Hurry uppa now."

"Alright, I'm going," she bravely said. Rosie picked up the bag of garbage and slowly walked out of the house. It wasn't that she minded the simple task of walking to the alley. It was the rats that hung around the garbage and the darkness of the night that frightened her. The last time she threw out the garbage, a big black rat jumped out as she lifted the lid off the garbage can. She trembled as she remembered the ugly squinted eyes that glowed in the dark, and how she ran screaming with fright back into the house. Rosie invented a little game along the way each time she had this unpleasant chore. She would sing loudly, hoping the noise would scare the rats away or whatever else that was out there. Today she chose to sing the song, "Figgah Bella." It was a cute Italian song Mama sang to her when she was a baby. She opened her mouth wide and started singing loudly: "FIGGAH BELLA DELLA MA!"

She could hear the echo of her voice as she sang in the dark alley, so she continued walking and singing loudly to take her mind off her fears. The silence was eerie, and she could hear her heart beating loudly, as if it were a huge drum keeping a rhythmical beat to her little song. As she neared the garbage can she slowed down her pace, dreading the frightful task of opening the lid. As she sang, she heard a sound of a cat meow somewhere in the night. The familiar odor of garbage was getting stronger as she slowly approached the old tin garbage can.

Suddenly an arm reached out to grab her. Rosie thought her heart would jump out of her chest as she stood in fright. A big black sedan was parked on the side of the alley and, to her fright, there stood a gangster with a gun. She suddenly realized that she had walked right in the middle of a shoot-out, and she was being held hostage as the gangster frantically tried to save his life.

"Yuh better let the kid go or she'll get it too," she heard the man with a gun say. Before she could think of a way to get loose she was being thrown, and her small body flew up in the air, then landed only a few feet away with a sickening thud. She heard the loud blasting of the gun as she watched the scene in front of her, mesmerized with fear. The gangster who had grabbed her was being shot repeatedly with a machine gun. His body finally fell onto the ground, knocking over the garbage cans with a loud crash.

The murderer jumped into the big black sedan and charged off, squealing tires as it sped down the street.

Rosie lay in the alley only a few feet away from the victim, and she was afraid to move. At last she summoned up enough courage to sneak a look at the victim. His body was lying in an awkward position, the lower half partially covered by garbage. Blood was splattered almost everywhere, dripping onto the cobblestones where she lay. His face was turned toward the sky, looking up with his eyes staring vacantly. The shock of the horrible scene delayed her reactions. Suddenly she found her voice and started screaming! Finally she saw people running toward her. At first glance the spectators thought that she was shot. Her leg had been badly scraped on the cobblestones and was bleeding down her leg. She was still screaming when Luigi appeared. He slowly picked her up and carried her inside their tenement house.

Once inside, Giroloma was hysterical, hearing her screams. "*Oh, madre mia*! What has happened to my *beechadeeda*?"

After some time it was understood that the only real damage Rosie received was a badly bruised and scraped leg and hysteria due to the trauma of the incident. Thereafter, she never had to worry about that unpleasant chore again. After this incident Giroloma made sure all her children stayed close to home. Rosie, Fannie and all the younger children could play outside close by the stoop where she could see them. Sometimes Giroloma would go outside and sit on the stoop, keeping a careful watch on them, as she exchanged the daily gossip with her neighbors.

Roebling Street was a major amphitheater with so many interesting things to observe, and it was fascinating to just sit and watch. Every few minutes a store on wheels would pass by. It was always better to buy from them because their prices would be cheaper than the stores, which had more overhead to account for. The horse-driven carts would sell everything from vegetables to pots and pans. Then would come the variety of pushcarts, some with vegetables and fruits. Some pushcarts would sell ice cream or Italian ices. Next the silver-colored "rolling ovens" would journey down the street, causing mouths to water with their tantalizing delicious aroma. They would offer submarine sandwiches, corn on the cob, fresh nuts, seafood, frankfurters and sweet potatoes. Some of the venders went on foot. One could sometimes encounter the vacuum cleaner salesman or the Fuller Brush Man. Sometimes the rag man would appear, selling old clothes, or the neighborhood handyman, who usually carried all his supplies in an old baby buggy. Occasionally a photographer would appear driving a cart led by a Shetland pony. This would be exciting for the children because they always got a chance to pet the pony.

Everyone knew the Irish policeman who could be seen walking his beat. He would inform the parents of any mischievous deed their child had been involved in. It was not uncommon to see the fire department arrive because of a mischievous child who couldn't resist the temptation of pulling the handle of a fire alarm box. The angry firemen tired of this game of false alarms. The questioning would not be "Where's the fire?" but instead, "Who pulled the alarm this time?"

Sometimes when Giroloma had some money she would take her small amount of change and sit on the stoop to wait for the right vendor to do her shopping.

The children of the block entertained themselves with group games such as jump rope, hopscotch, jacks and marbles. Sometimes they would become more creative, inventing competitive games such as who could whack a ball the furthest or who could roller skate he fastest around the block, or simple games of walking on the sidewalks trying to avoid stepping on all the cracks. Occasionally the entire neighborhood would become involved by blocking off the street and playing kickball, baseball or stickball. Basketball could be played by removing the bottom of a fruit basket and hanging it from a telephone pole. The telephone poles could also be useful for climbing, or playing Johnny on the pony. On hot summer days a mischievous child would open the Johnny pump so the water would gush into the streets and everyone would enjoy the fun until the water department arrived.

Giroloma was sitting on the stoop when she heard a commotion. Sally, her ten-year-old son, came running across the street, stark naked. He kept on running, his face red, almost crashing into the lady with an old baby carriage, and not stopping to be reprimanded by his mother. She was shocked to see such a sight. Apparently some game Sally had been playing with his gang involved him losing his clothes to the top of the telephone pole. Giroloma started yelling at the kids to get his clothes down from the pole.

Mama Russo had finished her morning chores and spotted Giroloma on the stoop. Giroloma looked up to see her lady friend join her.

"It's a nice day," Mama Russo commented as she sat down next to her, ready for their daily gossip and friendly conversation. Her daughter, Connie, joined the kids playing in the street.

Pretty soon a redheaded young woman was seen walking down the street. She was wearing a tight dress that was cut low in the front, exposing her ample breasts. Her tight dress outlined every inch of her curvy body. She walked past a young man slowly, teasing him with her provocative wiggle and giving him an inviting smile. Mama Russo could hardly contain her disgust as she said in Italian, "Look at that *puttona* (whore)! I have a large cross to bear; my son must have lost his brains marrying that woman. She sleeps with every man in the street. I'm so ashamed I could die." Just then the redhead spotted Mama Russo sitting on the stoop. "You comea over here!" Mama Russo yelled out. When the redhead walked over, Mama Russo could contain her temper no longer. "What's a matter, you walka around ina that tight dress and disgrace my son. You no good *emporko vistazo* (dirty pig), you nothing but a *puttona*!" Mama Russo yelled, shaking her fist at her. "You go ina the house ana wash your face ana change your clothes or I gonna give it to you good!"

The redhead looked scared and came rushing up the stoop running past Mama Russo into the house.

Pretty soon Luigi was walking home with his special unique march. He had just finished visiting his friend, Joe the Barber. He passed the bakery where the elder racketeers were sitting outside playing cards. They all knew Luigi and waved as he passed by. Today he spotted the neighborhood 'Godfather,' Mike Stellenti, while he was visiting Joe at the barber shop. Pretty soon Luigi reached the stoop where Giroloma was sitting and sat down by her.

After a while they saw the small figure of a man coming towards them. The man had a slight sway to his walk and was wearing a white Navy uniform. As he neared, Rosie recognized him. It was her big brother Jimmy. She horridly ran to greet him yelling, "Jimmy's home, Mama!" Pretty soon the rest of the children followed suit, knowing he always emptied out his pockets, giving them change. When Jimmy saw the kids, he reached in his pockets and threw small change at them, laughing as they jumped and scrambled to catch it. Then as if right on cue came the ice-cream man peddling his cart. Rosie and Fannie bought a double-dip cone with strawberry ice cream. Rosie sat back down on the stoop next to a kid nicknamed Jackie Donuts. She made faces at him as he watched her lick her ice cream. He was a chubby kid whose father owned the flower shop. His family was better off financially than most in the neighborhood, so he would spend all his money on donuts, then would sit next to Rosie, tantalizing her with the delicious sweets but never offering her any.

"Yuh owe me a big lick of yuh ice cream cuz of yesterday," he angrily said, his mouth watering as he watched her take a large lick, twisting her tongue all around the top of her cone.

"You had it coming to yuh, never offering me any of your donuts," Rosie laughed. "You were sure funny-looking when yuh was mad; you looked like a pig the way yuh squealed when I ate yah donut."

"That wasn't fair, yuh grabbed my bag when I chased that kid who made fun of me," Jackie replied.

"You are a pig. Yuh always have powered sugah and jelly on your face. All yuh need is a curly tail, ha-ha," Rosie laughed.

"Aw come on, just one lick and I'll give yuh a donut tomarra when I get my allowance."

Rosie thought about it for a minute, and said, "Okay, just one lick, but if yuh don't give me a donut tomarra, I'll get my brudder Sally to beat yuh up."

Giroloma was talking in Italian to Luigi and Jimmy when a strange sight took form. Someone was walking up the street toward her, an ugly lady walking awkwardly, trying to hurry. She was huge, with hairy legs and a *babushka* (scarf) on her head. She had a huge nose protruding from the face that

43

was practically covered with the *babushka*. She had a rough face like a man. On second glance, Giroloma recognized it was a man. It was Mimmie Sabbela, the gangster. Mimmie usually rode in his big black sedan with the safety glass about two inches thick. He was never seen without his personal bodyguard. It was said that he was a killer, as a story had circulated that he killed a man in cold blood.

"Hurry Giroloma, please hide me; I'm going to be killed!" he pleaded. Giroloma hurried inside the house with him. Mimmie was practically like another son to Giroloma, as she had known him and his family back in Sicily when he was an infant.

Once safely inside she asked, "Now what's the matter that you have to look like a woman?"

"I'm in a lot of trouble, but I can't explain now; I've gotta hide somewhere," replied Mimmie. "If anyone asks, you haven't seen me."

Giroloma was shocked, as she had never seen him so scared. It must have been something terrible. On second thought, she didn't want to know; she was in deep enough already by hiding him. She said, "Go under the bed, and I'll sit outside to watch."

"Oh, thank yuh. When I get outta this mess I'm going to reward yuh. I'll never forget how you yuh helped me."

"I don't want any reward, just your life. You are like a son to me. Now go under the bed."

Giroloma walked outside to regain her place on the porch stoop. Luigi and Jimmy looked at her inquisitively but she just remarked, "You didn't see anything."

Soon a few well-dressed men were rapidly walking toward the stoop and looking straight at her. One of them recognized her as being Mimmie's friend.

"Did you see Mimmie?" he asked.

"No, I haven't seen anything. I haven't seen him in months," she replied in Sicilian.

"If you do see him, tell him a friend was looking for him. It's important," he said.

"If I see him, I will give him your message," she replied.

The gangster tipped his hat and they walked on by.

"What'sa de matter with you? We could all be killed with him ina the house!" Luigi scolded.

"I can't let them kill him. I would do the same for my own children," Giroloma announced.

When everyone finally returned inside the house, Mimmie was still under the bed, so Giroloma went into the bedroom and said, "You can come out now. They were already outside asking about you and they walked down the street."

Mimmie crawled out from under the bed. He looked relieved they were gone.

Jimmy, who came into the bedroom to watch, said, "You are the ugliest broad I ever sawr, especially yuh legs!"

Mimmie laughed back and remarked, "Well, I better get outta here while the coast is still clear."

Will you be alright?" asked Giroloma.

"Yah, they won't catch up with me now...I'll stay dressed like this until I get to Manhattan," replied Mimmie. He then kissed her cheek, saying, "*Grazie* (thank you)."

"May God be with you, and come back to visit when you are out of trouble," Giroloma replied as she stirred the pot of chicken soup she had been cooking on the stove.

Luigi, looking over her shoulder, sniffed the delicious aroma of the soup and the freshly baked bread, then said, "I better call all the kids in." Luigi stuck his head out the window and put two fingers into his mouth, giving a loud whistle. This was the signal for everyone to come inside. He smiled and waited a few minutes then heard a loud echoing whistle; that was Rosie answering him back. Soon the house was filled with noise from all the children as they came running in.

After dinner Sally said, "I gotta work pushing wagons for the Jews tonight, Papa."

"You be back ina one hour. We gotta go to see Doctor Friedman. He isa giving us a free medical exam for his political campaign," Luigi warned.

Sally met his friends and walked to the Jewish section of town, where the marketing district was located. The carts and wagons were lined up and down the street. The wagons remaining on the streets at night had presented a problem because of the vegetables and fruits that would roll off the wagons. They would accumulate after a period of time and rot by the curbs of the streets. The city had an agency called the D.P.W., which would enforce a curfew for all wagons to be off the streets at a designated time. Then the D.P.W. would wash the curbs, sending all the rotted vegetables and lettuce leaves down the drain. Sally's job was to pull the wagons into the garage for the nightly storage. He would get paid two cents for each wagon. When he arrived with his friends, the merchant yelled, "Hey you kids, get busy and make sure you pull the wagons to the back of the garage first!"

Sally grabbed the wagon that was prepared by the merchant for storage. It was covered with canvas and had wooden lattice fencing around its exterior. Sally knew that these wagons had contained merchandise, usually toys or clothing. His gang of friends then got busy storing the wagons, starting from the back of the garage. The merchant would pull them up to the door and return down the street. After lining up the back row, the boys devised a system where a couple of the boys could do the actual pulling-in of the wagons while a couple of the boys would check inside the wagons for the merchandise. They would swiftly fill their pants pockets and the inside of their coats with toys, clothes, watches or whatever they could manage to steal. Sally climbed into a wagon by the back wall, and when he pulled off a section of the canvas he was surprised to see some jackknives, which he quickly put into his pockets. Then he saw some pens and cheap custom jewelry, which he also stuffed into his pockets. Then he saw some expensive looking wristwatches, which he knew he could get money for in the hock shops, so he quickly grabbed all of them and stuffed them into his pockets. Lastly some clothes were stuffed under his coat when he was finished.

When they were through, he snuck out of the garage, making sure the coast was clear. He walked down the street away from the section of the wagons, to wait for the rest of the boys. He was happy. Today he did well. Soon he saw his friends running up the street to meet him, and he could tell something was wrong by the way they were running. He ducked around the corner just in time to see the merchant chasing his friends. The smallest boy didn't quite make it. He saw the merchant was about to grab him by the shirt collar. The man proceeded to shake him and some merchandise began falling out of his shirt. The merchant was about to sock him when Sally interceded. Sally jumped in front of the kid and started dancing around the man.

"Yuh little thieving bastards, I'll teach yuh a lesson for stealing!" yelled the man.

"Aw go straight ta hell, yuh old fat son-of-a-bitch!" yelled Sally as he appraised his opponent. The man was short, fat and out of breath. Suddenly Sally swung at him, landing a blow right in the eye. The man lost his balance and crashed against a wagon filled with vegetables. The vegetables started rolling off the wagon.

"Let's get the hell outta here!" yelled Sally. The boys ran down the street to meet the rest of the gang, who were waiting for them.

"Boy dat was close," said the little boy, out of breath.

"Did any of yuh get anything?" asked Sally.

"Yuh, a couple of us made out pretty good," answered one of boys. "We was coming out, ready ta be paid by da Jew, and he was paying us when a ball fell outta Spike's shirt," commented Merc, the tallest boy in the gang.

"Hey, look, dere spoinkling da street, so let's go fishing," said Sally. They knew when the streets were cleaned, along with the garbage and debris, coins would sometimes be washed into the drains.

Merc took out a small pail that he stole from a wagon. "Foist, let's empty our coats and pockets then we'll wrap all the stuff we got into our coats. Then later we'll divide all our stuff."

Each boy emptied their clothes and wrapped everything tightly in their coat. Finally, when they accomplished this chore, they started their game they called *Fishing*. One boy removed the grate by the curb drain and Sally stuck the pail into the slimy drain scooping out all the slime until he could find a coin. Sally kept trying to scoop out money, until he finally found a dime.

"Dere must be more money down there," Sally said curiously as he stuck his head down closer to the drain to look. "Yah, I see some quarter's way down. I can't reach dem with my arm. Somebody is gonna hafta hold my legs and lift me down, so's I can reach dem," Sally added. Sally was the skinniest of the boys, and he could fit into the small opening of the drain, so he always had the job. The boys lifted him and grabbed his legs.

"Don't drop me like yuh did the last time; I almost fell in!" he ordered. Sally stretched and grabbed the coins. "Okay, lift me outta here," he said. Sally was lifted out and he fell on the curb laughing. "I got tree quarters!" he shouted.

"Let's go get a soda and split the money!" yelled Merc.

When the boys finally got back to their neighborhood they ran down the cellar of their tenement house, where they divided their stolen merchandise. From Sally's stuff, they each had a jackknife. They divided their money, then they decided to bury all the merchandise for a later date, to sell on the streets.

"Let's wrap an old coat around it before we bury it," said Merc. When they emerged upstairs Sally could hear the whistle from Luigi, his signal to go inside.

"I gotta go home; see yah tomarra," he said.

When Sally was inside the house he was met by Luigi's angry stare.

"Why you taka so long? What'sa that smell? You been ina the sewer again. Just looka at your shirt! Dirty sewer slime alla over it!" Luigi raged.

Giroloma walked over to him to inspect. "Oh *madre mia*, you're going to get it now!" she yelled.

She grabbed the broom in the corner of the kitchen and started swinging it at him.

"Now go washa up—you smell lika pig!" yelled Luigi.

Later, Luigi gathered together the whole family for the walk to the doctor's, but Rosie didn't want to go, as she hated getting shots. "Mama, gee, I don't wanna go, do I havta?" she asked.

"You are the sickest one, so don't give me no trouble," Giroloma countered. Before long they arrived at the doctor's office, and all the kids got examined first. The nurse at the desk took down their names before, one by one, they entered his examining room. Each visit was repetitious. First he took out his stethoscope and listened to their heartbeat, then he checked their eyes and ears with the little light. Then he put a stick on top of their tongue and made them say "ahhh" while he looked down their throat. Giroloma's visit was last, so Luigi went in with her to communicate with the doctor. After her though examination he looked at her gravely and translated the conversation through Luigi.

"Giroloma, you are a very sick woman; your cancer is advancing rapidly, and you should be in a hospital."

No hospitals, that's where you go to die. Besides, my children still need me at home; they are all very young," she argued.

"Well, at least let me give you something for the pain," Doctor Friedman said, handing her a bottle of pills. "Only take these at night before bed time, just one pill each time, as they are morphine and very strong. If you get any worse, you must promise to let me know," he instructed.

At the end of their visit the nurse gave them a bottle of Exlir Citrate for coughs. This bottle of pink medicine was his customary donation to every patient who visited him.

The night air was fresh and mingled slightly with the city odors caused by the factories and gasoline. As they walked they greeted all their friends and neighbors who they passed on the street. The barbershop, with its red and white striped pole outside, came into view, and Joe the Barber was just locking up. He waved, recognizing Luigi and the family. Next came the florist and the grocery store, where some people were sitting outside. Then they stopped at the bakery, where some older influential men were sitting. Luigi waved and they waved back.

"Nica night out tonight," Luigi remarked.

"It'sa good to taka your family for a little walk," said one older man. Luigi stopped to chat, lapsing into Sicilian. One man was waving his arms around, telling a funny story, and using his hand to give more details and impact. After the short interlude, they continued their walk. Roebling Street was still active even at night, as people sat in chairs by all the store fronts or on the stoops of their tenement houses, enjoying the night air and the company of their neighbors. Some families had decided to take walks, as the case of the Finazzo family, where each family member had their own distinct style of walking: Luigi's unique march, Giroloma's slow, painful steps, Fannie's toddling, Frankie and Sally's stroll, Mary running ahead of everyone to practice her cartwheels and Marianna's limp from her shoes that were too tight. Rosie lagged behind, playing a sidewalk game while she skipped.

"If yuh step on a crack, yuh brake your mother's back," she sang.

Chapter 3—THE SICK CHILD

Rosie's first memories were of her sister Mary. Giroloma had so many children that she assigned the older ones to take care of the younger ones. Mary's assignment was Rosie, who was six years old. Mary possessed the infinite patience of a saint when it came to Rosie's inquisitive mind.

"How come you can do all those tricks bending and twisting and I can't?" asked Rosie.

"Because I am double-jointed and you ain't," Mary replied as she was brushing Rosie's hair.

"Why ain't I?" Rosie asked.

"Because God made me special that way," Mary explained. Then Rosie asked for the millionth time, "Mary, why are you so pretty and I am so ugly?"

Mary's exasperated reply was always the same: "You are pretty, Rosie. I keep telling you all the time. Why don't yuh believe me?"

"Because the kids make fun of my nose," Rosie said sadly.

"Rosie, did anyone ever tell you that you have the most beautiful large round eyes in this world?"

"I do?" And with that new knowledge Rosie jumped out of the bed to look in the small cracked mirror on their dresser.

"Yah, I do have beautiful eyes," she said with wonder. She stared at her refection, realizing that for the first time in her life that she had something special.

"Now, come on, let's get to bed," Mary ordered.

Rosie jumped back into bed, happy with her new discovery. She snuggled up next to the person she adored, ready for their night time chat. Mary started it off by saying, "Wait til yuh hear what happened to me today. When I was outside doing my stunts, a strange man in the crowd introduced himself to me. He said his name was Tom Henderson and he was a talent scout. He said, with my unusual talent, I should be in Hollywood." Mary laughed at the utterly ridiculous thought. "Imagine me a movie star!" Then she did a somersault, rolling off the bed and landing on her feet, then proceeded to act out the part. "Would yuh like my autograph, deah? Oh, my big boy, come up and see me sometime." She was doing her Mae West impression. The hilarious expression on her face, with her lip spouted out, set Rosie into giggles. Mary did a quick flip and landed back in bed, joining her with the bad case of giggles that overtook them both.

A loud banging on the wall silenced them when Luigi yelled, "Sons of a bitchy, I gotta get some sleep!"

His sudden interruption sobered them out of their hilarious mood. Rosie, not wanting the fun to end, jumped on top of the bed and did her impression of Charlie Chaplin. Mary flew into hysterics. Rosie was so funny with her little stick arms and legs.

Another bang on the wall sobered them up. They knew Papa would be in with his belt. Mary's mood shifted, worrying about how she was going to ask Papa if she could be in the talent show. Mary was double-jointed; she was born with the ability to twist any part of her body without any effort or strain. It was as natural for her to curl up in a ball with her head protruding out from between her legs, as it was for most people to walk.

"I know Papa won't let me go, I just know it," she worried out loud.

"Maybe he will," Rosie soothed, suppressing a yawn.

"I'll ask him in the morning, and, please let him say yes," she prayed.

The next morning Mary awoke with a start; she smelled the fresh aroma of coffee brewing and then she heard Luigi's voice in the kitchen. She jumped out of bed, doing one of her somersaults, and in the process awakened Rosie. Once in the kitchen she asked, "Papa, can I talk to yuh?" Luigi looked up from his paper, puzzled. Mary crossed her fingers behind her back. She took a deep breath before she lost her nerve then plunged forward with her story.

"I have a chance to go to a talent contest next week and, if I win, I will get an audition for a screen test in Hollywood, with all expenses paid. Please, Papa, let me have this one chance," she rushed. She studied Luigi's face for any sign of encouragement, but to her dismay, there was a stony expression. His face turned a dark color as the vein along side of his forehead started pulsing.

"Hollywood, that's where the *puttonas* go! No, never will you getta my consent." He pounded his fist on the table, causing the coffee cup to turn over and go crashing to the floor. The loud sound of the crash had a sobering effect on him. He then grabbed his lunch pail and on the way out of the house added in a softer voice, "You stay around the house today and helpa your mother. She'sa not feeling well today."

Mary looked at Giroloma for support, but her face lacked emotion. She was in the family way again and looked ill.

After Luigi left, Mary begged Giroloma, "Please let me go, Mama...yuh know how much this means to me."

Giroloma looked at her child. Mary's violet-blue eyes against her almost white porcelain skin were captivating, contributing to her exquisite beauty. Giroloma knew this beautiful child was destined for greater things in life. Mary was holding her captive with her fierce expression of expectation. Finally Giroloma broke their spell and found her voice, "I'll talk to Papa maybe I can change his mind."

Mary in her gratefulness hugged Giroloma. "Oh, thank yuh for being so understanding." Now relieved that she had Mama on her side, she did a cartwheel, exposing her long muscular legs. As she tossed her head, her dark gold ringlets resembled little springs ejecting the same energy and the vitality that her tall slim body possessed.

Giroloma knew that Luigi was overly protective toward his daughters; he was very old-fashioned in his ways, but Mary had never caused her any trouble. She was as strong as a man and would gladly do all her housework and shopping without a complaint. Mary's cheerful light-hearted personality always melted Giroloma's heart, so she would help her daughter as much as she could. If show business was her dream, then let her dreams come true. Giroloma secretly admired movie stars, and she knew her daughter had talent.

The next morning after Luigi left for work, Giroloma smiled and said, "I have good news for you Mary...Papa gives his permission for you to enter the contest."

Mary gave a long grateful look at Giroloma's tired looking eyes until she could no longer hold in her excitement. "Yahoo, I'm gonna be a movie star!" Mary sang out. Then she did her imitation of Mae West, sticking out her lip and rolling her hips. Rosie got in the act with her little stick arms and legs.

Giroloma momentarily forgot her tiredness and pain and gave a hearty laugh. "Oh, stop! You girls are too funny!" '*They don't know how hard it was trying to convince Luigi,*' she thought. Giroloma was worn out from arguing with him all night and trying to persuade him, but he knew when Giroloma was not going to go his way. In the end he finally threw up his hands in pure exasperation. "I give uppa!"

Finally the big day arrived, and Mary awoke with eyes shining. "Rosie, wake up, today's the day," she happily announced. Rosie's eyes flew open. She was just as excited as Mary.

The arrangements had been made for the entire family to go. Tom Henderson had paid a visit with tickets for the entire family. He patiently explained all the advantages Mary could have if she had this one chance in life. The entire morning was in chaos, preparing Mary for her big debut. After searching in the closet for half an hour, along with Rosie's opinion, she managed to put something together that would be acceptable. She found a white lace scarf she could drape over her shoulders, a white shirt and her brother Sally's white boxing trunks. Rosie managed to find a blue ribbon to tie around her hair, then she stood back to admire her outfit. "It's perfect, yah beautiful," Rosie said. Mary accepted her opinion with a laugh. Soon the whole family was out the door, ready for the big adventure.

The contest was held at R.K.O. Theater, a long walk of five blocks. It was a hilarious sight, and even Luigi was there, carrying the baby as he walked along side of Giroloma. All the other children had to keep pace with Luigi's unique march. Everyone was dressed in their Sunday best, presenting a parade like appearance. Finally, they were there, and the neon theater sign read *Major Bowes Amateur Show*. The competition was tough. A lot of real talented people got their start here. Mary looked around nervously, until she spotted Tom, the talent scout. He was a slim man with a pleasant face. He was looking to make a name for himself and he felt Mary was his ticket. He couldn't take his eyes off this beautiful girl. Besides her talent and beauty, she had that extra something. He knew that she was an once-in-a-lifetime special with star quality.

Mary followed the other contestants behind the stage, and the good luck cheers from the family had boosted her self-confidence as she disappeared behind the faded pale green velvet curtains.

The family had tickets for the front row. Rosie could smell the delicious aroma of the fresh buttery popcorn that seemed to dominate the room. She was annoyed that she had to take a seat next to an ugly bawling baby. Soon the velvet curtains opened. The otherwise noisy crowd was suddenly quite except for the baby crying. The young mother was really getting aggravated trying to quiet him. Her embarrassment provoked her to slap him across the face, which in fact didn't solve the problem, but made him cry all the louder. Rosie stuck her tongue out at him and made a funny face, then he forgot what he was crying about. The lady was so grateful that she gave Rosie the bag of popcorn she held.

Rosie watched the talent show with admiration. Some contestants were tap dancing, some were singing, and a fat man did an Italian opera, which evoked the baby to start bawling again. Everyone was shushing at this lady to shut her brat up. Rosie thought the house would shake; she didn't know which was worse, so she held her ears through it all. Some people did comedy acts or did scenes from plays but when it came time for Mary's performance, she had the most originality of them all. Rosie remembered how she tumbled, twisted, rolled and gravitated her body into so many different positions. Mary had managed to sing and work in a dance routine along with her acrobatics. The combination of the three was unusual and extremely effective; the audience was spellbound and they cheered loudly when Mary took her bow. The finals were between Mary and a tap dancer. Mary then came in first place and was presented with a trophy; she was ecstatic! It was the best moment of her life. She loved the excitement of being on stage. She somehow knew she was destined for show business.

After the show, Tom Henderson approached Mary and congratulated her. He explained that he was going to try to talk to Luigi to get his consent for her to go to Hollywood. Even though he agreed to let Mary be in the competition, he was still against her actually going into the entertainment business.

When they got home they couldn't stop talking about the show, and Mary's violet-blue eyes were filled with excitement.

"Someday I'm going to be a movie star," she sang as she proudly held her trophy. "Mama, the first thing I'm going to buy yuh is a big house with servants, so yuh won't have to work so hard. Then I'm going to buy yuh a long mink coat." Giroloma laughed, enjoying the fantasy.

"What about me?" Rosie asked.

"I'll buy yuh beautiful dolls, toys and roller skates," answered Mary. The fantasy went on and on, everyone imagining being rich.

"Oh, thank yuh, Mama, for letting me go. It was the most exciting day of my life!" Mary said, kissing her, then she started looking around the kitchen to find a chore. "I'll do anything yuh want; what do yuh need me to do?"

Giroloma smiled; the happiness was catching. "Nothing…just be happy," she said.

That night a very excited Mary and Rosie lay in bed and talked, whispering half of the night and going over all the details of the talent how. Then the usual bang on the wall quieted them down.

"Sons of a bitchy, I gotta get some sleep!" Luigi yelled.

Soon after the contest, life was pretty ordinary. Mary busied herself helping Giroloma as much as she could; Giroloma was getting bigger with child and was tired a lot. The boy down the street was having a party at his apartment and invited Mary to go. Mary was quite about it, afraid to ask Papa. Finally, after supper when he was rolling his cigarette, contented because it had been an uneventful day—all the children had been good, no complaints, nobody to hit with the strap tonight—Mary knew this was the best time to ask.

"Papa,……..a friend of mine is having a party tonight…can I go?" she asked, her voice shaky with nervousness.

"Who isa this friend?" Luigi inquired.

It is a boy, Mario Danato," Mary answered.

Luigi lifted his brow. "A boy? No, you can't go to boys' parties."

Mary stood there ready to cry; she was young and she wanted to have fun.

Giroloma finally said, "Luigi, I know the people, and they are a very respectable family. They come from Castleammare, our hometown. Mary is sixteen and she should have friends."

Luigi was shocked at Giroloma's interference; it was the first time they ever had come close to an argument.

"She'sa too young, and no more, I don't want to heara no more. First you wanna her to be a movie star ana now you wanna her to be with boys."

Luigi was aggravated; he wasn't trying to be mean. Giroloma knew that single girls in Sicily never went anywhere without chaperones, so he was doing what was expected. Mary was a good girl, but she was too pretty and he had to watch her even closer.

"I hava to go to the meeting at the Italian club tonight." Feeling no need to say more, and upset at Giroloma, he put on his hat and left.

"Mama, please, please, let me go," cried Mary. "I've never been to a party. Yuh know the family. I want this as much as I want to be a movie star."

Giroloma sat and thought, '*Luigi is too hard on her and they are a good family*,' so finally she nodded her head. She was very angry at Luigi. She never interfered when he disciplined the boys, but the girls should be her department.

"Go ahead, but be home in a couple of hours, so Papa don't have to know."

Mary squealed with excitement. She started to sing and turn somersaults all around the house. Giroloma smiled at her energy and enthusiasm. Mary ran into the bedroom to find something to wear, ending up borrowing her older sister's party dress.

Rosie, her shadow, asked, "Can I come too?"

"Not this time; it's just for young people, no kids, but I'll sneak yuh a treat when I come home." As she was leaving she said, "I'll tell yuh all about the party tonight in bed." Rosie was content; she was going to get a treat and a story.

Later, when it was getting dark and Mary hadn't gotten home yet, Giroloma became worried. Besides worrying about Luigi getting home before Mary, a fierce thunderstorm had developed. Every time she heard a noise she jumped, then suddenly her worst fears were confirmed—the door opened and Luigi was home.

"What'sa the matter? Why are you uppa so late?"

Luigi sensed something was wrong. Before Giroloma had opened her mouth, the door opened again and there stood Mary, dripping wet in a party dress. Luigi was in shock! Giroloma had defied him and let Mary go. He grabbed the strap off its hook and started beating Mary. Mary was crying and screaming for him to stop. Giroloma was screaming, but his rage was too deep. After his anger was spent, he stopped, laid the strap down and bent his head, crying.

Mary flew off to the bedroom. Rosie had heard the commotion. In her concern she forgot about her treat that Mary had promised her. She was too busy consoling Mary.

"I had so much to tell yuh," sobbed Mary, "but now I can't talk," and broke down crying.

Rosie was gently patting her, saying, "It's alright Mary as long as yuh had some fun. Tomarra, when yuh feel better, yuh can tell me all about it."

Mary didn't feel better the next day. Giroloma discovered that she wasn't up and tumbling around the kitchen that morning. This was so unlike her she was instantly worried. Giroloma went into her room. "Mary, are you alright?" she asked.

Mary was lying on the bed. "Mama I don't feel well today, so I can't go to school," she answered in a low voice that was barely audible.

Giroloma sat down on her bed and patted her cheek, noticing that Mary looked flushed and felt feverish.

"You just rest in bed, and you'll feel better in a little while," Giroloma said with sympathy, then she left the room and went about her morning chores. She checked on Mary a few times, noticing that she was sleeping soundly.

After Giroloma worried a couple of hours, she heard a commotion and looked toward the door. It was Marian, her oldest daughter, and her boyfriend, a young physician named Paul Cruso she was dating. Marian immediately sensed something was wrong after seeing her mother's tired and worried face.

"What is it, Mama?" she asked.

"It's Mary…she's sick," Giroloma replied.

"Mary sick? Mary never gets sick!" Marian exclaimed, her eyes full of concern.

Paul said, "Let me have a look at her," and he walked into the bedroom, with Marian and Giroloma following.

Mary lay on the bed with her eyes closed. Her normally fair porcelain skin looked even whiter. Paul didn't have his instruments, so he put his head by her chest to listen to her breathing. Mary's breath was long and labored.

"I can't be positive, but it sounds like she's got double pneumonia," he said, alarmed. "She should be in a hospital right away. Let's help her out of bed and into my car outside," he added,

"You stay home and wait for Papa," Marian ordered. Giroloma was in shock; she barely could nod her head.

"I'll be there as soon as Papa comes home," she said while wringing her hands.

Later, when Giroloma and Luigi arrived at the hospital, Mary lay very still, barely moving, then she sensed their presence in the room. She made a feeble attempt to lift her head.

"Papa, I'm sorry," she barely whispered.

Luigi stood looking at her with tears in his eyes. "There is nothing for you to be sorry for; it'sa all my fault. You have always been a good girl. It'sa my fault. I justa worry too much, you such a pretty girl. I been wrong ana I'ma gonna maka it all uppa to you. Whena you get home we are gonna hava party for your sweet sixa teen," Luigi added tearfully. Mary's eyes opened for an instant and it looked as if a shadow of a smile crossed her face.

Giroloma bent over and kissed her cheek. "By tomorrow, you'll be home doing your somersaults in the kitchen and we will laugh and plan your party," she said, squeezing her hand. Mary's eyelids fluttered and Giroloma felt a weak twinge of life in Mary's hand.

Just then the nurse quietly entered the room, announcing, "It's time to let her rest now; you can visit her later."

Giroloma slowly left the room, saying firmly, "I'm not going to leave this hospital until Mary comes home."

They stayed in the waiting room all night, going in Mary's room when they were allowed. Members of the family came and went all night long.

The next morning Giroloma woke up with a start. She had fallen asleep in the hard leather chair. She stretched, feeling the pain of all her cramped joints. She looked over at Luigi. He was fast asleep in an uncomfortable position in a chair. Giroloma then remembered why she was here—it hit her full force: Mary was sick—so she jumped up and hurried down the hall. The nurses were nowhere about, and when she came to Mary's room no one was around. Giroloma said a silent prayer that Mary would be better today, then she entered her room and looked at Mary. Giroloma stood there for a very long time....... Mary was dead.

Giroloma couldn't scream, she couldn't cry, but another day stood still in her life. This pain was much worse. This was her child, the beautiful one. In her heart she knew she was her favorite. Giroloma heard someone screaming, not realizing it was her own voice. She ran down the hall and left the hospital. She was in the street, running and pulling out her hair.

The funeral was the saddest day on earth. Mary was laid out in the parlor of their house. Rosie saw all the people in black coming to their house bringing bowls of food. Rosie stood by the coffin wiping her eyes. She heard all the screaming and sobbing from her family but she couldn't cry out loud. She saw Mama fall screaming when they took her up to the coffin but she still couldn't cry out loud. Nobody grieved as hard as she did. In her heart Mary was her mother, her best friend and her world. She kept thinking, *'How could Mary die and leave me behind? Mary always took me everywhere she went.'* Then she remembered the white wedding dress and veil Mary was laid out in.

"Why is she wearing a wedding dress?"

"Mary was a virgin and she belongs to God now," came the reply. Rosie then overheard her mother sobbing and telling someone, "The doctor said she had double pneumonia. They did an autopsy and discovered she had an enlarged heart because she had rheumatic fever when she was a little girl." Then she heard her mother comment on how strong Mary was, how just the other day she carried two large sacks of potatoes home from the store, one on each arm.

A man appeared, saying his name was Tom. Rosie remembered him, the talent scout. He was crying and wiping his eyes. "She could have been a star," he kept repeating.

Luigi was inconsolable, and his sobs could be heard above anyone else's.

"It's my fault she is dead! I killed her! I'll never forgive myself to my dying day!"

"No, Luigi, you had no way of knowing that she had a bad heart," said John Coppola. "We all have to discipline the children. How could we control them otherwise? You have been a good father to all of them and everyone knows how much you loved Mary."

Giroloma heard the conversation, but she tended to ignore Luigi's pleading eyes. She could not forgive him. She loved him and he was a good man, but she would remain unforgiving for the rest of her life.

Rosie kept remembering the coffin in the parlor, and that night her nightmares began. It started in the middle of the night: Rosie woke up to see Mary in her bride dress, standing by the edge of her bed. Rosie started screaming, "Mary's coming to get me!" Every night she would see Mary standing by the bed even though she had she refused to sleep in that bed again, and every night she would scream, "Mary's coming to get me!" Everyone tried to comfort her but to no avail.

Marian, the oldest daughter, tried to comb her hair and help dress her. "No not you—Mary does it for me," she would say, and then fight everyone off.

Giroloma, in her grief, tried to console her, but she didn't even want her mother; she wanted Mary. Giroloma was worried about her, so one day not long after Mary died, she decided to try to keep Rosie busy to take her mind off Mary and sent her to the parlor with a broom to sweep. Rosie never liked that room anyway and especially since the funeral. While Rosie was sweeping she looked up at all the pictures of dead relatives hanging on the wall. She was staring at the pictures when suddenly she imagined that they were pointing their fingers at her in a gesture to come. Rosie stood in pure fright. When she was able to move she dropped the broom and ran, screaming, "Mama, Mama, they're coming to get me!"

Giroloma held her frightened child, rocking her and silently crying while trying to calm her down.

A few days later Giroloma lay moaning in her bed, the labor pains had begun. This was her eleventh child, but she never experienced this fierce excruciating pain that seemed to tear her body apart. The family doctor was on his way. The neighbor women were helping her at the present time. Luigi was shooed out of the room, and he was worried that something was terribly wrong. Fannie, the baby, was sitting on the table top while he was bracing her legs. His attention was on getting the kids gathered to go to an aunt's house. Suddenly the baby reached out, tipping over the coffee pot and spilling hot scolding coffee on herself. Luigi ran out of the house with a screaming baby.

"Marian, you take the kids over to Aunt Amelia's house and stay there until I come to get you!" he yelled.

"Come on, Rosie," Marian said, shoving her. Rosie shoved back. She resented Marian telling her what to do. She wasn't Mary, and besides, she wanted to stay home to see the new baby when it came. Marian was bossy and she wasn't taking any of Rosie's tantrums. Rosie had no choice but to be dragged down the street by the scruff of her neck. When they finally got to the aunt's house Rosie walked in the door with all the other kids. She waited and as soon as the coast was clear she ran out of the house. She ran all the way home, not stopping to catch her breath, afraid that Marian was going to catch her. When she finally ran into the house, she caught her breath and looked around. No one was in the kitchen; everyone was in the bedroom with her mother. She heard her mother moaning and crying out.

Suddenly the door opened and the doctor was there. He glanced at Rosie with a look of surprise to see that a child was in the house. Then he walked into the bedroom carrying a black doctor's bag. Rosie waited for hours, anxious to see her new baby. She smiled, remembering Mama telling her that this baby would be hers. She was being assigned to help take care of this baby as soon as it was old enough, just like Mary was assigned to take care of her.

"I wonder what is taking so long," she said. Pretty soon the doctor came out of the bedroom, and he looked tired.

"Is my baby here?" asked Rosie. The doctor nodded his head and left the apartment to go to the bathroom to wash.

"Where is my baby?" she kept asking, but the doctor couldn't hear her. Then she spied the black bag he had carefully laid down on a chair. Her curiosity getting the better of her, she opened the bag, and there, lying in the bag, was her dead baby brother. It looked like he was in pieces, and Rosie started screaming. She couldn't remember much after that!

Giroloma knew that something was terribly wrong with Rosie, but it was the appointed day the welfare lady would come calling.

"Mrs. Finazzo, I'm Miss O'Neal," said the social worker who was at the door.

"*No capesha englisha, venica, aspettare, uno momento* (I don't speak English, come in, wait a minute)," Giroloma said in Italian, then she yelled, "Sally!" Giroloma had to depend on her children to translate for her. The young thin lady with the thick horn-rimmed glasses entered the apartment.

All the children, as usual, were lined up so she could make a careful inspection. She observed the shabby railroad-style tenement apartment with the sparse furnishings. The curtains that were hanging were worn and frayed. The walls had pictures of saints and a cross was on the kitchen wall. She looked in the kitchen and there was a large pot with some vegetables steaming, creating a pleasant spicy aroma that had mingled with the musty odor of too many bodies enclosed in the small space. She had a list which she marked as she walked around, making notes of everything she saw. Then she looked at the children again for a closer evaluation. She started calling off their names. As each one answered their name, she observed that they were dressed in shabby clothes, but they were clean; their hair was still wet and had been combed and arranged in severe styles. They looked as if they had just been cleaned up before she arrived.

When she came to Rosie's name there was no response. Giroloma was saying something in Italian, wringing her hands, so Sally interrupted and said, "She's sick."

"Let me see her," ordered Miss O'Neal. She was led to a small bedroom, where her swift glance took in two double beds and a small religious picture on the wall with a rosary draped over it. Then they lingered on the small form that lay on the bed. She walked closer and knew that this child was seriously ill. The small child's eyes fluttered open for a second, exposing large dark round eyes, but they did not acknowledge her presence. There was a small bucket by the bed that contained vomit which dominated the putrid smell of the airless room. Giroloma was trying to explain in her native language, "We have called for the doctor." Miss O'Neal was growing red with anger.

"I don't understand, why in the world can't these ignorant foreigners realize this child should be in a hospital?" she mumbled to herself. Miss O'Neal was a dedicated person and she hated the poverty in which these poor people had to live. They had her sympathy, but she also had strong opinions on how they could improve their lives. They had their old country customs, like the garlic that poor child had around her neck. Miss O'Neal then told Sally, "Tell your mother that I will be back in a little while with transportation to take your sister to a hospital."

After she left, Sally hesitantly had translated her message, and Giroloma was terrified, as hospitals were places you go to die in. She made the sign of the cross, going into a long prayer, including three Our Fathers and three Hail Mary's, ending her prayers with, "Please God, please don't take another child away from me."

When she had finished with her prayers she sat holding Rosie's limp hand, worrying about the changes in her. Her naturally bright, inquisitive mind and her zest for life were missing. Instead, she had turned into a frightened nervous child who would go into hysterical screaming fits. The trauma she experienced was too much for her mind to accept, and Giroloma knew this had left Rosie emotionally and physically affected. Rosie's health begun to deteriorate; she had no appetite, her sleeping habits were irregular, and she would wake up screaming during the night with nightmares. Giroloma suddenly saw Rosie squirm in her sleep, mumbling, "Is that you, Mary?"

A little while later Rosie saw a shadow picking her up, and she caught a glimpse of Giroloma's face.

"Why was she crying?" she wondered. Then she was whirling as the car sped toward the hospital. All she could remember was the gray building. There was white all around her and the septic smell of medicine. She saw people in white looking at her worried. There was Mama crying and Papa talking, but she couldn't understand him. It seemed like a long long time. Then one day she woke up in a bed. The nurse was real pretty, she thought, as she was smiling at her.

"Where am I at? Where's my Mama? Where's Mary?" she asked.

The nurse shushed her. "Not so many questions, little one. You were real sick, but you're getting better now."

Many days and nights still went by, and she remembered glimpses and shadows but nothing was clear. Mary wasn't visiting her much anymore. One day Papa was there looking sad. She must have been getting better because he was saying, "We'll coma to see you every week."

"Why can't I go home?

"You were a sick, Rosie, very very sick. Whena you are completely well then you can come home," answered Luigi.

"Why are all those people asking me questions all the time?" she asked.

"They justa want to makea you well," was Luigi's reply.

Then the nurse was telling him to leave. He kissed her and waved goodbye.

Luigi then sat in the cold, unfeeling room, and Doctor Goldberg, who was sitting across from him, said, "Your child had a nervous breakdown. She also was in a deteriorated state of health. You almost lost her, Mister Finazzo. She is getting better now but the state has stepped in. The unfortunate death of your other daughter severely traumatized your daughter's well-being. I cannot interfere with the state's recommendation that she should be placed in a foster home when she is released from here.

"Also I'm curious about something...she talked about seeing a dead baby in a doctor's bag. Is there any truth to his?" Doctor Goldberg added.

Luigi sat twisting his hat, then he nodded sadly and cleared his throat. "My wife, she wasa in labor. I thought all the children were outta the house. Rosie went back into the house. The doctor, he saw her ina the kitchen. then he went to the bedroom to deliver the baby everything went wrong. The baby boy, he weighed about eleven pounds an she couldn't give birth to him. The doctor, he said the baby died ina side of her in labor. So anyway, the doctor, he dida the best he could. When it wasa delivered, he had to take it out ina sections. He remembered my daughter, she wasa sitting ina the kitchen an he didn't want her to see. So he cleaned outta his bag, wrapped the baby in a blanket and placed the baby ina his bag. He told another old lady who wasa helping to bring all his instruments to hisa office later. He went to the washa room to washa his hands and laid the bag on a chair ina the kitchen ona his way there. He never think that she would look ina the bag."

The doctor sat and thought for a few minutes, shaking his head.

"That experience, along with the death of her sister, attributed to her breakdown. We also have to consider her physical condition. Besides having diphtheria, she was undernourished. The lab reports showed anemia, plus she even had head lice. I am sorry but you're going to have a hell of a time trying to get her back," he added with disgust.

Luigi looked stricken as he said, "Me ana my wife, we try to do the best we can, but we gotta so many kids."

"Mister Finazzo, I can sympathize with you, and I know we are going through a Depression, but did you ever stop to think about letting another family who is not so unfortunate raise your children? You know it would be for their best."

"No, never, our children are our life." Luigi was angered. *'Whoever heard of giving your children away?'* he wondered.

Doctor Goldberg could see that he was getting nowhere with this case so he looked at his watch. *'Time for rounds,'* he thought.

"Well, you think about it and see me again," he concluded, dismissing Luigi.

The nice lady had come in to see Rosie again.

"Yuh always smell so nice," Rosie said, smiling.

"I just happen to have some perfume in my purse; would you like it if I put some on you?" asked the lady, smiling back at her. Rosie nodded.

"My real name is Margaret Wright, but you can call me Maggie," she said, as she was applying the perfume on her. "I bet you are getting very bored here." Rosie nodded.
"Well, I just happen to know of a nice couple who don't have any children, and they are real lonely and would love for you to visit them for the weekend."

Rosie's round eyes looked surprised. "Why me?" she remarked.

"Because they used to have a little girl, long ago," said Maggie.

"Oh, then she died like my sister Mary," replied Rosie.

Maggie was very shocked for a minute, but she recovered immediately.

Progress was now being made if Rosie could acknowledge her sister's death. Maggie was a social worker who had studied Rosie's case.

"Yes, dear, their little girl died a long time ago."

"That's too bad. Maybe I could visit them to make them feel better," Rosie replied. Maggie was pleased it had been so easy.

"Well, I had better go and make arrangements."

Rosie looked around her room, but she was not in the hospital room anymore. They had moved her to a different place. She had a bed in this room, and a desk with papers and crayons. Sometimes she would be asked to draw pictures of her family by different people who came in. She didn't think they liked her pictures, especially the one of Mary in her bride's dress lying in the coffin, or the one of her dead baby brother in the black bag.

The next day Maggie came to see Rosie again, only she was not alone. There was a man and a lady with her.

"Hi, Rosie," she said. "I want you to meet Mr. and Mrs. Rosenberg."

Rosie looked at the two smiling faces. The lady was pretty. She had black hair cut short and styled in large waves. She was dressed in a pink dress with a big floppy hat to match, but what really amazed

Rosie was the little fur coat she wore. The small animal still had a head and tail. Rosie was wondering if it was real. Then she looked at the man. He was sort of heavy and was dressed in a brown suit. When she studied his face, she liked him immediately. He had rosy cheeks, smiling eyes and a little moustache, not a big one with curly ends like Papa.

"Would you like to go on a weekend visit with us?" the lady with the animal on her neck asked.

"It would be okay," answered Rosie. Then she piped up and asked, "Is that a real animal yuh have on your neck?" Everyone burst out laughing.

"Oh, I can tell we're going to have fun," the man with the rosy cheeks said.

They did have fun. The Rosenbergs lived in a big white house in a city called Long Island. They had a long front yard lined with trees and flowers. When they entered the house a lady in a black dress with white trim took their coats. They told Rosie she was the maid. She did all the housework and answered the door. Then another lady was the cook. Rosie's big round eyes took it all in. The lady said to call her Sarah and the man Jerry. They showed her all around the house, and outside was a swing with a trestle of flowers around it. The man working outside was called the gardener. After they had dinner on a long table with huge candle sticks, Sarah showed Rosie her room, and it was the most amazing sight Rosie had ever seen in her life! She thought a princess must live there. The room was decorated in pale pink and green colors. The canopy bed was draped with pink satin material. The walls were decorated with a pattern of tiny rosebuds and a pale green background of leaves. There was a tiny dresser just her size, with perfumes and toiletries and a little golden brush and comb set. Rosie thought she was in heaven. Sarah then opened a closet and it was filled with beautiful dresses. She found a white satin robe and a matching silky night gown and dressed Rosie in them.

"Now I have a special surprise for you," Sarah said, as she pointed to the wall which was shelved with dolls and toys.

"Did all this belong to your little girl?" Rosie asked. A look of sorrow passed over Sarah's face, and it took some time before she could compose herself. "Yes, dear, but that was a very long time ago. My little girl's name was Julie and she died of a sickness."

Rosie felt instant sympathy for this kind person. "Are yuh looking for another little girl?" she asked.

"Yes, I can't bring Julie back but I would love to have another child. The doctor said I can't have any more babies, so I would love to adopt a little girl just like you."

"Yuh can adopt me," Rosie chimed in.

Sarah looked at this adorable child with the beautiful eyes and said, "I would love to." She then twitched Rosie's nose and said, "But you better get busy playing...these dolls and toys haven't been played with in a long time."

The next day after breakfast on the patio, they became much more acquainted. "Let's do something special today," Jerry announced. He then looked at Rosie and asked, "What would you like to do?"

Rosie thought for a minute. "How about getting some ice cream?"

Jerry laughed at her simple request. She had eaten everything with such zest, muffins with honey and strawberries. She couldn't fill up and now she was thinking of more food.

"I know what we can do," he added cheerfully. "We will go to the park."

Rosie wore one of the pretty dresses the maid dressed her in with matching hair bows. Soon they were off. Jerry rented a horse and carriage and they rode through a beautiful park. Jerry called it an enchanted forest. They sang songs and laughed all day. Rosie got her ice cream and later hot dogs from a stand. She even got to see a puppet show which was hilarious.

The weekend sped by, and before she knew it, it was time to go back. It had been the most thrilling weekend Rosie ever had. She didn't have to fight for anyone's attention. For once in her life she was the center of it. She saw life through a different world, a world she never knew existed. It was a fairytale and she was the princess. A new door had opened up in her life, erasing all the sorrow from her past. She wanted to stay in this fairytale world forever, but all to soon it was time to go back to the institution. They were saying goodbye and she was sadly waving back, fighting off tears that were threatening to escape through her big round eyes.

Rosie couldn't wait until the following weekend, and she kept counting the days. Finally it was Friday evening and they were back again to pick her up. She couldn't hold back her joy at seeing them again. Rosie had two more weekends with Sarah and Jerry and they had fallen in love with her. She was such a charming child, full of spunk and life. Rosie learned that they were Jewish and they owned a jewelry store. Sarah asked Rosie if she had any misgivings if she changed her religion. They had taken her to their synagogue. *'It was different, but just as nice,'* she thought. Rosie was happy, really happy for the first time in her life. She didn't think about her life with her real family; she just blocked them out of her mind.

Rosie was dressed and waiting for the weekend visit with Sarah and Jerry. She was anticipating what surprises they had for her this time. Sarah had mentioned taking her to a beauty parlor to have her hair styled. Rosie was waiting in the long hallway watching the door, then she spotted someone walking through the door, and he looked familiar. Her heart sank. It was Papa and he said, "I come to takea you home."

Chapter 4—THE GANGSTER WARS

"ORGANIZED CRIME WARS IN BROOKLYN, read all about it in the newspaper!" yelled the newspaper boy. The date was September Thirteenth, Nineteen Twenty-eight. Luigi was taking a short walk next door to the bakery at 115 Roebling Street to buy some stale bread. When he stopped in front of the bakery he glanced at the display of freshly baked cannoli and cream puffs in the window front. As he opened the door, the pleasant aroma of freshly baked bread and pastries filled the room, causing his mouth to water. Nick, the baker, spotted him entering and said, "Hi Luigi, how's everything?"

"Everything isa fine, I justa needa some stale bread today," Luigi answered.

"I've got some donuts for you today they've left over from yesterday and I can't sell them."

"Well, letta me pay you something for them. I gotta some change."

"No, I won't hear of it. Times are tough and you need your money," he answered. Just then two well-known gangsters, Tony Marino and Paul Como, entered the bakery and nodded to Luigi. Since they knew Luigi for years and knew they could trust him, they talked freely in front of him.

"Do you still have the inventory sheet, Nick?" inquired Paul.

"Yeah, here it is all filled out. Business is thriving, as usual." Paul stood studying the sheet and adding up how many bottles of booze were being distributed to the speakeasies. The demand was endless, as every private club, party, or anyone requesting booze for any reason was on the delivery list. Bottles of whiskey were hidden in the trucks along with the bakery items. The bakery shop was just a store front looking quite innocent by day, but behind the carefully concealed doors at night it was anything but innocent, with bootlegging, mobsters, crime, and wild parties. The bakery was actually a lot larger than it appeared, since the store had an extension on the back where the trucks were stored and one side of the building was an extension of the bakery with no storefront. The most interesting aspect of the building was the underground tunnel that extended around the corner to another store, the floral shop. This was concealed by a phony door in the bakery's kitchen. The phony oven was located next to the real oven and often was referred to as the escape hatch. This enabled the transfer of booze, weapons or people to go unrecognized.

Tony Marino was immaculately dressed—he always wore silk suits with a fresh boutonniere flower everyday. Tony said, "I remember your brothers back in Castellammare. Luigi, you Finazzos are a tough lot. We can't let Joe Parrino's men think we are soft. Remember we are Castallammares and they don't like our power; they are afraid of our kind. We know how to fight; we had to do that since the beginning of time, when just about every nation tried to conquer our island in Sicily."

"Everybody wanted our land froma the English, Irish, Greeks, and Arabs," replied Luigi.

"They detest our people because we got balls and connections with the old country. We are a threat to them because we are taking over," added Paul.

"The castle on the sea was our watch tower. That was what Castellammare was named after. We watch out for each other. We never go against our own kind," Nick remarked.

Tony looked at his watch. "Come on, Paul, we better go upstairs and attend to business. We've got a lot to do today."

After they left, Nick leaned over and whispered to Luigi, "I hear that a big shipment of machine guns are coming in from Chicago, from Big Al himself. All hell is breaking loose with this war. They are going to hide them all in the delivery trucks with the baked goods. They'll be distributed out to our people."

As soon as Luigi arrived home he entered the kitchen and was greeted by Louie, the third oldest son.

"Hi, Pa, you're just in time. We're teasing Moe." Moe was a Jewish friend of Louie's. Moe was a skinny short guy with a huge hook nose and thick glasses. His smile was his only becoming feature. When he smiled, his homely face took on a radical change. His eyes lit up, almost camouflaging his uneven features.

How's Jew Town?" asked Rocco, the oldest son. Moe just laughed, as he was used to being teased by Rocco.

"Hey, look at that schnozzle," Louie joked.

Moe looked at Louie. "You grease balls are funny-looking too!"

Giroloma changed the subject by saying, "We got racks of dresses and clothes to sell today."

81

Louie and Moe were small-time thieves. They always had a scam going, through Moe's connections. Moe Levee was a funny, pleasant guy, always laughing and telling stories. Giroloma took a liking to him, and when he had no place to go, she always made a place for him to sleep. Moe felt comfortable with these people even if they weren't from his ethnic background. They were warm-hearted and gave him a feeling of family life that he lacked at home. To show his appreciation he always helped her with her cooking and chores. He was a good cook and he started showing her how to make Jewish food. Today he was giving a lesson on pickles.

Rocco spotted them in the sink and laughed. "Pretty soon we'll be Jewish." It wasn't long before the kitchen was filled with laughter from all the little children. They loved it when Rocco was home. Rocco was the replica of his father, Francisco, except for his rougher features and stockier build. He had joined the mob as their "Hey Boy," delivering messages and doing deliveries for them. Most of the money he made he used to help support his family. He was always playing with them and tossing them around. Rosie's big round eyes adored him and she had every right, because she was his favorite. She was spunky, a true Finazzo, he always said. The fat little round-faced baby started to cry. Rocco picked her up from the floor where she was sitting. He was making faces at her when Jimmy entered the room in his Navy uniform.

"Here he is, soldier boy," teased Rocco. Jimmy's answer was a few punches thrown in the air at Rocco. Rocco made a pretend-duck with his head and threw some punches back.

Giroloma interrupted by yelling, "Oh no, no fighting in my kitchen or I'll go get the broom!" Everyone knew what the broom meant. At one time or another they all experienced her temper with a few whacks from the famous broom. Everyone humorously eyed the broom, still standing in the corner waiting for the attack.

"We better watch out for Mama's broom," cautioned Jimmy. Everyone laughed, joining in on the family joke.

Jimmy's small five-foot-two stature was the underestimated mistake of too many fighters. He was mean, fast and wiry, causing many men a painful surprise. Jimmy's street fighting had rearranged his otherwise nice features. His nose had been broken so many times it was flattened where a bridge should have been. His ears were what fighters refer to as cauliflower ears because they were so deformed from punches. Jimmy had run away at age fourteen to join the Navy, forging papers to join. He was always in and out of the family's home, either involved with the Navy or boxing. He had changed his name to Jimmy Valentine and became The Light-weight Champion of the Navy. Jimmy had a detached love for his family. When he was around he would do everything possible to help out, but before anyone realized it, he would mysteriously disappear. He was the family entertainment. He could tell them stories of every part of the world. Jimmy was always interesting and the family listened to his stories for hours.

Giroloma started running water in the tub by the kitchen wall. It was time for her never-ending chore of washing clothes.

Rocco handed her the baby, laughing. "Here Ma, I think she has a surprise for yuh." Giroloma gave him an exasperated look and threw a wet rag at him. He ducked and the wet rag hit Moe in the face. They all burst out laughing. A few days later Luigi and all the family were sitting down to dinner. The sweet spicy aroma that filled the room was coming from a large bowl with a huge mound of pasta and meatballs that sat on the center of the table, along with a bottle of 'Dago-Red' wine and a loaf of homemade bread. Each place setting had a mismatched cracked plate with a small wine glass. Everyone was about to dig in when they heard the funeral procession coming down the street. The band had started its slow, depressing funeral march. The children all ran to the window.

"Look, Mama, it must have been a famous gangster," piped Marian. She was the one most moved by the drama of a gangster funeral. She enjoyed a good cry every time one passed. The funerals were becoming more frequent, usually on the average of one or two a week, with the gang wars between the organization of Joe Parrino's men against the organization of Sam Galanti's men. They were fighting because of the 'Castellammares' taking over Brooklyn. The war become popularly known as the 'Castellamarese War.' The flamboyant funerals were more like parades. The white horses led the funeral wagon holding the elaborate casket covered with flowers, followed by the long endless row of expensive cars. Marian started wailing louder, until Luigi could stand it no longer.

"SHUT UPPA!" he yelled, covering his ears.

Everyone sat back down at the table, expecting the usual speech from Mama. "He might have been the one who killed my dear Francisco; now we must all pray real hard that his death has been avenged," she stated. Everyone bowed their heads and crossed themselves for the lengthy prayers that were always expected.

Several days later another funeral was about to take place, only this one was quite different. It was a young beautiful girl in the prime of her life. Jimmy had went out for some groceries and when he reached the stoop to the tenement house where they lived, Giroloma was sitting out there with a few other neighbor women. She looked up at Jimmy with a very sad expression and made a motion with her hands for him to sit down by her.

"Settee Jimmy, I'm sorry but I have some very sad news for you," she said, wiping her eyes with her handkerchief. "I just heard Gina died."

Jimmy felt the blood drain from his face. He had a big crush on Gina, as far back as he could remember. He finally found his voice and asked, "How did it happen?"

"It'sa strange how it happened...." Giroloma started her story, lapsing into her native Sicilian language. "She went to bed and they just found her dead in her sleep. No reason why; she was never sick. Now we must all show our respect by going over to her family's house this afternoon to see her laid out. I must comfort my poor friend, her mother Vita Farsetti; she was my friend from childhood."

Jimmy, was still in shock and shook his head in agreement, too choked up to answer.

Later in the afternoon the Finazzo family had taken the silent short walk to the Farsetti's to show their respect. Everyone had dressed in their finest clothes and had subdued expressions of sadness that were appropriately required at such sad occasions. Marian was slowly working her emotions up to the trauma of the event. Her sobs were getting louder as she walked. She was saving her final theatrics for the dramatic moment when they would view the casket.

Finally the family had reached their destination and entered the Farsetti's home. It seemed as if the entire neighborhood was there, dressed in black. The crowd was so thick that they had to push their way through to be welcomed by the grieving family. Giroloma found Vita and they hugged each other and cried. Vita's husband led them into the parlor where the aroma of fresh flowers dominated the room and pointed to the casket where the young beautiful woman was laid out. Marian had inched her way up to casket. After taking a very long look, she started wailing, letting her theatrical performance take hold.

Jimmy stared in sadness at the beautiful young woman in the casket. Louie was openly sobbing. "It looks like neither of us can have her now," Louie said, wiping his eyes. Jimmy stood staring at the beautiful face, sheer perfection, with white skin like porcelain. He stared at the tightly closed eyelids that concealed her lovely aqua-colored eyes and the long eyelashes that almost touched her high cheekbones. "What a shame someone so beautiful had to die," he whispered.

Jimmy remembered how every young man in the neighborhood had tried to win her affections. He remembered bringing her flowers and cream puffs with plump red cherries. Then Louie brought her presents, but she was fickle; one day she would smile at him and the next day she would ignore him and give her attentions to Jimmy. He remembered the arguments they got into, trying to compete with each other. Then came the day she ignored them both for the rich guy, who bought her expensive jewelry. It seemed she broke every young man's heart in the neighborhood, at one time or another.

Jimmy, still mesmerized by her beautiful face, imagined that he saw her eyelashes flutter, then her

86

hand move. Suddenly she seemed to come to life and sat upright in her casket. Marian, who was up close to the casket, let out an earth-shattering scream and promptly fainted, almost knocking over the casket. All the mourners started screaming, some of them fainting. Most of the mourners were fighting to leave, they were bumping into each other and walking over the unconscious people in their haste. Hysterical screaming, chairs being overturned and the rumble of feet like a stampede were the dominant noises of the room. The chaos continued for some time. The mourners in their fright had panicked. They ran, stumbled and fell as they fought to leave the room.

All of the Finazzo family finally managed to make their way out of the house. Luigi was half carrying Marian, who was partially conscious by now. She was still screaming during the short walk as he half-dragged her home. Everyone else was still in silent shock. Jimmy carried Fannie and Rocco carried Rosie, thankful they didn't get hurt in the stampede. Louie was holding up Giroloma, who was in a daze.

After finally arriving home, Jimmy put on a pot of coffee. Luigi sat everyone down, placing the cups in front of each person and pouring the coffee. When he was sure everyone was calmed down, he said,

"She wasa not dead. I seen thisa happen before one time in Sicily. She justa in a deep sleep likea coma."

Giroloma shook her head and spoke in Sicilian: "It's going to be hard on her now. Nobody is going to accept her. They will think of her as a spirit."

"Yeah, your right" added Jimmy, "I could never be comfortable near her now. You can have her now, Louie, she's too spooky for me."

"No thanks, maybe Rocco will have her."

"She is going to have a hard time finding a man, poor girl," said Giroloma sadly.

"The one thing I can't understand is, who pronounced her dead? Isn't it a law that a person has to be embalmed?" Rocco inquired.

"Many Italian immigrants come over here illegally, and even if they have papers, they don't trust the law," Luigi explained, lapsing into the familiar ancient Sicilian as he talked. "Maybe the Farsettis have no papers and they were scared to call the coroner. Even in the old country many people take matters into their own hands. It goes back many years. There has always been a mistrust in the law. For many centuries our people had been beaten down by the conquerors who tried to overtake our Island of Sicily," added Luigi.

Jimmy thought about Luigi's explanation for a few minutes. Then he said, "Yeah, I understand their fear but wouldn't they have to make arrangements with somebody to bury her?"

"They probably went to the Godfather to make the arrangements," Luigi went on to explain. "Our people don't trust the law. The Mafia takes care of everything. If they want a favor or justice, their law is the Mafia. Did I ever tell you the story of how the name 'Mafia' originated?" Luigi added, as he poured himself another cup of coffee.

"It is a legend that was told to me as a boy and handed down for many generations. Sometime in the year Twelve-Hundred Eighty-Two, in Palermo, Sicily, there was to be a wedding. The young girl and her lover went to a church to be married, but when they entered the church, the priest was not inside. The young man left his bride-to-be at the altar to search for the priest. While he was gone, the bride was raped by a French sergeant who was hiding behind a stone arch. As she fought him off she slipped and hit her head against the church wall which had a stone protrusion. She died of a skull fracture before the return of her groom. In his grief he shouted 'Death to the French' and attacked the French Sergeant. This incident caused thousands of angry Sicilians to shout, '*Morte alla Frencia Italia angela* (Death to the French is Italy's cry)!' Soon this saying caught on. For the next seventy-two hours the Sicilians attacked the French soldiers but eventually the French overcame them and killed them. Soon after this incident, a secret organization was formed by the many angry Sicilian men to fight back injustice. The password was 'Mafia,' which was made up of the initial letters of the tragic death cry."

Rocco looked at his watch. He had promised his girlfriend, Annette, that he would see her play tonight. Soon he was inside the RKO theater to watch the play that starred his girlfriend Annette. The faded maroon curtains had not opened yet. He was secretly glad he hadn't missed the show. Suddenly the lights lit up the stage and the curtains opened. The Italian play was a dramatic scene where two lovers had to part because the man was going to America. He had to marry a girl in America so he could become an American citizen. His family had promised the matrimony. Family honor had to come before his own wishes. He was chosen to pave the way for other family members to eventually migrate to America. The young girl was beautiful, with her innocent heart-shaped face. She started singing an opera, revealing her rich, clear voice. She was on her knees begging him not to go. Rocco thought she sounded like an angel. The scene was a tear-jerker, reminding many in the audience of their loved ones back in Sicily. A few sobs escaped from the audience, where grown men were crying. In the last scene, the beautiful girl committed suicide because she could not bear to let her lover go. She stabbed herself with a knife. Her last words singing out, were: "I would rather die than go through life without you." The young man was crying, cradling her dead body in his arms.

"What have I done?" he sang his anguished cry.

Rocco sat mesmerized, a small tear escaping from his eye. He quickly wiped his eyes, hoping his inner emotions weren't exposed. Rocco had built a reputation of being a tough guy, carefully concealing his generous and warm heart.

After the show Rocco was backstage with a box of candy he had brought earlier and concealed under his coat. Annette's eyes lit up and her little red bow mouth made a pretty smile of pleasure at seeing the man she loved. Within minutes she was in Rocco's strong arms. It had only been two days, but to her it was a lifetime since she last saw him. Rocco knew that he was in love. She was different from any woman he ever knew.

A few days later in the backroom of the bakery Tony Marino and his organization held a special meeting. They were all there—Tony, Big Jim and Vito Allecia. Vito was a slim, gaunt-looking younger guy who had a habit of blowing his ever-running nose.

Tony announced, "Legs is meeting us here, and we don't want him to get suspicious because he is going to get whacked tonight. We found out that he has ragged us out to the Perrino gang. We are all going to the Italian restaurant and afterwards we'll whack him."

Soon they all heard the slow movements of a wooden cane that was making a clumping sound as Legs slowly reached his destination.

"How are yuh, asshole?" Tony was grinning.

"I haven't been well; my stump's been hurting with this weather," he replied. Legs had been shot in the leg and groin several years back in a shoot-out. His real name was Pete D'orazio, but the nickname Legs was tagged onto him because he was always complaining about his leg. Tony was getting sick of him anyway, always whining and sniveling. He thought, *'Well tonight he will be out of his fucking misery!'* Tony had no mercy on a rat.' Tony was smiling as he thought, *'He even looks like a rat with his beady little eyes and pointy nose.'*

"Well, let's go to dinner. I'm hungry for some seafood," said Vito.

"Not me; I'm craving some good old style Italian food," Big Jim argued. Big Jim was always hungry. He ate constantly, and filling his large frame was his passion for life. His 300-pound body stretched out over his large six-foot-two frame which still left him unproportioned with flaps of fat hanging from his double chin .

"We'll go to Joe's Seafood Inn at Shepphead Bay; they have everything there," said Tony, settling the dispute.

It wasn't long before they were seated at the restaurant. Legs had no suspicion that they were wise to him. What news he told a member of Parrino's organization supposedly was in strict confidence. He had made a deal to start working for them, so he told them about the warehouses where their trucks were supplying whiskey and booze. It was planned to have a car follow them tonight for a shoot-out. *'They are dead men,'* Legs thought as he laughed out loud.

Tony caught his humor. "You're in a good mood tonight, my friend?"

"Just a private joke," Legs replied.

Sicilian tradition was to treat your victim well—the best of food, best cigar, best conversation before the kill, which was usually brutal and savage without mercy. It was usually a shock to the victim because he never suspected it coming. They ordered the best wine off the wine list, the best Italian food, seafood, and everything was delicious. Now Tony, gave Legs a serious look and being a sentimental man, he stared at his old friend Legs.

"Remember in the old days when we were boys together," Tony reminded him.

Legs nodded, and remembered the beautiful paradise, Castellammare.

"I will never forget how we swam in the ocean together and collected all the seashells, and our pet lizards," Tony went on.

"Castellammare was heaven a *paradiza*," Legs commented.

Tony's face took on a sad expression for a few minutes, then his dark eyes hardened. "That is why it is so important to stick to your own people; they are your heritage, your life," he said.

Legs was getting uncomfortable; he didn't like the drift of this conversation. '*If Tony would have given me my fair cut from the last job, things would have been different, he thought. The son of a bitch sits there and talks of loyalty. Where are Parrino's men anyway? It is time they got here, he worried.*' Legs was nervously looking around. Sweat had started to form on his forehead, so he took a napkin to wipe it off.

Tony was carefully observing him. '*Let the son of a bitch sweat*,' he was thinking.

Big Jim was eating, enjoying the delicious dinner, then he noticed Legs nervously glancing out of the window every few seconds. That's when it suddenly hit him that this was a setup by Legs. Big Jim's appetite suddenly left him, realizing that any minute Parrino's men could come shooting through the door, or be waiting outside. Big Jim kept trying to catch Tony and Vito's eye without being too obvious. They were too busy talking the ancient Sicilian language that they always easily lapsed into. Soon Tony ended the friendly chat by saying, "Did yuh enjoy your dinner, my old friend?"

Legs hands were shaking, he was trying to be inconspicuous as he dipped his bread into the sauce. He just nodded.

Tony made the motion that it was time to go, then he caught the warning look in Big Jim's eyes. Tony scanned around outside before he decided to venture out. "Is everybody ready? Let's go to the theater and see the new Italian play. We'll enjoy ourselves tonight," Tony announced. Vito got into the driver's seat of the big black Lincoln sedan.

"You can ride in the front seat, too, Legs; it's easier on your stump," remarked Tony.

'*What could have gone wrong?*' Legs was fretting. He was still uneasy, wiping his face.

"What's the matter, Legs?" Tony asked. "Yuh look like you're expecting someone."

Legs felt the cold gun on his neck, and he knew he was a dead man.

"Did yuh really expect to see Parrino's men coming trew that door tonight, Legs? Do yuh really think they give a rat's ass about a rat like yuh? Yuh really disappoint me. Yuh misjudged my powers. I know some people in Parrino's group—word gets out. Yuh know my boss, Sam Galanti, he is a very intelligent man," Tony explained.

"Please don't kill me," Legs pleated, sniveling. Vito was heading down Emmons Avenue, toward Ocean Avenue.

"Drive over to Gowanus Bay," Tony ordered.

They were soon entering the tough neighborhood of Red Hook, where the shipping canal and the boating docks came into view. Crimes were ignored in this area, as nothing was ever seen or heard in this tough section of town. The rest of the ride was silent, except for an occasional outburst from Legs.

"Stop the car!" came the dreaded order. They were in a deserted section by the ocean. The car came to a stop. Tony and Big Jim got out of the car.

"Get out!" Tony ordered. Legs attempted to move and stumbled out of the car, causing his cane to fall. Tony grabbed his cane. Five shots rang out, causing his body to jerk with each one.

"Turn him over and pull down his pants," Tony ordered, handing Big Jim the cane. Big Jim gave one strong thrust and shoved the cane up Leggs' rectum. One last scream was heard and then there was silence. Vito looked at Legs, who looked ridiculous with his hind end up in the air and the cane protruding from it.

"Assholes get treated like assholes, only this one's got a bigger one now," Tony joked. Everyone saw the humor in it and joined in laughing.

"If I would have stuck that stick up his ass any further, we coulda had barbecued rat and shit on a stick," added Big Jim, and he started chuckling. That remark really set everyone off laughing. Vito laughed so hard his nose started running again. He pulled out his handkerchief to blow his nose.

A couple of days later, another gangster funeral procession was going down the street with all its flamboyancy. The kids all rushed to the window to observe the parade-like funeral. Marian started in wailing until Luigi yelled, "Shut uppa."

"I wonder who it is this time. Maybe this was the gangster who killed our poor Francesco," remarked Giroloma while making the sign of the cross. Soon she had everyone praying that her husband's death had been avenged.

All the bosses of the Mafioso were there at the funeral. The elaborate arrangements of flowers outdid each other. This strange tradition was never questioned. It was the traditional way of life. Tony nudged Rocco. "Tomarra night meet us at the warehouse on Grand Avenue at eight o'clock. We got to take inventory of our shipment of guns. All hell is breaking loose with this Castellammarese war."

Rocco was dressed in his new black pinstripe suit and shiny alligator shoes when he entered the barbershop after the funeral.

The old barber was a long-time friend of the family. He, migrated as well as about everyone else on Roebling Street, from Castellammare. Unlike the younger ambitious people, he was satisfied to have his little barbershop and live in peace. He felt he had the American Dream. Even though he was a relative of the Godfather and his shop was patronized by the most powerful and famous gangsters, he preferred to stay out of family matters.

"Hi, Joe, how's business?" Rocco greeted.

"What'll it be today?" Joe asked.

"Just a hair cut today," replied Rocco.

"Settee." Joe motioned for him to sit down. Joe's shaky hand held the barber shears ready to start clipping at the thick bushy hair. Joe noticed a change in Rocco. His flamboyant lifestyle showed. "You know ifa I wasa in the flower shop business, I'd be rich." He gave Rocco a long warning look. "You father my best friend; I don't want to see you dead. Everyday something happens, somebody got to die. You watch yourself."

Rocco liked and respected this man, but he wasn't really in the organization and he was wise enough to keep his nose clean. He assured himself that the few messages and deliveries he did were innocent of any real crime. He was referred to as the "Hey Boy" and was not that involved. Besides, he reasoned, the little money he made was helping the family out, and times were hard. They needed the help.

Finally Joe was done with his hair and was dusting off his neck with a cloth. Rocco looked at his watch. It was getting late. He had a hot date to go ballroom dancing today, so he gave Joe some change and hurried out.

As he entered the street he bumped into Luigi, who was on his way to visit Joe the Barber. Luigi eyed Rocco's new clothes, and his only remark showed his disapproval: "Bigga shot, bigga shit!"

Rocco was at the warehouse, and he checked his watch: he was on time. He went around to the back and gave a code knock. The door opened and the watchmen led him in. The large room was stocked with barrels of olive oil. Off to the side was the row of delivery trucks.

"Hey, Rocco, over here," yelled Paul. Rocco spotted Tony, Vito and Big Jim.

"Look over here in this truck," Tony said. The truck door was open and inside it was stocked with machine guns and ammunition. "These were sent from the Chicago organization........beauties, aren't they?" Tony raved.

Big Jim was smiling as he said, "Rocco, you did pretty good at practice the other day; a few more lessons and you'll be ready the defend your—"

It happened so fast no one had a chance to immediately react. The big door opened with a bang and the shooting had begun. Rocco jumped into the truck, swiftly pulling out his gun. Tony followed immediately after him. Big Jim didn't have a chance. His body was dancing to the rhythmic sounds of the machine gun. The men were shooting from behind the barrels, and oil began squirting out of the barrels as the bullets flew. Vito had found sanctuary behind the truck and was blasting away. One man was hit and he fell, knocking over the barrel and spilling oil over himself, then slipping and falling on the dirt floor. He clutched his groin in agony before he twitched and lay still.

Rocco and Tony were shooting back now, having grabbed a couple of loaded machine guns in the truck. Another man was hit and fell face-first onto the floor. Vito felt a sudden hot blast of excruciating pain and went still forever. He was shot between the eyes. A third man fired a shot which hit Tony's shoulder, then the man fled, knocking over a barrel, but not soon enough for the bullet to hit his back.

Before Tony could recover, the sound of police sirens filled the warehouse. The police came running in by the dozen, taking refuge behind the barrels.

"Come out with your hands up!" they shouted.

A few days later Giroloma sat in the kitchen chair crying. Another funeral procession was going down the street. It was another gangster funeral in all its elaborate flamboyancy. The band was playing the funeral march and Marian was wailing. Giroloma could stand no more, so she got up, walked over to Marian and, WHAM, smacked her across the face. This was not the time to worry over other people's troubles; she had enough of her own. Her poor Rocco was in jail and they were going to deport him because he was not an American citizen. He was a small infant without citizenship papers when they arrived in America.

She was ringing her hands with tears streaming down her face. Someone was knocking at the door, so Louie opened it and there stood a pretty woman. Everyone was in shock to see this strange woman standing there crying.

"I have come to try to help Rocco," she sobbed.

"How can you help?" asked Louie.

"I am an actress at the B.F.K. Theater and my family knows a lot of influential people.

"Luigi was staring at her. To him, all show people had low morals, especially women; they were called *puttonas*. On closer inspection she had a made-up face, eye shadow, red lips and rouge. Luigi walked away, disgusted, and he thought,' *It I sad enough that*

Rocco is in jail, but now he has his whores coming to the house.'

She turned away to go, but Louie said, "Wait, tell us how we can stop him from being deported."

She smiled, as if in gratitude that someone would listen. "My family has influential friends who work in the immigration department and I might be able to persuade them to help him."

Louie turned and spoke rapidly to Giroloma in Sicilian. She instantly perked up and said, "I would do anything to prevent my son from going to Sicily. The prisons there are horrible. Please tell her to try and help." Louie was a very level-headed person who always relied on logic and good manners, which had brought him many advantages in difficult situations, so he studied this woman. Under her make-up she was very young and pretty. She had the heart-shaped face of an angel. Her long wavy hair set off her large gray eyes. He judged this woman a very good-hearted person who must care deeply for Rocco.

"Please accept my apology for questioning you, and my family's behavior. As you can see we all are upset about Rocco. Please sit down. Can I offer you a cup of coffee?"

She smiled, showing a very small dimple near her cheek.

"My name is Annette Lorenzo. I do the Italian plays with my family," she said in ancient Sicilian, smiling at Giroloma.

A few more months had passed since Rocco's conviction—a twenty-year sentence and he was ordered to serve his time in Sing Sing State Penitentiary. Annette had proved to be helpful by her family's connections to prevent Rocco from being deported. Giroloma had made friends with her, realizing how much Rocco had meant to her.

Family life had gone on as usual, except without Rocco's financial help, conditions were much worse now, especially since Luigi had lost his job at the shipyards.

Louie, the younger son, tried to help out as much as possible whenever he could get odd jobs. Moe still came around with his hot stuff. Giroloma made a little profit by selling the clothes to the neighbors.

Moe was always a welcomed sight. Besides his good humor, he helped put food on the table. Louie was sitting at the kitchen table when he heard a horn honking. Looking out the window, there was Moe in a shiny new car. Giroloma stood amazed. "What is Moe up to?" she asked, and again came the honking.

"Hey Louie, come out and see my new car!" Moe yelled.

Louie ran outside, his eyes lingering on the car, then he asked, "Where did yuh get this?"

"Come on Louie, get in and take a ride and I'll tell yuh!" Excited, Louie jumped in.

"Well, what do yuh think of my new car?" asked Moe proudly. Louie looked at him doubtfully. "Now where did yuh get it?"

"I borrowed it from a friend for a favor, but he's going to sell it to me."

"Come on Moe, now I know yuh don't make that kind of money."

"It's a long story, so come on; do yuh want to drive for awhile?" Moe offered, changing the subject. Louie had fallen in love with this classy 1928 cream-colored Ford.

"Boy would I ever!" They stopped the car and exchanged positions, Louie now behind the wheel. He was not an experienced driver, so as he turned a corner he almost knocked over a fruit and vegetable cart. Oranges and heads of lettuce were rolling in the street. The man waved his fist and yelled as he sped by. Moe was laughing, "You're dangerous."

Louie was laughing. "This is the life!" They were heading down North Fifth Street when they heard the siren of the police car.

"Ah-oh, I must be going too fast," Louie said.

"No, you're not going fast enough," replied Moe.

"What do yuh mean?" Louie asked. Moe looked scared and didn't answer, so the truth dawned and Louie added, "This car is HOT!"

"I just wanted some fun. I was going to return it, honest," Moe apologized.

"I should have known how stupid and crazy you are!" yelled Louie. Soon the police car was alongside of him, motioning for him to pull over.

Giroloma was still shivering from the long walk in the rain. They had just come back from court, and she gazed out the window, watching the rain drops splash against the glass. It seemed that her sorrow was in harmony with the drops, as the tears rolled down her cheeks.

"Louie didn't know the car was stolen!" she sobbed.

"It didn't matter; the law said he was just as guilty," Luigi said sadly. "He was in the wrong place at the wrong time. He is eighteen and considered an adult."

Giroloma moaned, "Two years in prison for my baby. He is not like Rocco. Rocco can take care of himself with those criminals. Louie is too gentle and innocent to be there."

"Don't worry about Louie; he is the smart one. He knows how to reason with people. Rocco is the hot head," Luigi said.

"It's all my fault because I let Moe bring me those dresses and hot things to sell and now God is punishing me," Giroloma cried.

"No, you are a good woman. You did it for the children to eat. There is no crime in that."

"Now I've got two sons in prison, what next?" Giroloma sobbed.

"Soon things will get much better, you'll see," Luigi said affectionately. "You still got me and all the children. The time will go very fast. They may get out early, and before you know it, we will all be together again."

Giroloma's gray-hazel eyes stared back at him, holding onto his words and praying he was right.

Chapter 5—THE PSYCHIC CHILD

Little Rosie sniffed the musty smell in the hallway of the tenement house where she lived, and as always, she was amazed at how many different odors she could smell as she passed down the hall. She always could guess what each tenant was having for dinner by the many different aromas that she smelled as she passed by their doors. As she passed the bathroom she was also surprised to see that it was not occupied. One bathroom was shared for every two apartments and it was usually fought over. She laughed as she thought of the fat man down the hall. It seemed that he was always in need of the bathroom and she had beaten him to it the other day. Feeling mischievous, she run and slammed the door in his face, and he beat on the door while she took her time singing songs while she sat on the pot.

Rosie was now ten years old and she was street smart. Her life in the tenement house and on the streets of Brooklyn had educated her to a way of life where survival was the ultimate objective. Survival was more important then certain types of morals. It was alright to steal, lie and cheat; it was the way of life. In her small life she had seen enough hardship, cruelty and pain, and she was wise for an "innocent" ten-year-old child. Her overly large, round eyes had a haunted look. Rosie had now learned a way of self-protection; she played a game of blotting out all the ugliness that surrounded her. It didn't matter if other kids teased her and made fun of her. She would find a way of getting even. She would find a way to eat if she was hungry. It didn't matter if Mama was sick, she would find a way to make her better. She would find a way to get love and attention if she was ignored. Whenever she went through the stores or marketplaces on the streets she would steal; she would hold her left hand behind her and, as she called it, "work your back hand."

Sometimes she did it out of pure necessity; sometimes she did it out of pure rebellion. Like the times she would wander through the dime store and steal make-up and lipstick. Now she knew she didn't dare wear any of these cosmetics, but she could pretend. She had hidden them in a special spot in her room. She had one dresser drawer which was practically bare, but it was the only thing in the whole house she didn't have to share. She had three outfits of clothes two for school and one for church. One clothes closet would service the needs of the family's entire wardrobe. Sometimes she would receive some used clothing from relatives, but never anything new. Practically everything Rosie ever had in her life was used and handed down to her, except the beautiful doll her godmother had given her. This was the most magnificent thing she had ever seen. She had a porcelain face and long brown hair set in long locks. She had a beautiful dress made of a silky patterned material. Her shoes were patent leather high tops. Her dress and hair had blue silk matching ribbons. Rosie imagined that she was the doll and she was a princess. She was most fascinated with the doll's hair. Rosie's own hair was naturally straight, thin and stringy, with a homemade uneven hair-cut copied after the typical Buster Brown style.

"It is more practical to keep it short because of the head lice," Mama would say.

Rosie knew that this beautiful doll was too good to be true. As soon as she started playing with it, her younger sister Fannie wanted it. Soon they were both fighting over the doll, so Giroloma came and took the doll away.

"If both of you can't have a doll, then neither one of you can play with the doll." That was her psychology. So the beautiful doll was put up in the china cabinet. Sometimes Rosie would longingly look at her up in the shelf. She knew she could never play with her again, no matter how much she begged her Mama.

The familiar cracked and crumbling ceiling led to the front of Mrs. Lafretti's apartment where her journey ended. Rosie rapped loudly on her door. Soon the door opened and there stood old, frail Mrs. Lafretti with her grocery list ready.

"Rosie, you be sure to check the fruit over.....I don't want any over-ripe peaches like the ones you bought me the last time. You be sure to stop at the bakery, fish market and butchers afterward. Save two cents for yourself and don't take so long," she added in her high-pitched voice, shaking a bony finger at her as she talked.

It was a hard job because Mrs. Lafretti gave her a large list, about two shopping bags full. Rosie was a small undernourished child and this chore took all her strength. Mrs. Lafretti's list was even longer today, but Rosie didn't mind. This money will help Mama; these pennies will be put in the sugar bowl for our birthdays and special occasions, she thought. Anyway, Rosie's mind was not on what Mrs. Lafretti was saying; she was thinking about the strange dream she had the previous night. She vaguely remembered saying goodbye and hearing the old woman give last-minute orders. Rosie skipped down the hall past the bald baby in his buggy. She ran into the mean girl with the pretty dresses and hair bows, but today she didn't care; she knew something good was about to happen. She didn't pay attention to all the different noises the tenement house had—people yelling, babies crying; this was just a part of her life. Even the sound of her mother's screams would be ignored when she was outside playing kickball. The other kids would ask her, "Why does your mother scream all the time?" And she would nonchalantly reply, "Oh nuttin, she's got cancer," and continue bouncing her ball.

Rosie was not aware of what the word cancer meant, even though she was a bright child. She blocked it out of her mind; she never wanted to really know why Mama cried. Certain things were much too horrible to think about.

Rosie left the dim building and the bright sunlight suddenly hurt her eyes. The street was crowded and noisy, as usual. Rosie suddenly felt her stomach grumble. Hunger was something she was used to.

"I'll hurry and get to the bakery before I go to the fruit market; Mrs. Lafretti never knows I eat some of the food before I return," she said to herself.

As Rosie walked down the noisy street, noises diminished and she remembered why she had this good feeling today. It all started the night before when the mobster Degerio came over to sell the Italian lottery tickets. While the mobster sat at the table with the tickets, Rosie became intrigued. She knew she should be in the other room with the other children and by the looks Mama was giving her, she knew she was in trouble, but she suddenly had this hunch that couldn't be controlled. Beating or no beating, she must make them understand.

"Please mister, please play this number," she repeatedly said.

The gangster looked at her as if to say, "Scram brat," but she wouldn't let up. Finally, to get rid of her, he politely said, "Okay, kid, I'll split the ticket with yuh; now what numbers do yuh want to play?"

"I'll tell yuh if yuh let me keep half the ticket, so I know yuh won't gyp me," she replied.

He was already getting tired of humoring this ill-mannered little brat, so he reluctantly agreed. "It will cost a quarter," he grumbled.

"Papa, please give the man the quarter, please; I know we will win," Rosie begged.

Luigi gave her a quizzical look, then asked, "Whata numbers do you want to play?"

"Rocco's prison number, two-zero-seven-seven-three," she urgently replied. "Play it under the 'R' for Rome."

"Let me write the ticket out!" Sally interrupted, as he sat down at the kitchen table, shoving Rosie out of the way.

Rosie started fighting him, yelling, "I want to write it out," but Sally ignored her and began writing; however, instead of writing the "R" he wrote the letter "P" (which represented Palermo Sicily) and his mistake went unnoticed. So the agreement was made, with Rosie saving her half of the ticket. When the gangster left, Luigi was too tired to scold Rosie for her bad manners. She was such a problem child he didn't know what to do with her. Rosie was headstrong and one of the brightest of his kids. He knew she was sickly and over-emotional and he often worried about her because Rosie was no longer the baby of the family and didn't receive all the attention she wanted. A few years after her birth, another child was born, another girl who they named Felippa but nicknamed Fannie. This last child, unlike Rosie, was a big fat healthy baby with a sunny disposition. Since Rosie was a few years older, she already dominated Fannie as she tried to dominate her older brothers, and usually got away with it.

Luigi finally dismissed his worries about her and tended to his nightly chore of carefully tying up his long moustache behind his ears. He then put on his nightcap to retire.

"That quarter was a lot of money," he pondered out loud. '*Well, maybe she was right about her hunch,*' he thought as he pulled up the covers and drifted off to sleep.

"PAPA, WE WON, WE WON! MAMA WE WON, WE WON!" Rosie screamed. Luigi and Giroloma woke up with a start.

"What'sa the matter, what's going on?" Luigi said.

"My poor child Rosie, she has to be cracking up again!" Giroloma cried. They got up and went into the bedroom where Rosie slept. "She's having a nightmare," Giroloma sobbed.

"NO, NO, MAMA, WE WON; WE WON THE LOTTERY; NOW WE CAN PAY THE RENT! NOW WE CAN EAT GOOD FOOD! NOW LOUIE CAN MARRY THAT NICE POLISH GIRL AND WE CAN HAVE A BIG WEDDING! PROMISE ME; PROMISE ME THAT YOU WILL BUY ME A

NEW RED SNOWSUIT WITH LEGGINGS AND FANNIE A BLUE SNOWSUIT TOO!

"Okay I promise," Giroloma replied. "Now come to bed with Papa and me and go to sleep." Giroloma tucked Rosie into bed between her and Luigi, then Rosie immediately seemed to fall into a deep sleep. Giroloma hugged Rosie close to her and made the sign of the cross.

"Oh, dear God, my little girl has had too much hardship, so please don't let her lose her mind again." She hugged her child next to her, as if to protect her from all the ugliness that her little life was forced to endure.

Rosie had completed her marketing and was making the long walk back. Her little arms were tired carrying the two large bags of groceries. She was about to put them down and take a rest when suddenly she saw her four brothers coming down the street.

"Hey, Rosie!" they yelled.

Now they were coming closer, closing in on her, and Rosie panicked.

Ah, oh, what have I done now? She wondered. I haven't stolen anymore lipstick from the dime store lately. I hope that they haven't found out I smoked that cigarette the other day. Or was it that kid I beat up? Ah, oh, I can't remember, but I'm in big trouble. She remembered the last time she got spanked by her big brother Jimmy, and with that horrible thought, she dropped her bags and took off running.

If I can make it to the roof tops they can't catch me, she thought, but it took no time before they grabbed her. Her little skinny legs were no match for all her strong brothers.

Jimmy swung her up in the air and placed her on his shoulders. "We won the lottery, thanks to you, you little devil." They were all cheering her.

"Can you believe it? Our little Rosie picked the right numbers? Our little Rosie, the smartest one in our family, has made us rich. We won six hundred dollars!" The boys were hugging her and cheering her. Rosie never got this kind of attention and she glorified in the wonderful moment. Her eyes sparkled and she grinned. She was so happy; her otherwise thin, peaked little face actually looked full with the big smile and radiance that glowed from within. The boys carried her all the way home, cheering her all the way. Sally picked up her grocery bags; he didn't want her to lose her two cents even if they were rich. Rosie waved to all the street people as they passed.

When they reached the door of the tenement house, all the people were cheering her. The news had traveled fast. When the door opened to their apartment Rosie had a broad smile ready for the big rush of cheers she was expecting from her parents. Instead, to her disappointment, there was her mother sitting there with her big white handkerchief sobbing. Rosie immediately rushed over to her side and asked, "Mama, why are yuh crying? We have money now, we are rich!"

"*Oh madre, mia*," Giroloma tearfully replied, "I am crying because I am so happy!

I should have believed your dream. You have something special, a gift just like my mother has. I should have realized your powers, my special little Rose."

Then Rosie looked around the kitchen table and realized they had company. She recognized Degerio the gangster, but there were other men she did not know. Suddenly she was very frightened; in her imagination she thought that they were going to trick her. She knew they wanted her ticket.

"Come on now give me the lotto ticket, little girl," said Degerio in a low voice. She didn't like the expression on his face and she was filled with distrust. His small dark eyes were calculating. They had no emotion except a cruelty that knew no conscience. They stared out of a hairy lumpy, doughy face, a face that was slowly turning pink. This time he spoke again in a much louder voice. "Give me the ticket, child." Rosie stood frozen, as she could not find her voice. She knew his man was evil. Suddenly he rushed over to her within inches of her face. His voice was much louder and raspier this time. His voice had a strange choking sound, brought on by his anger. Rosie got a blast of his foul breath, which smelled like a combination of garlic and tobacco. She still stood frozen, unable to find her voice, then she heard voices coming from all around her.

"What the matter with the *beechadeeda*? Is she *potso* (crazy)?" Everyone seemed to start yelling at once.

"Grab hah and get the ticket." Before she knew it she was being whisked high in big muscular arms. "Give me the ticket!" Degerio yelled, and her teeth rattled as she was being shaken. She felt dizzy as the room spun around her.

"Stop that! You can't treat our child like that!" she heard Mama's angry voice. "Put her down!"

Rosie felt herself being lowered, then lying on the floor, she regained some of her wit. Her mouth opened and out came a loud cry of "No-o-o-o!" Then she jumped to her feet and ran, as fast as a rabbit, out of the room and down the hall. Mercifully, the bathroom door was open. She heard them running after her, the scuffling of many feet, and slammed the bathroom door just in the nick of time. She could hear the pounding on the door.

"You crazy girl, what's the matter with you?" Then she heard, "Open up!"

Rosie was out of breath, panting and holding onto the wall for support, but after a few seconds she regained her composure and yelled, "You give me your part of the ticket first. Give it to Jimmy and I'll let him in here to get mine."

It wasn't long before Jimmy was at the door, and he was exasperated with her dramatic imagination. "I've got their half of the ticket, sis, so open up."

Rosie knew she could trust her brother Jimmy to handle things from then on. "Jimmy, will yuh be the one to redeem the ticket?" she yelled.

Jimmy laughed. "Little Rosie, you know you can trust me. Nobody's going to swindle me!"

Rosie felt reassured. "Give me a minute and I'll open the door!" she yelled. Rosie pulled down her bloomers and grabbed the ticket. She had it hid in her bloomers where she felt it would be safe.

True to her word, Giroloma kept her promise to Rosie, and all of Rosie's predictions came true. Rosie remembered the gala atmosphere of the entire tenement house. She could smell the delicious aroma of food cooking as Giroloma and her older daughter bustled around the kitchen. The kitchen table was set with trays of fresh fruit and nuts, trays of Italian cookies, even cannolis and assortments of fig cookies and fancy candies. Rosie walked around smelling all the wondrous aromas and she had to pinch herself twice to make sure this was really happening. Mama also was smiling, a rare occurrence.

"Did you pay the rent?" she asked.

"Yes, three months in advance," answered Rosie proudly. Giroloma's cheeks were rosy from the heat in the kitchen. She chose to ignore the pain in her body. She was so determined to make this day a happy occasion. God knew how much her family had suffered and they deserved a day of happiness.

Friends and relatives came to help with the cooking, so she was advised to sit down, where she occupied a chair and started with supervising the kitchen, making sure the food was prepared to her liking. Feeling extravagant, she had sent the kids to the bakery next door for all the sweets. She was too happy to be tired. When she smiled, it brought her back to when days were good. She really had a good sense of humor and a hearty laugh. It surprised her when she heard the sound of her own laughter.

Rosie peeked into the kitchen again, and saw enough food for an army. She could smell the sweet spicy aroma; a blend of spices consisting of sweet basil, oregano and garlic, coming from the pasta sauce that was cooking in a large pot. She saw all the platters full of chicken, vegetables, olives, breads that filled all the space in the tiny kitchen. Her Sister Marian was singing, and Giroloma was laughing; happiness was everywhere!

"Mama, there is so much food. We can't eat all this."

Giroloma laughed such a wondrous sound to hear. "Rosie, we are fortunate, but others around us are not, so we are going to share our food with our neighbors and have a big celebration today."

Soon neighbors were at the door; they could smell the aroma of all the food throughout the whole tenement house. Giroloma already knew that they would be there, with a small excuse and hopes of being invited to eat. Giroloma had a big heart, and to everyone who came to the door, she would happily announce, *"Venica casa; settee, manga, manga* (Welcome to my house; sit down and eat, eat)." She knew that during this Depression people had very little to eat, and it didn't take long before the house was filled with hungry laughing people. Luigi had the homemade wine and was filling everyone's glass.

"Salute to our good fortune," he said. "Now we maka a salute to my little Rosie ana Sally, who maka all this possible," he added. "You see, Rosie had the right numbers, but ifa it wasn't for Sally picking the letter 'P' for Palermo, instead of 'R' for Rome, we woulda never won. So he deserves justa much credit asa Rosie" Everyone raised their glass and smiled at Rosie and Sally. Rosie's big round eyes sparkled, as she never got this much attention in her whole life.

Everything was happening just the way Rosie had prophesized in her dream. Louie was telling Giroloma about the wonderful girl he had recently been courting:

"Mama, she's beautiful: gold blond hair and light blue eyes. She has a figure like a movie star. The most important thing is her personality; she is an angel! I am in love and I want to marry her. I just know she is the right woman for me. I have never known anyone like her, or felt this way about a woman before."

Giroloma looked into the clear blue eyes of her third son, who was a good boy. He had a good job and was staying away from the underworld. Louie had his father's good looks, except he was finer-featured and had a more rounded shape to his face. In fact, he could be called a baby-face. He had a strong resemblance to Rocco, the oldest son, except

Rocco was more muscular and had a rougher edge to his features. Louie liked the finer things in life, such as going to shows, refined restaurants and ballroom dancing. Louie had class and he always said and did the appropriate thing for the occasion. He also had a detached smoothness about him that was so different from his brothers. Giroloma knew by instinct that she would never again have to worry about him. She was secretly glad that he wanted to settle down.

"There is just one thing, Mama; this girl is not Italian, she is Polish."

Marrying into a different nationality was not easily accepted at those times, and Giroloma was shocked for a few minutes, trying to find her true emotions on this subject.

"You are sure she is a decent girl, Louie?" she asked.

"Yes, Mama, she is all I'll ever want, and we want to marry right away."

"Then you have my blessings. You bring her over to meet our family and we will make special arrangements for the wedding. Since we are different nationalities, we must discuss how we can include our traditional customs, so both sides can be happy!" Giroloma said, smiling.

The wedding day had finally approached. Giroloma was getting ready for the happy event smoothing out her dress. She always wore long black dresses. The one she had on was a newer one that wasn't so worn. She looked in the mirror and was depressed by the malformed sight she saw. Both of her breasts had been removed because of her cancer, and she was still getting worse, so it was hard to hide the pain from her children and husband. She didn't want them worrying about her. Life was hard enough without that added worry. She was determined to live as long as she possibly could to raise her children. Sometimes she hardly got though the day because of her pain and discomfort but each day was another day to be with her family and she got though it by sure grit and determination. Still the sight that looked back at her from the mirror was shocking. Tears started to form in her eyes when she examined the area where her breasts used to be.

Rosie, who was always inclined to read her thoughts, sensed her unhappiness. "Mama, don't worry; me and Fannie can fix yuh up like we always do." With that thought in mind, Rosie ran to the bathroom to get tissue paper. Fannie was in the bathroom and knew immediately what Rosie was doing. They had helped Mama so many times with this problem.

"I'll help, too," Fannie offered. Soon Rosie and Fannie were padding Giroloma's breasts with the tissue paper.

"See, Mama, look how nice you look now," Rosie praised, as Fannie climbed up on her lap. Rosie resented it when Fannie got attention from Mama or any other kid for that matter. Rosie felt that she always had to fight the other kids to sit on her lap. On rare occasions, when she had Mama all to herself, she felt loved. Giroloma had so many children who needed her attention and she had so many chores to do. It was hard to give all the attention that Rosie seemed to need. Giroloma's mind was tired, tired of worrying about everything. She knew she was sick and didn't have long to live.

Everyone was excited as they left for the church. It was a beautiful day, Saint Valentine's Day. A perfect day for two people who loved each other to take their vows. Celia was a beautiful bride; she had a satin wedding dress that accentuated her curvy figure. The reception was at a hall and the food was catered. Rosie and Fannie had managed to get new dresses, which their sister Marian had made. This was one of Rosie's happiest days. The sun was shining through the high arched windows of the church, reflecting a steady stream of light over Celia and Louie as they said their vows. '*A marriage made in heaven*,' Rosie thought.

When they got to the hall, everyone was in a gala mood. The only thing strange was the people. All of the Polish people sat on one side of the room and all of the Italian people sat on the other side of the room. The music started the traditional Italian wedding march, and then continued on with Italian folk songs. Everyone there was dancing. Rosie and Fannie made a good couple. Even Giroloma and Luigi were dancing. Pretty soon the band changed players and some strange music started. It was a polka sung in Polish. It really didn't matter, though; the tune was catching on and soon the Italians were dancing to it. Then the food was served on a long table. It was a strange combination of Italian food and Polish food. Rosie noticed that some of the Italians were eating the Polish food and some Polish people were eating the Italian food. It was strange, as this was a time of prejudice. If one ventured out of their area in New York, they could end up in China Town, or the Irish side, or Jewish Town, or Polish Town, so everyone mostly stayed in their own barrier—it was an unspoken law. Each barrier or section could only be just streets away, but everyone wanted to live within their own ethnic background. That's why it was so extraordinary for this wedding to take place. The Italians were called Wops, the Polish were called Pollock's, and the Jewish were called Jews.

The barriers were being broken when these two very different nationalities attempted to mingle with each other. Everyone there was in a gala mood, and nobody cared who you were. If people couldn't

117

understand each other, all they had to do was smile or laugh with each other; that was the international language. They all had something in common today and yet they all knew that tomorrow they would be back in their own section of town.

Rosie's next prediction was also coming true. Giroloma, never forgetting Rosie's dream, kept her promise to buy Rosie and Fannie new snowsuits. It was cold outside and Rosie's legs were getting tired.

They had walked all the way to Shanty Town, which was referred to as Jew Town, the center of marketing and trade. The Jewish merchants had shops, stands and carts for just about everything one needed.

When they finally found a stand where they were selling clothes, Rosie spotted a red snowsuit and tried it on. It was made to order. Rosie felt like a princess in it and twirled around and around. Then Fannie found a blue snowsuit. They were both very excited, giggling.

"How mucha for these snowsuits?" Giroloma asked in broken English.

"Six dollars each and that's a bargain," said the merchant. "These snowsuits are of the finest wool material and trimmed in real velvet," he added.

"Oh no, itsa too much money; I no can afford that," said Giroloma.

It was customary to haggle over the price with the Jewish merchants at times. The merchant would start with a much higher price than he knew he could get. The old expression "to Jew" must have gotten started in this manner. Giroloma and the merchant haggled back and forth for about ten minutes and Rosie finally could take no more. "Please, Mama, pay the man; we have money."

Giroloma shot Rosie a murderous look, and Rosie knew when Mama looked at her that way she had better behave or else. Giroloma never had to say a word, just give her that look.

"Now you go sit down on that bench," she said sternly, and Rosie obeyed. She took Fannie's hand and sat down.

Time went slowly and Rosie grew bored and started drifting off to sleep. Finally, after it seemed like hours, the transaction was done. "Come on, girls, we have the snowsuits!" yelled Giroloma. Rosie jumped up, startled, and was amazed to see it was already getting dark. She nudged Fannie, who was fast asleep, and excitement returned when Giroloma said, "I know you are cold, so you can wear them home if you want." Rosie and Fannie hurriedly dressed in their new snowsuits, and it was the first new clothing they could ever remember having. Rosie never felt so rich as she did in her little red snowsuit with leggings. The very long walk back home was a picturesque sight. Giroloma's tired painful steps with a tired little girl on each side.

Last but not least, Rosie's last prediction was beginning to happen: Giroloma was finally going to Dannemora State Prison to visit her oldest son Rocco, she was smiling because she could barely control her excitement as she prepared for the trip. Mama and Papa were going, but not any of the younger children, and poor Rosie couldn't understand why. She wanted to go more than anything.

"We can't afford to take all of you. Our money is running out, and we have to be careful with what we have left," explained Luigi.

While Giroloma was dressing she caught a reflection of herself in the mirror. As always this depressed her because she looked much older than her age of fifty. Her hair had turned all white and there were lines of suffering on her face. Her figure was gone, she remembered how beautiful she looked in her youth with a tiny twenty-inch waist line and long honey-colored hair that reached her waist. The most difficult part of looking at her body was the flat area on her chest where her ample breasts used to be. This observation brought tears to her eyes. Her cancer had taken its toll on her body and aged her beyond her years. Giroloma sat down on the bed and started to sob, not realizing that Rosie was in the room.

Rosie put her little arms around her and cheerfully said, "Mama, don't worry; me and Fannie can fix yuh up real nice

like we always do." Soon Rosie and Fannie were padding Giroloma's breasts with the tissue paper.

"See, Mama, look how nice you look now," Rosie praised.

Giroloma knew that she was dying and that this trip would be the last time she would probably see her son, but it was her little ones that worried her the most, her two little girls. How would they live without her? She made the sign of the cross." Oh, dear God, please, if you have to take me, please take my two little girls with me," she silently prayed.

Pretty soon they could hear Luigi's precise foot steps."

Are you ready, Giroloma?" he asked. "We don't want to miss the bus!" Luigi appeared, immaculately dressed in his best suit and hat that he reserved for special occasions.

All the children lined up to say goodbye, and they bent and kissed each one, giving last-minute instructions:

"Marian, please take good care of the girls," Giroloma said.

"Sally and Frankie, don't get into any trouble; Louie isa going to check on all of you later," Luigi warned.

Soon they were on the bus heading to Dannemora State Prison to see Rocco. It was lucky that he transferred from Sing Sing State Prison, which was further away. Giroloma's mood now changed to happiness, as the last prophecy from Rosie's dream was coming true.

"I'm going to see my son!" Giroloma's heart sang.

Chapter 6—THE ROTTEN CHICKEN

Giroloma looked around her kitchen. She had everything neat and orderly. Today was Thursday, not her day for washing. She looked at the pile of laundry that had accumulated since Monday, then she looked at the little neat bundle that she had agreed to wash for her sick neighbor, Maryetta. Giroloma, being a good-hearted person, had taken on this chore for a few dimes. Then she stuck her head out of the window and yelled in Italian, "Hey, Mama Russo, do you need the lines today?"

"No, I can wait until tomorrow; it looks like it might rain," replied Mama Russo.

'Co-operation is the way to manage your laundry,' Giroloma thought, as she pulled on the pulley that rotated the line, taking off the few clothes that remained.

"Mama, let me help you with the wash today," said Fannie, her youngest child.

Giroloma, grateful for some help even from Fannie, said, "Alright, honey, you can start by unwrapping this bundle." Fannie's chubby little fingers started to open the tightly wrapped bundle. Suddenly the force of the tightly wrapped bundle, once free, exploded open, exposing a huge pile. The force had knocked Fannie off her feet, making her lose her balance, and she tumbled on top of the enormous pile. Giroloma was angry that she had been tricked. She couldn't refuse because two dimes were all she had to buy food for supper.

"It's alright, Mama, I'll help you so you don't have to work so hard," Fannie offered. Giroloma looked at her baby, thankful that she had such a sweet child. At least God made this last child easier to raise with her sweet disposition. He must have realized when he gave her Sally and Rosie, he gave her a lot to contend with; those two were always getting into trouble.

"Fannie, let me look at your forehead," she said, and Fannie came closer for the inspection. Giroloma felt Fannie's forehead where two huge bumps had emerged. Giroloma began to feel her temper rise, remembering how Fannie got hurt the day before. Fannie was playing outside on the sidewalk when an older girl was doing some flips.

"I can teach yuh how to do this," remarked the girl. The girl took Fannie's arms and stood behind her to flip her. Instead, she pulled her upside down and deliberately cracked her head on the sidewalk. Giroloma heard her screaming and ran to see what the commotion was about. The girl's mother arrived at about the same time. The girl's mother saw Giroloma coming and started defending her daughter. Giroloma was like a mama bear with her cub; she back-handed the woman, knocking her down with a force. In her anger Giroloma yelled, "Let this be a warning...if your daughter ever hurts Fannie again, I'm coming after you!"

Giroloma's attention now turned to her wash, and she started filling the wash tub that sat in the kitchen corner. Fannie enthusiastically started to rub the clothes on the scrub-board using the bar of soap. Next Giroloma looked around her kitchen, which consisted of a sink, a few cupboards, and a long table surrounded by several mismatched chairs. It was time to think about what to cook for supper, so she took a brief survey of her food supply. Breakfast usually consisted of stale bread, which she could buy at the bakery for a few cents, and re-used coffee. The grounds were used several times over in order to stretch their use. Sometimes on rare occasions Luigi would bring home stale donuts. They were in the Depression and they had to stretch what food they had to feed seven hungry people. She had tried everything to be creative. Pasta was the main course. Every night it would be pasta with something, usually with some sort of vegetable that was starting to go bad that she had obtained from her brother's grocery store. She would cut the rotten parts off the vegetable and prepare the rest for their use. Today she was craving chicken. Not the kind of chicken soup she usually cooked, which consisted of chicken feet, heads, gizzards and, if they were lucky, liver. She would send Sally or one of the kids over to the chicken market, and there they would patiently wait for the discarded parts after the chicken was slaughtered. For a few pennies she could feed seven people with these precious chicken parts. First the heads would be tied with cheese cloth and boiled in the water for the flavor. The feet would be cleaned by burning them over a burner on the stove and then all the cheesy fatty tissue would be scraped off. Then they would be added to the soup along with the carefully washed gizzards and liver. The intestines would be split open and scrubbed in salt water, then wrapped in parsley and added to the soup. Adding some vegetables and pasta would complete the soup.

Today, though, she craved roasted chicken. Feeling extravagant, she remembered the two dimes that she was paid for Maryetta's wash, so she stuck her head out of the window and yelled, "Sally, Rosie!"

Rosie, hearing her yell, came running up the stairs. "What is it, Mama?" she responded.

"Go to the chicken market and buy us a nice big chicken," Giroloma instructed.

Rosie's large round eyes got even bigger in surprise. "Are we really going to have chicken to eat for dinner tonight?"

Giroloma walked over to the cupboard and took two dimes out of the sugar bowl. "Make sure you get a good chicken and don't get gypped."

After Rosie left, Giroloma looked over at the wash tub, where a few clothes were washed and rung out hanging on the side in a twisted ball. Fannie had tired of her play and had run off. Giroloma looked in dismay at the large heap of wash to be done. '*It can wait*,' she thought. Suddenly the pain was back. It was just a dull nagging hurt all morning. She tried to ignore it, concentrating on the work she had to do. Now, as a sharp reminder, it couldn't be ignored. She tried to suppress a scream, but failed, thankful that nobody was home to hear her.

Rosie skipped along to the corner of North Fifth and Roebling Street. She had another block to go. Even though she was starting to sweat in the hot day's sun, she was imagining how good that chicken was going to taste at dinner tonight. She could almost taste the tender chunks of white chicken. Her mouth was watering with the thought. Mama was an excellent cook; she made everything taste delicious, except pasta with broccoli. Papa would force her to eat it with the threat of his leather strap that was placed by his plate every night at supper. She shuttered, remembering how she would always gag swallowing it down and tasting the horrible, putrid taste. She felt the anger build up in her, thinking about the previous night. When she came into the house after playing, she knew Mama was cooking broccoli again by the evidence of broccoli sitting in the sink.

'Every Wednesday night is apparently broccoli night,' she thought, being a good detective. She wondered what Uncle John's family was having for supper tonight. Uncle John had a grocery store in the neighborhood. She laughed when she remembered when her younger sister Fannie stole an apple by sticking it in her underwear. When they were getting ready to leave the store Fannie was walking like a Chinaman taking small steps. Mama, growing impatient, yanked on her arm, causing the apple to roll out. Her underwear must have been too loose because the shiny red apple rolled onto the floor right from under her dress. Rosie laughed again as she thought of how funny Fannie looked with her face as red as that apple. Fannie was humiliated and started to cry very hard when Mama scolded her. Uncle John intervened, saying it was alright, and gave her a bag full of apples for all the children. Uncle John was kind, but he had four girls of his own so he couldn't afford to be too generous. *'That's it, Rosie thought, I'll go over to play with my cousin Justine today and hag around until dinner time and get invited for supper.'* Rosie remembered how smart she thought she was, until they were called in for supper. To her dismay, there on the table sat a huge bowl of pasta with broccoli, she realized that Uncle John was just as strict as Papa when she spied the leather strap lying right by his plate.

'I'll never go over their house for supper again.' she thought angrily. She remembered how she politely tried to get out of eating by making excuses

why she should be getting home. Uncle John would hear none of it as he served her a larger plate then the rest. "Your family already knows that you are here. Sally stopped in the store a few minutes ago. So eat up, we must be polite to out little guest," he said with an amused expression on his face.

At last the chicken market was in front of her; she had come to the corner of Fourth and Roebling Street. She then saw the large sign across the front of the building, which read, *Live Poultry*. As she entered the market she was overcome with the foul smell of a combination of wet feathers, rotten eggs and dead meat. She leaned over the counter for a few moments to recuperate from the horrible odor when a small man with shrewd beady eyes appeared.

"What'll it be, chicken or eggs?" he asked in his Jewish accent.

"Yes, sir, I would like the biggest chicken yuh have," said Rosie, proudly showing her two dimes.

"Well little girl, seems like your too high and mighty today for your regular request of chicken guts?" he chided.

"No, I want the whole chicken, and make sure it is the best one in the market," said Rosie, mustering up as much dignity as she could.

The man laughed and said, "I've got the perfect chicken for you."

Soon he was back with a large newspaper-wrapped bundle, so Rosie paid him and had skipped happily home, thinking of the good bargain she had transacted and how Mama would be so proud of her.

When Rosie got home she pasted a big smile on her face, anticipating the praise she would receive on her good bargain and proudly handed Giroloma the bundle. Giroloma unfolded the newspaper to get a look at the chicken.

"*Oh, Madre mia,* it's rotten!" she cried. "They sold you a rotten chicken. Go back to the market and tell the man to give you another one. We have no more money and we'll have nothing to eat tonight." Giroloma began to despair and started to sob into her handkerchief.

"Don't worry, Mama, I'll get another chicken or our money back!" A very angry and determined little girl left the house.

When Rosie was back in the chicken market she approached the man with the beady eyes. He was waiting on another customer and ignored her when she entered the market.

"Mister, yuh just sold me a rotten chicken," she loudly announced.

The beady eyed man was embarrassed in front of the other customer. He looked at the customer and said, "It must be a mistake," handing her the bundle.

"It's no mistake. If my mama says it's rotten, then it's rotten. Please give me another chicken, or my money back. My mama's sick with cancer and she's craving chicken. That was all the money we had and if yuh don't give me my money back, we won't have any supper," she rattled on.

The customer in the market was a lady who knew hard times, so she glared at the flustered chicken marketer and said, "You would stoop so low as to cheat a kid? Well, I won't do business with you," and she walked out of the store in a huff.

"Wait don't go...it's all a mistake!" he yelled after her, but it was too late. This little brat chased off his customer. Now he was really angry. His face was turning a bright pink.

"Let me see that chicken," he said angrily. Then he made a big pretense of inspecting the chicken, saying "There is nothing wrong with this chicken, now go home! Scram!"

"No, I won't go home until yuh give me another chicken," said Rosie stubbornly, folding her arms.

"I said to scram! Now get out of my market!"

"NO!" was Rosie's reply.

He looked at this grubby child and angrily thought, '*Another one of those dirty wops. They are taking over the neighborhood.*' He didn't want her hanging around, ruining his business. '*Well, I'll teach her to argue with me,*' he thought. "For the last time, SCRAM, YOU DIRTY LITTLE WOP!" he yelled.

"NO, NOT UNTIL I GET ANOTHER CHICKEN!" Rosie yelled back. The next thing she knew he grabbed her by her dress and marched her to the door and gave her a hard push with his shoe as kicked her in the buttocks. Soon Rosie and the chicken went flying out of the market and landed on the pavement in the street. Rosie was humiliated beyond despair. How could she tell Mama that they would have no chicken tonight? She picked up the now-disheveled chicken and slowly started home, rubbing her sore behind as she walked. Soon Rosie had reached the tenement house where she lived. She was still sobbing at the indignity of the chicken market man. She slowly sat on the stoop, wondering, '*How can I tell Mama? How can I bear to see the disappointment on her face?*' She began to cry, not knowing what other course to take. Pretty soon she saw her Brother Sally coming up the steps.

"Hey, sis, why are yuh crying?" he asked.

Rosie told the whole forlorn tale to her brother, and when she was finished with a final sob, she had all his sympathy.

"That dirty Jew kicked yuh in the ass! Why I oughta go down there with my whole gang and show him who he is messing with."

"No, it won't solve the problem; there must be a better way," Rosie reasoned.

Sally was a few years older than Rosie, but they had the same disposition. He was more than just a big brother. He was also her buddy. They were a team, both alike, partners in crime. Between the two of them they could outfox anyone in the neighborhood.

"We've gotta fix him," Sally repeatedly said.

All of a sudden Rosie jumped up as an idea struck her. "I know how to solve this," she said, immediately feeling better. Her spirits lifted because now she had a plan. "We will go to City Hall to the mayor and report that Jew."

"We'll need money for the subway," Sally said.

"Come on...I know where yuh hid your shoe shine money. It's under the carpet!" said Rosie triumphantly.

"Alright, I guess it's for a woithy cause," Sally said, a little disappointed. Sally went into the house to get his dime and off they went, carrying the rotten chicken in the hot summer sun.

New York was a complicated place to follow directions, even for an adult who knew his way around, so this trip for two young children was a highly complicated challenge. Sally and Rosie were finally on the right subway, but they couldn't understand why everyone was giving them strange looks and holding their noses. Then they heard some people gasping saying, "Pheew! Pheew!" Finally someone couldn't stand it anymore and piped up, asking, "What's that awful smell?"

Then it dawned on them what the awful smell was. It was the rotten chicken!" It was a hot day and that poor chicken was getting in an even worse state of decay, being dragged all over the city. Rosie and Sally looked at each other and tried to suppress a laugh. Just like the team they were, they chose to ignore the fact they indeed were the culprits with the bad smell. They looked around at people, indignant, as if to say, "I don't know anything about this bloody stinky mess I'm carrying around."

Finally they were off the subway, and after looking at the street signs, they found Fulton Street. They spotted the Kings County Court House, an oval shaped dome with a huge clock and flagpole with a long staircase of steps leading to the four columns that supported it. Next to it stood Borough Hall with its cupola. "That's the building we go into," said Sally.

Soon they were walking up the steep front steps of Borough Hall. When they entered the historical building they were facing a front desk marked Information Desk.

"Can we see the mayor?" asked the small blond boy. He was obviously the bravest of the two dirty kids carrying something smelly and putrid. The front desk lady, feeling appalled, answered, "The mayor is on the sixth floor but you can't see him." Then, "Hey, wait...you can't go up there!"

Rosie and Sally were already in the elevator and the door was closing, leaving a trail of something that looked like blood and feathers behind them. They weren't going to be stopped from seeing him, not after coming all this way. Inside the elevator they got the same reaction. That poor rotten chicken was really a soiled bloody mess, and by now, it reeked of the foulest odor imaginable. The people were gagging and holding their noses, saying, "Pheew! Pheew!" Finally, to the relief of the remaining people, they arrived on the sixth floor. Rosie and Sally got off, then entered the mayor's office suit.

"Can we see the mayor?" Rosie asked the receptionist. The lady looked shocked and then she suddenly started to realize that a foul odor was coming from something they were carrying. She was instantly nauseated and started gagging in her handkerchief. Rosie looked at the sign on the door. "James Walker, City Mayor," she read out loud. Before the receptionist had a chance to regain her composure, they were already in the office.

The mayor was a very big Englishman and considered a fair man to the people. He was, at the present time, trying to clean up the slums of Brooklyn. It must have been an extraordinary sight when he looked up from his papers to see these two funny-looking kids holding something bloody, but before he got a chance to react, he got a whiff of the foulest odor.

"Pew! Pheew! What's going on here? What are you kids doing here? And what is that awful smell?" he yelled. He immediately began opening all the windows in his office, not waiting for them to answer.

Rosie began to get afraid, as he was a very large man with an even larger voice. The long trip, the hunger pains she began to feel, and the whole ordeal had begun to take their toll. So she started to cry.

Then the mayor stared at them a few seconds, astonished at the strange sight before him. There stood a little boy and girl in tattered clothes looking forlorn, and the little girl's tears mixed with her dirt were making streaks down her cheeks. In her hair and on her clothes there appeared to be something fuzzy. On closer inspection, he realized it was feathers. Then he stared at the strange bundle that she was holding. It appeared to be bloody and loosely wrapped in some newspaper with something that resembled claws protruding from the unraveled section.

At first he tried to suppress a laugh, but found he couldn't control his outburst. It was the most comical sight he ever had seen, especially with that stinky thing they were carrying around. He was a jolly man and had a good sense of humor. He had a hearty belly laugh, and every time he would look at them he would burst out laughing again. Soon his laughter turned into chuckles, as he was wiping his eyes. Finally after several minutes, he regained his composure and asked, "Now do you mind telling me what in the hell is going on?"

Rosie started her sad tale.

"My mother, who's got cancer, sent me to the chicken market to buy a chicken. When I got home we found out the Jew sold me a rotten chicken. Mama told me to take it back and buy another chicken, because that was all the money we had and we would have nuttin' to eat for supper. I went back to the chicken market and asked for another chicken and the Jew refused. He then pushed me and kicked me in the ass, see," she said, and pointed to her behind, "right here! I couldn't make Mama cry again so we came here to report the rotten chicken to yuh."

The mayor was a kind-hearted man and it seemed like the saddest story he ever heard. "Where do you kids live?" he asked.

"On North Fifth and Roebling Street," Sally answered.

"What—you mean you kids came all the that way?" Now the mayor showed another emotion; he was angry. He picked up the phone and asked for the Department of Health.

"Give me the food commissioner, on the double." After the conversation, in which he told the food commissioner to accommodate him and check on a chicken market, he turned to the kids and said, "I'm going to take you kids home, but first we are going to the chicken market." Sally and Rosie were hesitant, and they looked at each other, both nervous.

"We don't know, sir.......yuh see, we are not allowed to ride in anyone's car. Our father would give us a beating," Sally said.

The mayor chuckled and said kindly, "Don't worry, kids, you are with the law when you ride with me." The mayor was impressed that these two little kids had more common sense, integrity and spunk then anyone he knew.

Rosie and Sally stared in awe at the shiny big expensive car. They had never ridden in a car in their entire lives. In the neighborhood where they came from, nobody had a car, except the gangsters. Cars belonged to rich people, and rich people didn't live in the slums. They climbed into the car and thoroughly enjoyed the ride. When they arrived at the chicken market, Rosie and Sally marched in a few steps ahead of the mayor.

"There he is, that Jew that sold me the rotten chicken!" Rosie announced.

The man's beady little eyes looked frightened at the two important men with Rosie. He recognized the one as the mayor, and it didn't take long to discover who the other man was. The food commissioner took out his badge and showed it to the marketer. Then he asked, "Are you the person who sold this little girl a chicken?" In his fright, all the marketer could do was nod.

"Well then, is this the rotten chicken?" The food commissioner opened the box that they had placed the chicken in for the trip. Again all the marketer could do was nod.

"Go in the back and pick out two of the finest chickens you have," the commissioner ordered. The nervous marketer hurried and soon was back with the chickens.

"Now wrap these chickens up for this little girl. By the way, I'm not only giving you a fine, but I'm also revoking your license. You are, as of now, out of business," said the commissioner, handing him some papers.

The mayor, who had remained silent, then spoke up and said, "If I ever hear of you striking another child, you will have me to contend with!"

When they got back in the car again, the mayor said, "When we take you kids home, I personally want to come in and meet your parents." Rosie and Sally glowed; it was their lucky day! As they neared their street, Sally recognized some of his friends and waved. Soon all the kids in the neighborhood were chasing the car. "Hi, Jacky; Hi, Merc; Hi, Connie!" Rosie and Sally yelled as they waved to all the kids. They felt like celebrities, riding in the big expensive car with the mayor. They were the talk of the neighborhood.

"Did yuh see that big limousine?" said one kid.

"They're riding with the mayor!" said another kid. Sally and Rosie had to push through the crowd of people that had gathered by the sidewalks and stoops, who had come to see the event.

Finally the mayor stood at the door of the tenement apartment with the two dirty, tired and now conceited little kids. When Luigi opened the door he was surprised to see his long-sought-after children. Luigi noticed the two important men standing with his children, and a look of surprise came over his face when he recognized the mayor. As they entered the tenement apartment, the mayor shook Luigi's hand and said, "I came all this way here to congratulate you on having two of the most brilliant children I have ever met. They saw a wrong and went to justice to rectify it. I hope that they will go far in this world."

Luigi very quickly translated the entire message to Giroloma in rapid Italian. Giroloma's eyes brightened, as she smiled at her children.

After they left, Rosie and Sally were celebrities again. Giroloma and Luigi were filled with happiness and smiled with pride at their two brilliant children.

Much later, the table was set with two large, plump, roasted chickens as their centerpiece. Giroloma called everyone to sit down and "*mangia*." After saying a long prayer and thanking God for sending them these two brilliant children, the Finazzo family had their chicken dinner after all, and everyone agreed it was the best chicken they ever ate!

Chapter 7—THE SHOESHINE BOY

"Come get yah shoes shined, five cents a shine!" yelled Sally. He had been yelling for twenty minutes, and still no business. '*Aw the hell with it*,' he thought, but just as he started gathering his supplies, a well-dressed man approached him.

"Hi, kid, how's business?" It was Pete Palazzolo, better known as Crazy Pete. He was a racketeer who worked for the bosses at the bakery.

"Business ain't so hot today; that little punk across the street stole my customers, and I'm gonna shut his big mouth!" Sally exclaimed, as he doubled up his fists. "He's gonna havta learn he can't invade my territory. Maybe dey didn't teach him about street etiquette over on Thoid Street."

"Yuh sure remind me of yuh brudder Rocco, splitting image of him, and yuh got guts like him. I like that. Keep up the good work, kid. Someday soon yuh might work for me," Pete laughed, his grin exposing the gap between his teeth.

After Sally had finished shining his shoes, Pete dropped him fifty cents. "Maybe this will make up for a slow day," he said as he strolled by.

As soon as he left, Sally went charging across the street. "Hey, yuh little punk, come ova here—I got something for yuh." The wide-eyed kid didn't know what hit him. Sally threw him with one punch. "Yuh gotta understand who the boss of this neighborhood is, see?

Yuh only work where I tells yuh, understand?" The kid nodded his head nervously.

"I'm gonna let yuh off easy this time, so just say yuh worked for me today, got it? Now hand over the loot and make it snappy; I got tings to do." The kid reached into his pocket and handed Sally twenty-five cents.

"Here's a nickel back. Tanks for the money; yuh catch on fast," Sally remarked.

Sally picked up his shoeshine box and headed home. He was laughing to himself. He had seen the kid earlier set up on his corner. The kid thought he could pull something over on him by cutting into his territory. His first inclination was to run over there and punch him out, but on second thought, he decided to let him work all day and then grab his money, a more profitable plan.

Pretty soon Sally was in front of his tenement house, and the familiar faces were all there playing. Rosie and Fannie were playing kickball, two older ladies were sitting on the stoop exchanging the day's gossip, and a woman with a baby carriage strolled past him with an ugly bawling baby.

"Hey Sally, over here!" yelled Racketeer Merc. His last name was Mercantelli, so the nickname stuck. Most kids on the block had a nickname, and usually it had something to do with his appearance or family.

Sally spotted a group of his friends standing on the corner across the street. "What have yuh been doing all day?" he asked. "Aw nuttin, just hangin' around," said Sonny, stuffing his chubby hands into his pants. He was a short chubby kid with a bad case of asthma.

"Let's take the long a walk over to my dad's poolroom; if there's an empty pool table maybe he'll let us shoot a game of pool," said Sonny.

The group of boys started walking down the street, a strange-looking group of all different sizes, from Racketeer Merc, who was tall and thin, to Sonny, who was short and chubby.

Just then a drunk, who was stumbling around between two buildings, yelled out. "Hey, you little thieving bastards, you want my money, do you?" He had a thick Irish drawl.

Sally recognized the man from the day before, showing off a handful of bills. "What's the hells the matter with him?" Sally asked.

"I tink he's crazy. Someone stole money off him yesterday and now he's tinking we did it," said Spike, the youngest one in the group.

"Oh yeah, well, let's have some fun," said Sally.

"Come on, boys, take my money. Here it is right in my hand," said the old drunk. He was trying to entice them so he could grab one of them and work him over.

"Hey, yuh old drunk, yuh got a score to settle with us?" Sally yelled.

"Come over here, you dirty little punks, and I'll teach you a lesson or two!" The drunk took the money he was waving around and put it into his coat pocket.

"Hey, yuh old fart, I'm coming over a punch yuh out, so get ready," Sally warned.

"Your really goin' ta be sorry, yuh wise crackin' little bastard!" countered the drunk, squinting one eye. The drunk was really angry now, so he yanked off his coat, threw it down on the ground, and started swinging his fists.

"I gotta plan; I'm gonna fight with him and you, Sonny, grab his coat when I say, 'Bananas,' " Sally instructed.

The group of boys then moved swiftly, running across the street. Sally, in the lead, approached the drunk and started dancing around him like a boxer. The drunk tried swinging at him, but kept missing. Sally kept dancing around him and ducking to his clumsy swings. Then he yelled, "Bananas!"

Sonny quickly grabbed the drunk's coat and hurriedly emptied out the front pocket where he stuffed his money. He then threw the coat in the drunk's face. The drunk lost his balance and tumbled over some garbage cans, making a clinging noise. By the time the drunk recovered from his fall, Sally and his gang were running across the street. They ran back to their tenement house and down the flight of stairs to the cellar. The drunk had given up the chase by the time they crossed the street; they were too fast for him. "I'll get you, you little wops!" he yelled.

"I hope no one sawr us," gasped Sonny, short-winded.

The boys lay on the dirt floor panting. Finally when they recuperated, Sally laughed and said,

"Let's count the loot." Merc counted the money and they had seventeen one dollar bills.

"What'll we do with it?" asked Spike, snapping his gum. Spike was the smallest one in the group, as he was about two years younger than the rest of the boys, with a pugged nose that always seemed to be snotty and a mouth full of chewing gum. His wide blue eyes showed excitement, looking at all the money.

"We gotta figure out how to divide it," said cock-eyed Jerry. One of his eyes was looking at the money, but the other eye was staring someplace else. His crossed eyes never seemed to focus on any particular person or thing.

"I tink we should save most of it and then later, when we need it, we'll always have some money," said Racketeer Merc.

"I know we gotta trust each other, so let's form a gang and take a blood oath," Sally suggested.

"Yeah, great idear," Racketeer Merc agreed.

"Everyone agreed, say aye."

"Aye," came the unanimous vote.

"Now we gotta become blood brudders," said Sally, pulling out his jackknife. "We'll all take a cut from our little finger like just dis," he continued, demonstrating by cutting his finger. "Now we pass the knife around and everyone takes a cut." The knife was passed, and everyone cut their finger grimacing at the pain. When it came Spike's turn he paled a little, trying hard not to show his fright at the sight of blood. Spike was always trying hard to keep up with the other boys. He earned their respect by being tough for a ten-year-old.

"Let's put our fingers together and say from this day forward we are blood brudders. We promise to stick together, and never cheat or rat on each other." The five boys put their fingers together, all looking solemn, each repeating his vow.

"Now that we're blood brudders, this here is gonna be our official club house, and our official password is gonna be 'Bananas,' " said Sally.

"I suggest that we hide our money and once a week take out a quarter each," said Merc. "We gotta figure out how to hide this money. Let's look around for something to put the money in," he added.

Everyone started looking in the dirt, and finally Spike found an old jar.Holding up the jar, he said, "Here's something we can use."

"Yeah, that'll work; we can bury it in the dirt, but first we take out a dollar each," said Sally.

"Now can I make a suggestion that we go to the movies tommara," Merc offered.

"Yeah, good idear, and we'll still have enough left over for a soda and goodies." Everyone agreed. Having formed their gang and hid the money, they all started laughing.

"We're rich!" yelled Spike, popping his gum.

"We gotta remember, whenever we have money it goes in the jar. Also, I'm the oldest, so I should be leader," said Merc.

"Yeah, well I'm the toughest so I should be the leader," remarked Sally, putting up his fists.

"Yuh ain't even thoiteen yet; I'm foiteen and I have the most brains. Yuh can be second in charge, how's dat?"

"Yuh, okay, no big deal," said Sally.

"We oughta get outta here, as my old man's probably yelling for me," said Step-in-half Joe, his nickname stemming from the malformed leg that caused his limp.

"Yeah, good idear, let's go," Spike agreed. He was worried about his old man, especially if he was drunk. Spike took many beatings when his old man's temper was up.

They returned outside by the stoop when Sally heard the familiar whistle from Luigi, which meant it was supper time.

"Gotta go now, but let's meet at our club house at ten o'clock tommara morning," said Sally.

When Sally entered the kitchen he could see that Luigi was angry. "What for you no come straight home with your shoea shine money? You leava your shoe shine box outside for someone to steal. It's a lucky thing, Fannie bring it in," Luigi scolded.

"Sorry, Papa, I met my friends," Sally said.

"Bulla-shita, you friends a bunch of bums. I oughta smacka you face for playing when you supposed to be working. How mucha you make today?" asked Luigi. Sally usually held out some money for himself. But since he had made so much money today he decided to be generous, so he pulled out eighty-five cents and gave it all to Luigi. He knew how much the family depended on every little penny they could get to survive. "I had a good day, Papa," he proudly announced.

"You are a gooda boy to help your family out," said Luigi, his anger now gone. "I justa worry about you when you no come home on time."

"*Mangia*," Giroloma loudly announced. She was anxious to get everyone at the table while the food was still hot. She placed a huge bowl of pasta with broccoli on the table, and Sally's hunger suddenly vanished, as he detested broccoli. After the lengthy prayers were finally said, everybody hurriedly started passing the pasta bowl, filling their plates. After a day of practically nothing to eat, their appetites were enormous. He noticed Rosie, who was sitting next to him, and she was looking at her dish disgustedly. One thing they had in common was they both detested broccoli. Sally took a fork wrapped with pasta and was ready to eat until he spied the putrid little green bunches of broccoli, then he put his fork down, disgusted. He was unable to eat it. He looked up to see Papa eating with his strap next to his dish. He then had an idea.

He pointed out the window and said, "Hey, Rosie, look out there." Rosie looked out the window, trying to figure out what it was he wanted her to see, which gave him his awaited opportunity as he quickly emptied his pasta into her dish. When she looked back in her dish she discovered what he had done. A huge mound of pasta was sitting in her dish. Sally was amused by the look on her face so he started laughing.

"Yuh son of a bitch!" she screamed. POW! She socked him in the eye with such unexpected force he flew off his chair. The silence that was momentarily dominating the room suddenly erupted like a volcano. Everyone immediately started yelling—first at Rosie for swearing, then at Sally for emptying his pasta in her dish. The yelling continued, reaching a louder pitch until Luigi could stand it no more. He jumped up, knocking over his chair, and grabbed the strap. He rushed over to Rosie, grabbed her off her chair and gave her a couple of good whacks. He then grabbed for Sally, but Sally was too fast for him; he took off running out the door and he didn't stop until he reached the candy store. Once inside he spotted the soda fountain.

"Gimme an egg cream," he ordered, referring to a mixture of chocolate syrup, an egg, milk and seltzer.

The soda jerk eyed Sally and said, "Boy, that'sa big shiner yuh have there, kid," while he placed his drink in front of him. Sally made no comment; slurping his drink was his reply.

Then a strange man sat down next to him and said, "Hey, gimme a cherry Coke!"

The soda jerk, recognizing him, said, "Hi, Mack, what's new?" as he started preparing his Coke, first squirting the glass three-fourths full of seltzer, then three squirts of Coke syrup and then a squirt of cherry syrup. Handing him the Coke, he said, "Hey, did yuh hear about the raid? I guess there's a lot of counterfeit coins being passed around. I hear they make these outta lead milk cans. Well anyway, yuh remember Paul Denato? Well, he was in on it."

"Yeah, I read about that yesterday; I hear that the police are dumping all that stuff in the East River by the dock," Mack replied.

"Not only are they dumping the counterfeit money, but the whiskey they confiscate, too," said the soda jerk.

Sally's ears perked up. '*Tommara I will tell the gang*,' he thought. After he had finished his drink, he dropped a dime on the marble counter top. The soda jerk listened for the ringing noise that told him it was real. Sally decided to stop on his way out at the candy counter, and after much deliberation, he picked out five cents worth of penny candy. On his way home he chewed on his favorite candy, the black licorice sticks.

Once home Sally hoped he wasn't in trouble. He snuck into the kitchen real quietly, hoping no one was around, but there sat Giroloma on a chair, with a few towels tossed over her shoulders. When she saw him, she started scolding him in Italian: "Where did you go? You're lucky your Papa had to go to a meeting tonight. The next time you take off out of here like that, I'm going to give it to you good." Then calming down after saying her piece, she noticed his black eye. "Boy, Rosie gave it to you good tonight!" Sally was embarrassed; it was the first black eye he ever had, and to think, a skinny ten-year-old girl gave it to him. *'If this gets out I'll never live it down,'* he thought.

"It's bath night; now get your clothes off so you can wash," said Giroloma, interrupting his thoughts.

Every Saturday night Giroloma made all the kids bathe. She would call in all the girls first, then the boys. The tub in the kitchen served as a laundry tub and a bathtub. Giroloma started filling up the tub. Sally was twelve but looked much younger because he was so small and undernourished. She looked at his skinny chest. Whenever Giroloma had extra money she would take him to the soda fountain for a malt, instructing the soda jerk to add an egg in the mixture. Being healthy meant being fat, to her old country ways. Girolma left the room, letting him take his bath.

After his bath was finished came the long ordeal of combing his hair. First she would mix up a concoction of strong vinegar in a bowl and take a fine-toothed comb to comb out all the head lice. Contacting head lice was a common problem of everyone in the neighborhood. It was extremely contagious and no amount of treatment could completely rid anyone of them, because wherever they went, the lice would invade them again. Once prepared for the lengthily process she would sit him down between her legs and comb each strand of his white blond hair, examining the comb each time. If she found the eggs she would squash them with her fingertips. His head fixed in one position for long periods of time, he would stare at the long black skirt of her dress.

After this ordeal he would have to endure the torture of swallowing the concoction of Citrate of Magnesia. Besides the horrible taste, on which he would gag, the effect was a bad case of diarrhea. Giroloma believed that to stay healthy you needed to be cleaned out once a week. The rest of the night would be occupied by all the kids fighting over the pot.

The next morning Luigi brought some stale cinnamon rolls home from the bakery, as it was Sunday and he always tried to have something special if they could afford it. The kids were all excited it had been a long time since they had a sweet. Giroloma turned on the oven before she placed the rolls in to warm them. Everyone could hear the loud familiar popping noise. It sounded like popcorn, but was in actuality the cockroaches exploding as the oven heat killed them. Being infested with cockroaches was just another common problem in the neighborhood. Cleanliness had little to do with the infestation, as they multiplied by the millions in the walls, cracks and crevices of the old buildings in Brooklyn. After a few more minutes the popping stopped and Giroloma opened the oven to wipe out the dead cockroaches. When the oven was clean, she placed the rolls inside to warm.

"It's Sunday, so while the rolls are heating, I want everybody to quickly get dressed for church," she ordered, and Sally groaned. He would much rather be with his friends, but he knew that nothing short of dying would convince Mama to let him miss church. They were strict Catholics, and religion was a big part of their lives. After church it was customary to visit relatives. Besides church Sunday was considered visiting day. After church Sally knew that he would take off, but by the time he got to the clubhouse it was eleven o'clock.

"Hey, yah late. We've been waiting for yuh," grumbled Merc.

"Yeah, I forgot today is Sunday and I had to go to church," mumbled Sally.

"Yeah, I had to go to the early Mass," Sonny grumbled.

"Where'd yuh get that shiner?" inquired Merc. Sally's eye was black and blue, and he could barely see out of it because it was swollen shut.

"I had a fight with my big brudder," Sally replied. He didn't want to admit that his younger sister Rosie gave him his first black eye. '*I'm gonna stop teaching that little bitch how to fight*,' he thought.

"Well, what do yuh want to do today?" asked Spike as he was taking his gum out of his mouth to inspect it.

"I dunno, but I found out some news about the counterfeiting raid." Sally then excitedly told them the story he had heard the day before.

"We gotta go to the docks and hide when they dump the stuff," suggested Sonny.

"That's a bad idear. Stealing that money is a federal offense and we could get into big trouble," remarked Merc.

"Today let's go to Jew Town and rent bicycles. I gotta idear," said Merc.

Soon they were on their way to the Williamsburg Bridge. The bridge was often referred to as Jew

Bridge because it made it easy for the Jewish to migrate from Manhattan to Williamsburg, a growing Jewish community. The bridge had three sections: one was for large trucks, one for cars and one was a boardwalk that people used to walk or ride their bicycles. Sally and his gang were soon across the bridge, and were now in a nicer section of Delancy Street. The New Law walk-up apartments were in view, and they were staring at the fancy apartments when Merc said, "Let's go into the lobby." They all followed him inside, wondering what he was up to.

"Now what we've gotta do is take the names we see in each mailbox and apartment number. Let's see. I'm gonna be Albert Steinberg at apartment one-o-five. Now you guys pick a name and address." One by one, they all selected a name off one of the mail boxes and an apartment number.

"Now we gotta remember our new names and addresses," cautioned Merc.

Soon they were walking into the slums of Delancy Street, past the rows of wooden-framed tenement houses. The strange neighborhood smelled of garbage and litter. When they came to the corner they encountered a gang of Jewish boys who looked pretty tough.

"We ain't gonna waist time fighting these guys; we got business to do. Besides we voyaged into their turf; we could get killed," Merc added.

As they walked past the gang, they heard the remark, "Hey, go chase yuhselves; no assholes are allowed around here." That could have been an opening for an argument, but Sally's gang chose to ignore them.

The tough gang of boys weren't ready to let their victims pass. "Hey what's the matter with the little sissies? Are yuh afraid we'll beat the shit outa yuh?" challenged the biggest kid.

"Hey, dese are funny-looking kids. Look at the ears on the tall one; dis one's got gouch eyes. Dat one walks funny. What's a matter kid, you got fucked-up legs?" The gang was taunting them to encourage a fight. Just then the biggest kid grabbed Spike by the collar and lifted him up.

"Hey, we got little peewee here. Why ain't yuh home with yah Mama sucking tittie?" Suddenly he started punching Spike in the face. Sally swung at the biggest kid, knocking him off balance, then he came after Sally full force. He landed a punch, hitting Sally in the nose. Sally was then ducking his swings and dancing around him, then he got an opening and clipped him an upper cut, landing a powerful punch in the jaw. The kid stumbled and fell, but suddenly another kid came at Sally with a switchblade knife. A nearby cop was walking his beat when he heard the commotion of the boys yelling, and he blew his whistle. The Jewish gang took off running and Sally's gang took off running in the opposite direction. After running a few blocks they slowed down, realizing that they were no longer in pursuit. Merc looked at Spike, and his nose was bleeding.

"Here, kid, wipe your nose," he said, handing him a handkerchief. Spike had his sympathy because he always got the worst of things.

"Yuh always git picked on foist cuz you're the smallest; that gang had no balls," said Sally, wiping his own bloody nose. "The only way they can fight is with a knife."

After a short while they were in front of a used clothing shop.

"Now we are going to go in this here rag shop and buy us some coats," said Merc. Sally was wondering what Merc had up his sleeve, but knew it had to be something good. Merc always came up with genius ideas. Having bought the coats for a few pennies a piece, Merc said, "Put on the coats. We are going to the bike shop to rent bikes. "

Finally they reached Abe's Bike Shop on Grand Street, but before they entered the shop, Merc cautioned them, "Now yuh just listen to me and remember yah new names and addresses." They walked into the bike shop and started looking over the bikes. The smell of rubber, oil and cigar smoke filled the air.

"Can I help you boys?" the shop owner asked. He was squatting down, repairing a bike when they walked in, his wide lower lip expressing a smile.

"Yeah.......we wanna rent some bikes," Merc replied.

"Well, I'd be glad to, but you gotta put down a dollar deposit and the fee is fifty cents an hour," said Abe, anticipating the profit he was going to make.

Merc knew that he was asking an exorbitant amount of money; fifty cents an hour was way over the rate. "We don't have the deposit money with us right now our father said he would give us the money when we bring the bikes back," Merc explained.

"Where do you boys live?" asked Abe.

"Over in the New Law apartments on Delancy Street," Merc answered. Abe thought for a minute. That was a nice Jewish section of town.

"We could leave our coats as a deposit," said Merc.

"Aw no, that's a bad idear; my dad would wallop me if anything ever happened to my coat," Sally remarked, catching onto the scam.

Abe thought about the situation. They would have to come back for the coats, so how could he lose? "Alright," he said, "but you all must sign your names and addresses on this sheet and hang your coats up on this hook before I give you the bikes. "

Riding the bikes back to their side of town was fun, and they were laughing how easy it was as they were riding back over the bridge.

"Merc, you're a genius," said Sally.

"Well, we can have fun on these bikes for now, but we can't bring them home," said Merc.

"Why not?" Spike asked, disappointed.

"Because our parents would know that they were stolen, stupid. What we gotta do is sell them over at East River," Merc remarked.

Soon they arrived at the river and started shouting to the kids, "Bikes for sale." They soon drew a crowd of kids who wanted a bike. A freckle-faced kid was admiring the red one Sally had.

"How much for yours?" he asked Sally.

"Two bucks," Sally replied.

"Wow, I havta go get my father. Can yuh keep it for me until I get back?" he eagerly asked.

"Yeah, but yah gotta hurry, I can't keep it for long," replied Sally.

It wasn't long before all the bikes were sold, and afterwards Sally's gang went back to their club house to count their money.

"Wow, look we've got over twenty-one bucks, including our money from the drunk," said Sonny. "I say we celebrate and do something."

"Yeah, let's go to the soda shop and then maybe roller-skating," suggested Sally. After making their decision, they took out enough money to enjoy the rest of the day.

At the soda fountain they each had two banana splits.

The next day while Sally was in school, Luigi took Sally's shoeshine box down to his corner and set up the stand, yelling, "Getta you shoes shined, fiva cents!" It didn't take long before he had ten cents enough for a couple of rolls of cigarette paper. Next he walked down the street by the railroad tracks looking for stray cigarette butts. When he had accumulated a bag full he walked home. By the time he got home it was lunch time, and he could smell the delicious aroma of the escarole boiling as he walked in the door.

"Ah,scar*cola* with *bonutzo*," he said appreciably. It was one of his favorite meals.

"*Mangia*," said Giroloma, handing him a bowl of the green vegetable along with some bread and a bottle of olive oil. Everything Luigi did was done precisely and systematically. He poured just the right amount of the olive oil into the bowl and broke up his bread evenly, dipping it into the olive oil a precise number of times. After eating, he looked forward to the pleasant chore of making cigarettes. He laid all the butts on the table and started cutting off the ends. Then he took off the remaining paper. When he was though with that chore he had a large mound of tobacco. He then fluffed it up with his hands and started rolling his paper with a little cigarette machine. This was how he could afford to smoke. His next job was gathering all the shoes that had holes in the soles. Then he would stuff them with cardboard.

The boys had met in their clubhouse on Friday, ready for the weekend's adventures.

"Tomarra is our day to scare those stupid Jew kids," laughed Merc. They all started laughing at the thought. Every Saturday for the last month they had been going to Bridge Plaza Park, a prestigious Jewish area, and scaring the Jewish kids. On their first visit they picked on a pudgy little red-haired kid as their victim and beat the hell out of him, then all the other kids were afraid of them after that.

"If you kids want to play in this park it will cost yuh a nickel," Merc threatened, so every week they faithfully paid their nickels.

Merc started smoking a cigarette and offering everybody one. Sally and the rest of the boys smoked except for Sonny and Spike. Merc offered them a drag and they ended up coughing.

When they emerged from their clubhouse, Sally heard Papa's whistle. "I gotta go now; see yuh tommara."

Saturday was the appointed day for the welfare to visit, so Sally had to stick around until after ten o'clock. The social worker was at the door at ten o'clock right on time. Giroloma had the children lined up. Each child was cleaned up, with their wet hair combed into a severe style. Mrs. Williams was their new social worker. She was a stern, heavy-set woman who never smiled and seemed to have a distain for them in general. She carefully observed each child, calling their names. Giroloma had told Sally to ask for new shoes.

"We need new shoes, my mama asked me to tell yuh," he translated. Mrs. Williams didn't answer right away.

"As I call your name, I want each one of you to sit in a chair and lift your feet," she explained. As she called each child she examined their shoes.

"This one's shoes are still wearable, this one needs new shoes," she went on. Out of all the children, she only ordered two pairs of shoes. Luigi took out his pocket watch to check the time.

"Let me see that watch," she said. Luigi reluctantly handed her the watch. She inspected it, noting that it was gold.

"You must realize that you cannot own anything of value, so I'm sorry, but I must confiscate this," said Mrs. Williams. Luigi's face dropped. It was his only treasure.

"This here watch come from my dead brother; itsa family keepsake," he pleaded.

"I'm sorry, but if you want assistance you cannot have anything of value. Come to think of it, you're dressed in an expensive suit, Mister Finazzo .How do you explain this?" Luigi was shocked; he was fastidious about his attire. He always made sure his clothes were pressed and clean, even down to his shoes, which he always kept shined. He took pride in his appearance, especially his thick moustache, which was carefully trimmed and curled every day. His beautiful thick, wavy hair was always styled and brushed to match his perfect appearance. His friend, Joe the Barber, gave him free haircuts. Even his fingernails were clean and clipped to match his immaculate appearance.

"Justa because I am poor, itsa no excuse to be looking like a bum. I ama dressed uppa today because I wasa looking for a job. Ifa you think my suit looks like new than I'ma complimented." Luigi then opened his suit jacket to show her the lining, which was frayed and tattered beyond repair. He then lifted his foot to show her the soles of his highly polished shoes, which had holes filled in with cardboard.

"Thisa here is the only suit I own. I hava two pairs of worka pants and two shirts," said Luigi.

"I'm sorry, Mister Finazzo, but I still have to take your watch," she said before she left.

It was time for Sally to meet his gang. As he started out the door Giroloma stopped him and warned, "You be sure to be home early, as today is Papa's birthday."

Sally, feeling depressed about Luigi losing his watch, said, "Mama, I'm going to work real hard so I can buy a boirthday cake for Papa. Don't start any party without me." Giroloma smiled and nodded; sometimes Sally really surprised her.

When Sally met his gang at their clubhouse he was in a bad mood, still thinking about the watch. He lit up a cigarette and was puffing angrily.

"Hey, Sally why the puss?" asked Sonny.

"Aw nuttin. Are we still going to Bridge Plaza Park?" he asked, changing the subject.

"Yuh, we're all here, I hope we get the chance to work over some Jew kids today," came the reply.

They took the long walk to the park, Step-in-a-half Joe limping behind with Spike. When they got to the park they spotted the same dumb-looking pudgy kid playing along with the familiar faces of about thirty kids. It was a beautiful day, a perfect day to be in the park. They noticed the kids already had started a game of softball.

"Hey, fatso, yuh got our five cents?" Sally demanded from his prime victim.

"Yeah, err ahh," the pudgy kid stuttered, then suddenly out of the bushes emerged about ten men. They were their fathers. They started yelling and coming after them.

"Hey, you dirty little wops, I'm going to beat the shit out of you!" one yelled. "Go back to the gutter where you come from!"

"Bananas!" Sally yelled. Everyone got away except Sonny and Step-in-a-half Joe. Sonny was getting slapped in the face by this huge red-faced man, before he decided to bite his hand, and the man yelled, "Ouch, you little son-of-a-bitch!"

Sonny finally wiggled out of the man's grasp and took off running, but poor Step-in-a-half Joe was getting walloped. Finally, with his good leg, he managed to give a swift kick between the legs of his captor, and the man bent over in pain, giving him his chance to get away. They soon caught up with the rest of the gang, and they never stopped running until they reached the subway train and jumped in.

"Wow, that was close," Sonny wheezed, trying to catch his breath.

"Are yuh guys alright?" Sally asked Sonny and Step-in-a-half Joe.

"I guess we can't win them all," said Merc.

"Yeah, this was the only time that I didn't get walloped," piped up Spike. Everyone looked at Spike and started laughing when they realized that Spike had been forgotten in their haste to escape from the angry fathers.

"You're getting much smarter, yuh little gum-snapping knucklehead," Sally commented.

"Yeah, dem doirty Jews. Let's get off at the next stop while were still in Jew Town; I gotta plan," said Merc.

Soon they were in the business district, the main trade center, with the merchants selling everything from fruit and vegetables to furniture. Stopping at the storefront of a deli, Sally's mouth watered at the delicious aroma of garlic and baked goods.

"I tink we should rest awhile and eat." Sally had nothing to eat at home that day. All they had was reused coffee so weak it was almost clear and some stale bread that he felt guilty to eat when he saw Rosie and Fannie eyeing it. He knew he could always eat something when he was on the streets. He hated being hungry and having to watch his little sisters starve. He hated going to bed hungry and not being able to sleep because of the hunger pains. At least hanging around with his gang he could make enough money to eat, but he wished he could master mind a plan where he could give his family more money without raising their suspicions. Well, he would think of a way.

"Hey, Sally what do yuh want to eat?" asked Merc.

"I dunno yet, let's go inside the deli for some sandwiches."

Inside the deli, the slanted display of every kind of lunchmeat was displayed, including hard salami, chicken salami, corned beef, roast beef, bologna and cow's tongue. A large sign read, *A nickel a shtickl*. This was called *knubivoorsht*, another word for garlic wurst. The aroma was making Sally's stomach grumble. Sally ordered a corned beef on rye sandwich, a cherry soda, and in the bakery section a large slice of cheesecake covered with plump red cherries. He carried his food over to the wooden serving bar to eat. The rest of the boys selected their sandwiches and stood over by Sally.

"Where'll we go from here?" asked Sonny. His mouth was full of food, some of it falling out as he talked.

"Look at yuh, I tink yuh was born a pig?" remarked Merc.

"Yuh want me to be the decoy again, Merc?" Sally asked.

"Yeah, yuh do a good job at distracting Moe."

As soon as they were done eating they were headed toward the area of the push carts. Each Jewish merchant had his stand with fresh vegetables and fruit, carefully cleaned and displayed. Sally and his gang had tagged every Jewish merchant by the name of Moe.

Merc spied the cash box that was filled with money on top of the cart of one of the merchants and he said, "Yuh know what to do, Sally," and he pointed to the victim. "When I yell 'Bananas,' yuh drop the orange."

Sally strode up to the merchant and said, "Hi Moe, mind if I take an orange?"

The merchant was annoyed and yelled, "Get outta here, kid! Scram!"

"Aw, yuh won't miss just one orange...come on, I'm hungry. Come on, just one orange," Sally begged.

"No, get the hell outta here," said the merchant, then Sally heard the password, "Bananas," so he grabbed the orange and rolled it under the cart.

"Aw gee, Moe, I'm sorry; it slipped," he lied.

"You're damaging my fruit, now get outta here!" the merchant yelled, as he crawled under the cart to recover the orange. Merc quickly ran over and grabbed the cash box, then they ran until their lungs hurt.

"I can't run no further," moaned Sonny, wheezing.

"Let's ride the subway...we could use the rest," suggested Sally, noticing that Step-in-a-half-Joe's limp was much worse.

Back at their clubhouse, Merc was counting the money. "Thoity bucks! We did really good today," he said.

Sally lit a cigarette, took a long drag and said," I gotta get my Pa a watch; he lost his today and it's his boirthday, so do you fellas mind if I take my cut now?"

"Naw, I don't mind; does anybody have any objections?" Merc asked around. "Tell yuh what, we will all take out five bucks apiece, that's what we made today, and do with it what we want." Everyone agreed and the money was divided. Sally soon left his gang to search for a pawn shop. He walked several blocks until he spotted a sign that read, *'Henry's Pawn Shop: We buy, sell, and trade anything of value.'*

Sally walked into the shop, and he noticed the musty odor of leather mingled with dust and stale air. The store shelves were piled high with old radios, phonographs, records, musical instruments, suitcases and miscellaneous merchandise. In one corner of the shop hung fur coats and clothes. A massive wooden showcase enclosed a large variety of jewelry, from necklaces to cuff links. Looking very closely, Sally discovered the display of pocket watches.

The merchant, a short husky man with a toupee parted in the middle, asked him, "Anything I can do for you, kid?"

"Yeah, I wanna see your pocket watches. It's for my Pa; today is his birthday."

The merchant lifted the box containing several pocket watches. "How much do yuh want to spend?" he asked.

"Two bucks," answered Sally, looking over the watches. "And I want one that works and is genuine foiteen karat gold."

"Not for two bucks," laughed the merchant, "but I got this one I'll sell yuh for five bucks: it's foiteen karat gold and keeps poifect time."

Sally looked at the watch. It was impressive, and the gold glimmered in the half-lit room. He admired the scrolls of fancy engraving on the cover, which flipped open easily. "Does it keep poifect time?" he asked.

"I'll even guarantee it and put it in writing for yuh. This watch is like new," said the merchant.

"I'll buy it, but I only got tree bucks."

The merchant looked doubtful, scratched his toupee and said, "Tree dollars and fifty cents is the least I can take. Yuh got a real bargain here; yuh don't find a better price anywhere."

"Alright, I guess I'll take it," said Sally, hiding his excitement.

"I'll find a real nice box to put it in," said the merchant, happy to make a sale. He knew he could have gotten more for it but business was slow and he liked the kid.

After the transaction was completed, Sally left the shop and walked back toward his house, happy with his bargain. He then walked into the bakery and greeted the baker with, "Hi Nick, tonight's my Pa's boirthday and I want a nice birthday cake and a gallon of ice cream."

"I have a nice cake made today that wasn't picked up," said Nick. "I can sell it to yuh for thirty cents and I'll trow in the ice cream for fifteen cents, since you're Louie's little brudder. He is my best buddy."

After Sally left the bakery, he went next door to his tenement house and he heard the commotion as soon as the door opened.

"Where you been all day when I whistle?" Luigi yelled.

"Papa, I went to get yuh a boirthday present," answered Sally.

"What's in the box?" Rosie interrupted.

"It a boirthday cake and ice cream," said Sally, smiling.

"Oh, look Fannie!" Rosie was elated as she opened the cake box. "A cake with pink frosting and strawberry ice cream!"

"Hey, stupid, dis is not yah boirthday," Sally joked.

"Where dida you geta the money?" Luigi was almost afraid to ask.

"Papa, an old drunk must have lost it. I saw him stumbling around and when he left I found five dollars on the coib," Sally lied. Luigi looked doubtful, but he hoped Sally was telling the truth. The gala spirit of laughter from all the children lightened his spirits.

Pretty soon the cake and ice cream were on the table, everyone having a dish in front of them, ready to eat, when Sally nervously said, "I have something for yuh, Papa," and he handed him the little box. Luigi looked surprised; he couldn't remember the last time he received a present. He opened the box and his eyes lit up when he saw the pocket watch.

"*Grazia!*" he exclaimed, his eyes shining with happiness at his present. "You are a very good son," he added, as his eyes filled up with tears. Luigi carefully took the watch out of its box and held it up to inspect it. It was a fine piece of jewelry, much more magnificent than his other pocket watch. Sally smiled. It felt so good to do something for his beloved Papa.

Giroloma gave Sally a knowing wink. She was proud of Sally's generosity.

The next day on a street corner stood a small boy with light blond hair, knickers and a cap turned sideways, yelling, "Come get yah shoes shined; five cents a shine!"

Chapter 8—CONEY ISLAND KIDS

It was one of the hottest days of the season and the tenement house apartments were suffocating, with hardly any ventilation. The people in Brooklyn would anticipate the coming evening, in which they could gain some relief by sitting outside on the porch stoops or up in the balconies or fire escapes in hopes of catching a cool breeze.

Sally and his gang of friends stood in line to go to the pool. It was a city funded pool which served the community. In order to swim in this pool they had several rules. There was a separate pool for the boys and girls; the boys had to wear gray bathing trunks and get their feet examined before entering the pool. Sally finally was admitted into the pool; he had been waiting in a line that was at least three blocks long in the hot scorching sun. Once in the pool, which was overly populated, he got fifteen minutes of fun. The lifeguard, a big burly man, pointed to him, who meant his time was up. Sally hated to leave the cool water, so he dallied a little longer, procrastinating getting out. The lifeguard hit him gently with the leather belt he had over his arm, and Sally knew that if he dallied any longer the belt would hit him again, but this time not so gently. Sally had waited at least an hour for this fast dip, and with regret, slowly got out of the pool. As soon as he was dry he would be back in the long line in the hot sun.

There were other ways of cooling off. The Johnnie pumps or fire hydrants could be a means. It was skillfully done, with usually an elder person showing the kids how. Someone would get a hexagon wrench to fit the fitting and open up the pump. Water would squirt out into the street. This would get improved on by another genius idea of placing a drum, which had the top and bottom removed, over the pump. This was the best idea yet. The water would come straight up out of the ground like a geyser.

Then all the neighborhood kids would have hours of fun cooling off. There was never a worry about too much traffic because the streets were usually considered play areas, and very little traffic would commute. Most of the traffic that did come down the street was usually someone who already lived in the neighborhood and would carefully park on the side of the street. It was comical to see the older people get into the act. It was a common sight to see a couple of elderly men or racketeers pull their card tables into the wet streets. There they would sit cooling off, playing a game of cards. Their bare feet would be covered by the cool water. This might last several hours until the fire department would arrive and spoil their fun. However, by placing the drums it took a little more time for the fire department to get to the pump to turn the water off. It wasn't long before the city installed a sprinkler system for the use of the people.

Rosie was over at her cousin's playing; she usually had fun playing in the streets with the Johnnie pumps going, but today she wished she could go swimming. She heard a neighbor kid tell her all about Coney Island. It was considered one of the largest amusement parks in the world. It was located in Brooklyn, an island off the Atlantic Ocean by Gravesend Bay. She wished she could go there. Papa was always promising her that when they could afford it he would take them, but that seemed impossible; they couldn't even afford to eat. Rosie looked at her cousins and said, "I have an idear.......let's go to Coney Island." Rosie's cousins were Uncle John's daughters. They were all younger then her and a few were quite young, the youngest a baby.

Justine, one of the older girls asked, "How will we get there?"

"Oh we'll find it," replied Rosie, who had all the confidence in the world for a ten-year-old. "I know the way, I've been there before and I can show yuh all the sights." Rosie knew this was a lie, but she did feel confident about how to get there. She had seen all the posters explaining which subway to take.

"Well, anyway, we don't have any money," said Justine.

"We won't need much, just enough to ride the subway, and we can pack some fruit from your dad's grocery store, so we don't havta buy food," Rosie responded.

"I do have seventy-five cents," remembered Justine, "I've been saving my money to buy a bike. But what about our parents? They won't let us go!"

"They don't havta know; if we leave now we can be back before supper and they will never miss us."

Justine pondered the idea, which was sounding better every minute. "Alright, let's do it," she said excitedly.

"Let's put all our money together and maybe we can have enough for some ice cream and candy when we get there," added Rosie. The excitement was rising...what a great day they were going to have!

Six excited little girls were at the B.M.T. subway station. The group consisted of Rosie and her younger sister Fannie and the four cousins: Carolina, Justine, Amy and the baby, Josephine.

"Here it is, the sign says Coney Island. This is the subway to take," said Rosie, pointing her finger to the sign. Justine paid the fare, a nickel for each girl, as they entered the subway. Soon they were settled on the subway car. Their destination was over ten miles away, but the ride was only about twenty minutes. A small sack with some apples and grapes were all they managed to steal from the store before they left. Rosie smiled to herself and thought,' *this is going to be a great day!*' She had two dimes tucked into her left sock and a quarter hidden in her right sock. Her left sock was her money for rides and hopefully goodies, but the quarter was her secret money. She thought about how she got that quarter and was almost ashamed of herself.

She remembered the stuck-up snotty girl, Isabella, who was always making fun of her. Isabella had long black curly hair that her mother always styled in long hotdog locks. She wore pretty dresses that were bought at 'Macy's Department Store.' Isabella was fortunate in being the only child of a well-to-do widow. Now Rosie heard talk of how her mother got so much money. She heard the word *puttona* before and she had a vague idea of what that Italian word meant. Sometimes, when there was no one to play with, Isabella would be nice to her. On rare occasions she would invite Rosie inside her apartment. Rosie always accepted because Isabella had dolls and toys to play with. A couple of days ago, such was the case. While they were busy playing, a man had knocked at the door, and Isabella's mother opened the door.

"Good afternoon, Mrs. Michaeletti," greeted the man. Rosie immediately recognized him as being the neighborhood florist. He was a very short stout man, holding some flowers, looking nervous. He looked embarrassed as his frog shaped eyes looked right at her. Rosie knew that he had a wife and children, so she couldn't figure out why he was here. She heard Mrs. Michaeletti whisper something to him, and he took out his wallet and gave her some money. Mrs. Michaeletti was making some silly eye movements, lifting her arched eyebrows, and Rosie was admiring how red her lips were when she said, "Why don't you girls go out and buy an ice cream?"

The short frog-eyed man then cleared his throat and reluctantly reached into his pocket and tossed each girl a quarter. Rosie couldn't believe her luck. '*A quarter could buy five ice creams*,' she thought.

Then he looked right at Rosie and said, "Yuh know, my brother looks just like me."

Rosie wasn't exactly sure of what was going on, but she instinctively knew she wasn't supposed to say anything about him being over there. When she went back outside, a few girls were playing Hop Scotch, and Isabella joined the other girls, abandoning her.

"What do yuh want to play, jacks and jump rope, hit the stick, double-dutch and Skelly or Potsy?" Rosie asked.

"We don't want to play with yuh, cuz yuh wear rags and yuh have a big nose," yelled Isabella.

The other girls joined in calling her, "Nosey Rosy!"

"I oughta beat the shit out of yuh all!" Rosie yelled, holding back her tears.

Then she heard Papa's whistle, so she didn't have time for an ice cream now or those stuck-up brats. As an afterthought, she didn't want to spend her quarter too fast anyway, so she stuck two fingers in her mouth and gave a loud whistle, her signal that she heard his whistle and was coming inside.

The hissing noises of the subway slowing down interrupted her thoughts.

"We're here!" the girls all shouted at once.

Once outside the subway they could see the carnival atmosphere. Coney Island consisted of many streets between West Nineteenth and West Fifth Street, and every street was sectioned off for a different amusement. The girls were standing on the notorious wooden walkway called 'Boardwalk.' This huge wooden walkway was over a mile in length and about eighty feet wide.

"Look at the funny rolling chairs," said Justine. The wicker chair was pushed by a boy along the boardwalk. A storefront close by read, *Boardwalk Rolling Chair Company: chair rentals fifty cents an hour.*
'I could never afford that; well, maybe someday I'll come back here just to ride in it,' Rosie thought wistfully as they continued to walk, taking in all the sights.

"Where are we going to go first?" asked Justine. Her wide opened eyes were taking in all the business establishments that were mainly built on the boardwalk, consisting of elaborate hotels, theaters, restaurants, stores and bath houses. They stopped to look at the sign, which read *The Prospect.*

"That's the movie house where they make motion pictures! My friend told me all about it!" Rosie said excitedly.

Rosie and all the girls were star struck. Everywhere they looked they saw something fascinating. A big sign read, *Albert's Stop In—everything for a nickel. Sausages, Frank footers, Hamburgers, Deli Sandwiches, Soda, Brew.* They had walked up to the corner of Stillwell Avenue, and Rosie made a mental note to come back by herself and buy a frankfooter. Soon they were at Serf Avenue there was a gate which had an arm post that turned when one paid their admittance into Steeplechase Park. This was the amusement park with all the fun rides. The very large yellow sign read *'Steeplechase the Funny Place'* directly underneath that sign was was a round sign with a strange evil grinning face reading, Admittance $2.00.

"We gotta figure a way to sneak inside," said Rosie, so together they sat down on the ground, thinking of a way to get past the barrier.

"We could sneak underneath the arm post, but we gotta do it when nobody is looking," said Carolina. They nodded in agreement and waited for the opportunity. They all eyed the ticket man, but the line was empty and the ticket man looked bored. Suddenly a young pretty lady came up to talk to him. She was wearing a yellow polka dot dress. It seemed that she had lost sight of her companions, and they had made an agreement to meet at this spot if they were separated. While they were engaged in this conversation, the girls knew this was their golden opportunity.

"Let's go!" Rosie shouted as they dashed to the gate. Each one of them hurriedly slid under the arm post, except the baby, who had to be pushed. The ticket man was so engrossed in the presence of the pretty lady that he didn't realize what that been transpiring, until he spotted the last one—a baby being pushes under the post.

"Hey, you girls get back here!" he yelled. The girls had heard him shouting and had run a good distance. He debated pursuing them further, but changed his mind, remembering the lovely lady with the yellow polka dot dress. As he turned his head, his glance caught the image of one of the brats sticking her tongue out at him.

'Oh, the sights are so magnificent to see,' thought Rosie as she walked through all the different stands. The smells were a mixture of cotton candy, popcorn and candy apples. When she spotted the hot-dog stand, after pressing her nose against the glass, she could understand why they called this place Coney Island. The plump hot-dogs were on a rotisserie wire being roasted over a hot grill, and scorching them just a little too achieve that juicy brown texture. The special sauce they heaped on top of them made it all worthwhile, she thought, sniffing the pleasant aroma.

"Hey look everyone!" shouted Amy, "over here the rollercoaster!" Rosie had never imagined seeing such a magnificent sight, and it was so high! She could hear the faint screaming voices as it coasted down the hill. She then caught sight of the huge Ferris wheel; its multi-colored lights were flashing all of its splendor as it was rotating and turning.

"The Four Horses Ride!" yelled Fannie, and everyone stopped to stare. There were the a row of steel racehorses ready for a new race on tracks. They would depart every few minutes racing through the park covered in a glass type pavilion. Each horse could only hold one rider. At the end of each ride a large crowd would gather to watch the girl's skirts blow up high around their waist and expose their underpants. This was caused by vents of compressed air. Rosie laughed at one girl, whose dress flew up, exposing her pink lacy underpants. The crowd was pushing, trying to get another look at the next victim when Rosie was knocked down.

"Hey, yuh bunch of joiks!" she yelled, but in her attempt to get up she noticed a round ticket. She knew what it was. It was the pass people paid two dollars for. On the ticket was a circular row of numbers, and whenever a ride was taken a number would be punched out. She was excited, as this ticket had ten rides left. She couldn't believe her good fortune. She started to yell, but quickly changed her mind, as everyone would want a ride, and in this instance she didn't want to share.

'No, I'll sneak back here later with Justine; she has some money left and we *can both go on rides.'* Then, feeling guilty, she thought, *well maybe it wouldn't hurt if we took Fannie'.*

"Come on, let's head for the beach!" Justine happily shouted. All of the girls eagerly agreed, anticipating the swimming and sandy beach. They grouped into a line, all holding hands as they walked through the heavily crowed area. Soon they walked to a section where all the stands were.

"Hey, little girls, watch me trow the ball; anyone can do it!" yelled the man in the pink-striped shirt. "Look here see how easy it is," he continued, as he demonstrated the easy game. "Just knock the bottles down and yuh win a teddy bear." Fannie broke her grip as she was fascinated and mesmerized by the fast-talking man, but Rosie grabbed her hand pulling her along.

'Maybe later, I'll come back here and win her that prize, she thought,' feeling generous and very rich with that quarter in her sock.

Soon they were near the beach, and they could smell the fresh fishy scent of the ocean.

"Look at the water," yelled Fannie. They could see the blueness of the water, making ripples of small waves as it hit the shore. As Rosie looked out she could see tiny ships, like miniature toys floating in the blue waters. Pretty soon they were walking by all the huge, powerful magnificent yachts.

Why do these people have so much? I wish I was rich, thought Rosie. She sadly kicked her shoe into the sand, suddenly realizing that the hole in shoe was letting in the sand from the beach. At last they had come to the their destination, and she forgot her wishful thinking. She was caught up in all the excitement of the beach.

" Yahoo, we're on the beach!" everyone shouted harmoniously, as if they were in a chorus. Rosie kicked off her shoes and then carefully tucked her socks into them. Then she joined the others twirling round with bare feet in the sand. The beach was filled with people in bathing suits, playing or sun-bathing. Some people had umbrellas stuck in the sand by their blankets. Rosie noticed a few kids playing with a multi-colored beach ball. It looked like they were having lots of fun.

"Let's head for the water!" Justine shouted, and Rosie followed the group, splashing in the cool water. The clear water was refreshing after the long walk in the hot sun. Rosie was not a swimmer and after a while she tired of being in the water, so she waded back toward the shore. Once she was out of the water, she walked through the sand until she spotted the beach ball sitting all alone on a blanket. She quickly grabbed the beach ball and blanket, happy with her good fortune. After a short walk Rosie found a spot to claim on the sand. She spread the blanket out and lay down, waiting for the girls to come back. When the girls finally emerged from the water, she waved and gave a loud whistle with her two fingers in her mouth. They spotted her at once, hearing her loud, distinct whistle.

"Look what I found!" she yelled, pointing to the beach ball and blanket as they approached.

"Yeah, okay yuh just happened to steal it from somebody," commented Justine, secretly glad they had something to play with.

"I didn't steal it; they were sitting all alone, with no one to claim it, so I did," Rosie reasoned.

After they had their fill of playing with the beach ball, the girls realized their hunger and happily spread out their lunch on the blanket, enjoying their little picnic. Then they played in the sand, making sandcastles. Rosie finally grew bored, remembering the amusement rides. She quickly nudged her cousin Justine and made plans.

"We're gonna bring yuh back some cotton candy and soda." By now everyone had grown thirsty. "We'll be back in a little while so yuh all stay here right in this spot. On second thought, come on, Fannie, yuh can help," said Rosie.

Now they were off to see the sights, and Rosie, Justine and Fannie were soon aboard the roller coaster and after that the Ferris wheel. Fannie spotted a ride where everyone got into a huge rolling barrel. The last ride was the most fun, The Four

Horses. The saddle was large enough for two of them, but since Justine was quite heavy she had to go on one alone.

"Make sure yuh hold onto yuh dresses when yuh get off," Rosie warned. Soon the tickets were gone, so they headed for the hot dog stand.

'*This must be heaven*,' thought Rosie. They had pooled enough money for a hot-dog, a couple of sodas and a cotton candy, which they could share with the long waiting other girls. The frankfooter was too temping with its tantalizing aroma, so, on Rosie's insistence, they shared it, each girl taking a large bite. Rosie was savoring the delicious taste of her portion. Soon they passed the fast-talking man with the pink-striped shirt at the game stand.

"Come over here little girl, I'll give yuh a free trow,"said the man, throwing the ball to her. Rosie couldn't resist the temptation. She threw the ball, missing the bottles.

"It will only cost yuh a nickel for tree trows, so try again; no luck, yuh missed. Try again, try again," said the fast-talking man. This time she knocked a bottle down.

"Gimme my prize," she yelped happily. To her disappointment, he handed her a small ceramic Kewpie doll. '*It isn't woith my nickel*,' she thought. "Hey, where's the teddy bear?" she angrily asked.

"No, yuh didn't knock one down tree times in a row," he replied, smiling that he had scammed her.

"I'll stand here and scream and say yuh did something dioty to me if I don't get the teddy bear," said Rosie angrily. His round smirking face took on a shocked expression as she opened her mouth to scream. A high-pitched piercing scream escaped her lips before he clamped his hands over them to smother the sound. Looking around nervously, he handed her the Teddy Bear.

"Now scram!" he snapped angrily. She grabbed Fannie's hand and skipped away, turning around to stick out her tongue at him.

Luigi stuck his head out of the window and he gave his familiar whistle. Pretty soon all the children came rushing in. It was his custom to count heads before they ate, so after he counted, he realized there were two missing. He looked again, visually seeing that the black one was home—that was Frankie; he had coal black hair, dark eyes and a dark olive complexion. Next he noticed that the white one was home. The white one was Sally; he had white blond hair, blue eyes and a fair complexion.

"The girls are missing...Rosie and Fannie are not home," said Giroloma, wringing her hands. Shortly after this realization there was a knock on the door, and it was his brother-in-law, John Coppola. After comparing stories they discovered that six girls were missing. The last time anyone had seen them was early in the morning. John remembered seeing them around the store, catching Amy stealing some grapes. They were all together in the store. They said they were playing a game. He was angry at them and chased them out. Everyone looked worried as this was close to the time of the famous Lindbergh baby kidnapping. Luigi assigned each kid an area to go out searching. Soon everyone in the family was scouring the neighborhood. Word caught on and even all the neighbors pitched in for the search.

Rosie and Justine joined the girls at the beach and gave them their treats. They played some more and decided to swim again. They were enjoying themselves so much that time was totally lost to them.

'*This is such a nice place,*' Rosie thought. '*I never wanna go home.*' "HOME? OH NO!" she gasped. It suddenly hit her, and she looked up at the sky; it was getting dark!

"We havta start for home!" she yelled, then suddenly realized she had spent all of the money. She looked at all the girls. The baby was crying, and her diaper was hanging down past her knees, as she had messed her herself early in the day. The girls had forgotten to bring diapers. Anyway, no one really wanted to change her, even if they had diapers.

Rosie, feeling scared for the first time, said, "I don't know how we are gonna get home; I spent all the money!" It was too far to walk, miles away. Soon all the girls began to cry, including Rosie. The beach was bare; all those people, they just seemed to disappear. They started walking on the boardwalk and everything looked deserted. The once blue water and sky looked black by now.

'*It's getting spooky out here,*' thought Rosie. She was crying hard by now and all the girls had joined in the chorus of wailing. Rosie stopped crying long enough to hear all the wailing from the other girls.

"That's it," she said. "Let's go find someone, and I'll tell them we lost our parents and maybe they will give us enough money to take the subway home. We all have to keep crying real loud and maybe they'll feel sorry for us." All the girls nodded that wouldn't be hard, as they were both hungry and scared.

As they walked on the boardwalk they could hear the sound of the trampling noise as their shoes hit the plank boards. It sounded like the marching of a small band, and even their crying and sobs had a musical sound. It was pitch-black out by now, but at last there appeared a man in blue. It was the security guard, employed by the park. Rosie turned and said, "Now start crying real loud." The guard heard the crying and rushed over.

"What's the matter?" he asked, his voice filled with concern. A kind word was all it took, and the wailing increased in volume. It wasn't an act, like their plan; it was genuine.

"We lost our parents!" wailed Rosie.

The man was sympatric and kind, so he said, "We better get yuh girls over to the station to talk to the park manager."

Soon they were in a small office. After they explained their plight more than twice, the manager's bushy eye brows blended together to make one large eyebrow when he frowned. He gave a very long, concentrated stare at the girls. They looked a sorry sight, with their tired, dirty faces that had scared expressions. He observed that the cotton candy stuck to the hair of one of the smaller girls resembled a spider's web. He didn't quite believe their story.

'Why haven't their parents looked for them?' He wondered. This would be the first place they would come if they lost their children. It happened every day. The little girl with the big round eyes kept telling him all they needed was transportation money to get back home. It was getting late, and he had had a hard day and wanted to end this problem. Finally he decided that they would give them whatever fare they needed, along with an escort to the subway. He reached into his pocket and pulled out some change.

"Here," he said to the security guard, "take them to the subway, get them on the right train and if this isn't enough money, just add some more. We'll be compensated for it later when we file our report."

At last the girls were on their way home, tired, hungry and anxious to get there. Then it hit Rosie like a bolt of lightning, waking her out of her drowsy slumber. She had been so relieved at finally getting a way home that she hadn't thought it was pitch-black outside and they were certainly missed by now. Mama and Papa would be looking for her and the girls. Now she really started to worry. Boy, was she in trouble! She tried to think of some excuse to give them. She could say that they were kidnapped; no, they wouldn't believe that story. She could say that one of them got sick and had to go to the hospital. No, they wouldn't believe that either. You only went to the hospital when you were dying. Her otherwise foxy bright mind was too tired to think up anything to tell them, so she decided to accept the consequences. She knew she was in for a beating, so out of despair she began to cry.

"What is it?" asked Justine.

"Mama, Papa and Uncle John, they are gonna wallop us when we get home. It's too late now. They probably had supper hours ago," Rosie sobbed.

All the girls then began to cry again, and this time for a very different reason. The subway train stopped, and when they got off, Rosie said, "Let's all go to my house; we're in trouble anyway, so we might as well all stick together." They made the long walk home, crying and sobbing all the way. The little baby was trailing behind, toddling and tripping over her long-soiled diaper.

Giroloma, Luigi, Uncle John and his wife all sat at the table looking worried and defeated. They had every kid in the neighborhood search everywhere possible.

"Why would six little girls just disappear?" Luigi questioned.

"We havea to seea the Godfather; something terrible has happened to them," Giroloma sobbed. She could feel the hysteria building up inside her. "They never were this late and all of them missing."

Just then they heard a small noise at the door. The little noise was a very faint tapping, almost like someone was afraid to come in. Luigi flew to the door and flung it open.

There stood five crying little girls and a baby. Shock made then all speechless. The girls looked tired, dirty and terrified. The baby was a disheveled mess with her diaper half off, and she was crying too. They were all still crying, knowing what was in store.

Luigi found his voice first. "They are home and they are safe, oh thank God!"

Rosie could hear her mother crying out in relief. She lapsed into her familiar Italian language, using all the "*Grazias*" she could. The girls were all hugged and kissed many times over and over. Finally when the excitement of knowing they were safe died down, there came the dreaded question. "What happened?" It was repeated: "What happened?"

Finally Rosie found her voice, which was barely audible, and she whispered, "It was hot and we decided to go to Coney Island." The room full of noise suddenly became very quite as everyone tried to comprehend her simple explanation. In only a matter of seconds she had seen the transformation of concern turn into shock, and finally anger, as the realization of the situation dawned on them.

Then finally the big explosion came that she had dreaded. Mama, Papa, Uncle John and Aunt Francis and all her brothers and her big sister started yelling at once. The yelling hurt her ears. She stood with her head bent low as she suddenly realized that she deserved her punishment for causing them all the worry and pain.

Luigi placed her on his lap while he spanked her behind with his belt. Uncle John followed suit and started spanking his girls. The room was filled with emotion as all the spanking, crying and yelling continued.

Afterward when things had calmed down a bit, Giroloma set the table for the girls to eat. The sobbing girls ate the pasta set before them, not appreciating the delicious taste as they normally would under happier conditions.

That night in bed Rosie said her prayers: "Please God, bless Mama, Papa and all my brothers and sisters. I am heartily sorry for having disobeyed my parents. I know how much worry I have caused them today. I know how much they love me, even though they walloped me, and God, thank yuh for the most wonderful day of my life!"

Chapter 9—TEACHER'S PET

What is the worth of anything, but for the happiness 'twill bring?
Richard Owen Cambridge, *Learning,123*

Fannie sat at her desk. The teacher was taking roll call. When she read "Phyllis Finazzo," she looked flustered and then angry. "Is Rose Finazzo your sister?" she asked.

"Yes," replied Fannie.

"I will warn you that I will not tolerate any misbehavior, is that understood?" Miss O'Conner challenged in her sternest voice.

The girls sitting around her snickered and whispered, "Yuh rag-mop-wop."

Fannie noticed that most of the girls in her class at the all-girls school were Irish girls with red or auburn hair and pretty dresses. She looked down at her old homemade dress that was a hand-me-down and felt ashamed. Her heart fell, as it was going to be another year of being disliked because of Rosie.

Fannie was a year behind Rosie in school and had the misfortune of having the same teachers. She felt the resentment and the apprehension of the teachers in teaching another Finazzo. They all seemed to think that she would be another problem child.

This year, however, Fannie was determined to have her school teachers overcome their prejudicial misjudgment of her. In reality, Fannie was the opposite of her sister. Where Rosie was outspoken, Fannie was quiet. Where Rosie was mischievous, Fannie was obedient. Where Rosie was domineering, Fannie was recessive. Even for sisters they had very little resemblance. Where Rosie was skinny and small for her age, with a narrow, peaked face, Fannie was a pretty child, healthy-looking with a round face and apple cheeks. It was unfortunate the teachers never seemed to look beyond her name; if they did, they would discover that Fannie was a very sensitive girl who wanted to be liked and accepted.

After school Fannie walked home with tears in her eyes. It seemed so unfair that she should be treated this way because of Rosie. Fannie thought back to this past summer when they had summer school. They were offering a special class on etiquette, and she was really interested in learning fine manners and proper behavior, but Rosie seemed to think it was a joke. Giroloma had encouraged them to go because the program offered free lunches everyday. Besides learning some manners, they could at least receive a decent meal once a day. At home food was scarce. There never seemed to be enough to satisfy their appetites.

The first day at summer school they were taught how to set a proper table. After they sat down, the teacher explained when to use each utensil during the course of the dinner. Fannie could hardly contain her appetite when the delicious aroma of roast beef filled the air. Then they had something called mashed potatoes and gravy. The next day even Rosie was anxious to go back, envisioning the delicious meal. The teacher explained the proper way to eat soup. After the delicious soup was eaten with the proper spoon, the next entree was dessert. There was a huge bowl of an assortment of fruits as a centerpiece. The bowl was passed around as each girl daintily took one fruit. Rosie had selected an apple. She was craving that apple all through the long torturous ordeal of the teacher's lecture.

When Rosie bit into the delicious apple, the teacher reprimanded her, telling her to take smaller, daintier bites. Suddenly Rosie discovered a worm in her apple, and she started spitting it out, gagging.

"Teacher, there's a woim in my apple!" she exclaimed.

Miss Donohue walked over and examined her apple, discovering a half eaten worm protruding from the section Rosie had bitten into. She then gave her speech, "Proper etiquette is never to insult your host, even if you dislike the food. As in your case, Rose, you must eat the apple."

"I ain't eatin' a woim, and yuh can go to hell with your uppity manners!" Rosie countered, throwing the apple at the teacher. Miss Donohue was aghast at Rosie's table manners and language.

"Either you eat this rotten apple or you will be dismissed from school and receive an 'F.' Also I expect a sincere apology from you for your bad language, immediately," declared Miss Donohue.

"Go to hell! I might be poor, but my mama never expects us to eat woims. Come on, Fannie, we're gettin' outta here." Fannie couldn't side with Miss Donohue in this case, so she left with Rosie, indignant that she would dare to go to the extremes of forcing bad food on them. When they got home, Giroloma was in the kitchen washing clothes.

"Why are you both home so early?" she asked in Italian. Giroloma was happy to hear about all the different varieties of food they were offered everyday at school. She was anticipating another conversation today with the girls, learning about another strange food.

"I'm never going back to that school again," said Rosie indignantly. Giroloma stopped scrubbing the shirt she had been so diligently working on before they got home, looking shocked and waiting for the explanation to come.

"Mama, she tried to force me to eat an apple with a woim in it," said Rosie.

"I have never heard of such a thing; what's the matter with that teacher? I'll go back with you girls and tell her a piece of my mind," Giroloma said furiously.

When they reached the school, Giroloma headed straight for the principal's office with her two small daughters in tow. The principal, a small man with a receding hairline and bow tie, looked shocked when he saw Giroloma approaching him. "My daughter isa in summer school class ana the teacher wasa trying to maka her eat an apple with a worm in it," Giroloma said in broken English. "We area poor and I don't hava any fancy food ona fancy plates, but we don't eata any garbage."

The principal was astonished that a teacher could expect a child to do such a thing, so he said he would straighten things up with the teacher. The teacher was finally called into the office and had the embarrassment of being chastised. As they were leaving the teacher snuck a glare in Rosie's direction.

As Fannie approached the tenement house she heard voices inside. When she walked in she noticed that her brother Louie was visiting. Louie smiled and asked, "How's my baby sister doing in the fourth grade?" "Alright, but I don't think the teacher likes me because she had Rosie last year," she replied in a small voice.

"Don't worry, kid; your good disposition and pretty smile will win hah over after she gets to know yuh," replied Louie. Then he turned to Giroloma and said, "That Rosie is so bad; Mama, can't yuh do anything with her?"

"I try, but she is so strong-minded, just like Sally. What can I do......beat them all day?" she replied, exasperated.

Fannie was the youngest of the family, so everyone over-protected and babied her, yet, surprisingly, she was not spoiled. Her good nature and happy outlook was untarnished. If anything, having Rosie for an older sister really hurt her self-image. Rosie was domineering and constantly over-shadowed her. Rosie was always telling her how to act, who to play with, what to say. Rosie was also very protective. If Fannie had a problem, Rosie was the first to defend her, and woe to any kid who dared to give her trouble. All the girls were afraid of Rosie; Sally had taught her how to box and she was good enough to beat up even most boys.

"Why can't yuh be more like me?" Rosie would say. "Beat the hell outta them. I can teach yuh how to box, it's all in the footwork," Rosie would add.

The next day at school Miss O'Conner never looked at Fannie, except when she took roll call. Fannie had studied her lessons and raised her hand several times, but she was ignored. Fannie studied Miss O'Conner and thought she was pretty when she smiled, which was seldom. She had thick auburn hair which framed her face in waves. Fannie already knew that her hair was really just a wig, as she remembered how Rosie had told her all about it.

"I fixed that bitch! I stuck a wad of chewing gum on the blackboard when she was giving a lecture. As she backed up, the wig stuck to the chewing gum, lifting the wig off her head at a lopsided angle. It was hilarious; her almost bald head was exposed with little straggles of hair. She looked like a monster!" Rosie laughed. Fannie remembered how she laughed when she heard the story, but now she was made to pay for Rosie's pranks.

As the school year wore on, Fannie tried her best everyday to get Miss O'Conner's attention. She studied her lessons, but only received fair grades. When they had an essay, each student was supposed to read it aloud in front of the class. Fannie had chosen a subject about nature and animal life which she carefully prepared. When it was her turn to recite in front of the class, she knew she had the best report.

She read it aloud, never stumbling or missing a word, and each word was emphasized with the proper emotion. When she had finished, some of the students clapped. She knew she had done her best, but Miss O'Conner never gave her the well-deserved compliment she had worked so hard for; instead she gave her a cold glare and said, "You may sit down now." Fannie was so let down she couldn't hide her tears.

When the next student had recited her essay, Miss O'Conner smiled and said, "That was very good." Fannie knew that girl wasn't as prepared as she was. When the essays were handed back, she was shocked to see that she only had an average grade.

One day, as Miss O'Conner was passing out papers, she stopped by Fannie's desk and said, "Hold out your arm!" Fannie held out her arm, not quite understanding why the teacher asked.

"Do you write on your arm like your sister does?"

"No, Miss O'Conner, my sister's got derma graphical skin; it's very rare." Miss O'Conner just huffed and said, "You probably find other ways to cheat."

Fannie was mortified, as she had worked long into the night getting her lesson just perfect. She was so humiliated that she ran out of the classroom. It was useless, she thought; no matter how hard she tried she just couldn't win. Maybe Rosie had the right outlook on these teachers: fight back and make them miserable. Fannie had thought about how Rosie was born with derma graphical skin. All she had to do was press a bobby-pin or toothpick on her skin and in two seconds it would start to swell and rise about a half of an inch. She had fun demonstrating this trick. The kids called her the human slate. She cashed in on it at school, too; she would write all the test answers on the back of her arm and cheat.

When Fannie got home from school she looked as though she had been crying, and Rosie noticed how upset she was.

"You should treat hah like she teats yuh. She only likes the rich girls in class," Rosie went on, and just then Luigi came in the kitchen. "You girls get ready. We are going to the shoea store to get new shoes," he ordered.

It was the politicians' way of getting the poor man's vote. They would sponsor stores to give away items to the needy, in return for their support. When the family arrived at the shoe store, there was a crowd of people already there. The used restored shoes were displayed on three shelves for men, women and children.

Rosie looked over the shoes, and they were ugly, with big black buckles. She tried a pair on and they were uncomfortable.

"I don't like these. Fannie, yuh watch me and do just as I'm doing," she said. Then she spotted the tennis shoes and they didn't look too bad, so she grabbed two pair; one for her and one for Fannie. The store was in chaos, as people were trying on shoes everywhere. The sales clerks were so busy they didn't pay close attention, so Rosie kicked off her worn-out shoes and pushed them under a shelf, Fannie doing the same, then they walked quickly over to the new shoe section. Rosie spotted the shoes she liked, a pair of red leather shoes with a little bow on the front and a tiny strap buckling across the ankle.

"Do yuh like these shoes?" she asked Fannie. Fannie had never seen a more magnificent pair of shoes, and her eyes were glued to them as she nodded.

"Now all we havta do is put them on," she said excitedly. They searched around for the right sizes, four and five.

When they were finally walking home, Giroloma noticed their new red leather shoes, and she didn't remember seeing them on the shelf.

"Where did you get those shoes?" she asked.

"They were there by mistake, only two pairs," Rosie lied. Giroloma noticed that they were also carrying tennis shoes. She opened her mouth to reprimand them, but changed her mind. They needed the shoes, she thought even if they did something wrong, so this one time she choose to ignore it.

The next day Fannie wore her new red shoes to school. She wished she had a new coat to match. She shivered and tried to wrap the old, thin, ragged coat around her for protection. It was getting cold, only days away from Christmas. By the time the school was in view it was starting to snow. White snowflakes were dancing to the ground with the slight wind. When she looked up at the sign it read, *Public School Forty-Three.* It was barely visible with the layer of snow that clung to it. When she entered the school the sudden warmth felt good to her cold shivering little body. The familiar smell of chalk and fresh ink hit her nostrils as she entered her classroom. When the class had begun, after taking roll call, Miss O'Conner made an announcement: "We have some sad news. An unfortunate family had a fire over the weekend and they lost everything they had. I think it would be a good idea to have a special drive to donate some clothes to these children. They cannot attend school until they have clothes to wear." Miss O'Conner directed her plea to the rich girls in the classroom, staring at them for a full minute before changing the subject to their school work.

Fannie felt terrible. '*Those poor kids,* she thought, *how can I help them?*' At school the next day Fannie had brought a small bundle—it was her Sunday dress. Her whole wardrobe consisted of three dresses.: two for school and the best one for Sunday. She decided that she needed her school dresses, but could sacrifice her Sunday dress. Fannie tried to make the best of her meager wardrobe by looking clean and neat for school every day. Every night she washed out her dress for school and hung it from the clothesline. When she would come home from school each day she would take the clean dress off the line and iron it. She always combed her thick dark hair in a becoming style. She took pride in trying to look her best.

Suddenly all her attention focused on Miss O'Conner as she entered the room. After roll call, Miss O'Conner asked, "Did anyone remember to bring some clothes for the clothes drive?" directing her attention to the rich girls in class. The class was silent and no one raised their hand. Fannie looked around, realizing that she was the only one who brought something, then she awkwardly raised her hand.

"What is it, Phyllis?" the teacher reluctantly asked.

"I brought something for the poor kids," Fannie proudly announced. "It isn't the best, but maybe they could wear it until they get something new."

Miss O'Conner walked over to her desk and picked up a pretty pink dress with ruffles around the sleeves and collar. On closer examination, she noticed that it was neatly mended and repaired in several inconspicuous places. Miss O'Conner knew, even though this dress was repaired, this was Fannie's best dress and it was too fine to wear to school. All she had ever seen Fannie wear to school was the same two washed-out old dresses that she recognized from the year before on Rosie. Suddenly Miss O'Conner realized that the well-to-do girls that she had expected to help had brought nothing, while this poor girl who had nothing unselfishly gave her best dress. Feeling the guilt mount up inside her, she realized how wrong she was to judge this poor child who had tried so hard all year to win her approval. Miss O'Conner finally walked back to her desk, her head down, ashamed to face her students because of the tears that couldn't seem to stop. She sat at her desk and sobbed. Then she wiped her eyes one final time fighting to regain her composure before she finally said, "Phyllis, I want to make an apology. I have misjudged you. I am so sorry not to have noticed what a nice person you are. Please forgive me."

Fannie could not believe her ears. She had tried so hard to be accepted and now she felt like a celebrity. All the girls who had ignored her before were suddenly smiling at her and showing friendship. She was overwhelmed with happiness. Fannie smiled back, trying to suppress a nervous giggle, with her little round face and rosy apple cheeks expressing happiness at finally being excepted. It was one of the happiest days of her life.

Walking back home from school, Fannie heard a commotion in the schoolyard where Rosie was taunting some girls.

"Hey yuh little twit, yuh think yuh can talk to me like that? I'll beat yuh face in like a punching bag!" she yelled. Just about every day Rosie got into an argument, and she seemed to thrive on fighting. She was always a little braver because she had her two-hundred-pound cousin, Justine, to back her up. If things got rough, Justine would jump in and sit on the poor victim. The fight had already begun. Rosie was out there with her little stick arms up in a boxer's position, dancing around her victim. Her victim was usually much bigger than her and would laugh at her funny position and little stick legs. That was usually how they got surprised. Rosie somehow would land a punch with such force that her victim would be knocked down, then it would be free sailing from that point on. Only this day, three much bigger girls had ganged up on her. Justine, who observed what had transpired, jumped in, landing on some poor girl's back and flattening her out. She then jumped on another victim until Rosie could get away from them. Fannie dismissed the excitement of the fight, which after all was an everyday occurrence.

She walked on home, happy to be alone with her thoughts.

The next day on her way to school, she thought, '*today is the last day of school before Christmas vacation.*' School seemed to go a lot easier for her today, she noticed. The girls who sat around her gave her a welcoming smile as she sat down in her seat. During class, Miss O'Conner smiled at her a few times and let her answer questions when she raised her hand. The day had gone beautifully. At the end of the day, Miss O'Conner wished everyone a Merry Christmas and told them all to enjoy Christmas vacation. Then she said, "Phyllis, would you please stay after class; I have something to talk to you about."

Fannie wondered what Miss O'Conner had to tell her, suddenly feeling apprehensive, praying it wasn't something derogatory. When the bell rang, dismissing the class, she reluctantly waited for all the other classmates to leave before approaching her teacher. Finally when Miss O'Conner looked up from grading her papers, she gave Fannie an encouraging smile. "I asked you to stay after class because I have a Christmas gift for you," she said, handing her a beautifully wrapped package with a big red ribbon made into a bow. Fannie was flabbergasted, unable to speak.

"I hope you will except it," Miss O'Conner said. Fannie had never received a Christmas present in her life. She was close to tears as she slowly unwrapped the big bow and carefully unwrapped the paper. Inside the large box was a beautiful red wool coat. It was soft and warm as Fannie excitedly tried it on.

"Oh, Miss O'Conner, how can I ever thank yuh for such a beautiful gift!" Fannie exclaimed, tears running down her cheeks.

"You can thank me by accepting my apology at being so mean and thoughtless," said Miss O'Conner. "I hope you can accept my invitation to come over to my house during the holiday." Fannie was overjoyed. Never in her life could she want anything more.

"Oh, I'd love to! I'll ask my mother, but I'm sure she will say yes," Fannie rushed on.

"Oh, another thing Phyllis.......there is more in the box," said Miss O'Conner, smiling. "I noticed that you had new red shoes, so I bought the coat to match." Fannie rushed to look into the box, and there was a beautiful white hand crocheted scarf and mittens to match.

"Oh, thank yuh, thank yuh again; I can't wait to show this to my mama!" said Fannie excitedly.

"Well go ahead, and I can't wait to meet your mama. I will come over during the holidays to get permission to take you home with me," said Miss O'Conner smiling.

Fannie put on her new coat, scarf and mittens, and she felt like a movie star. '*This just can't be happening to me*,' she thought as she happily waved goodbye to Miss O'Conner.

"I'll see you in a few days," she sang as she ran out of the classroom. Fannie ran all the way home, anxious to show off her new coat. When she got home, she ran into the tenement house like a whirlwind, slamming the door behind her.

"Mama, look what Miss O'Conner bought me!" she exclaimed.

Giroloma looked up from her baking—she had flour all over the table in preparation of the cookies she was baking for Christmas—and she looked shocked when she noticed the new coat. Then she said as she was rolling the dough mixture, "I told you that your nice personality would win her over, but I never expected this!"

"Mama, she wants to come over to meet yuh and she asked if I could come to her house for a visit. Please can I?" asked Fannie.

"After I meet her and talk to your papa, I'll give you your answer," Giroloma said, smiling.

Christmas day finally arrived, and everyone was filled with the holiday spirit. Laughter and happiness filled the tenement house. Giroloma had baked mounds of Italian fig cookies, which she had kept hidden under her bed the night before. When the children awoke, they were surprised to see the large tray of cookies on the table. Each child had a cookie and a special treat of an orange by their plate. These were their Christmas presents. After the excitement wore down, then it was time to dress for church. Each child would put on their one outfit reserved for Sundays. After the long special Christmas Mass, the rest of the day would be spent visiting relatives. Giroloma somehow would always manage to have a special Christmas dinner, and this year they had a turkey donated by the church. Early Christmas morning, before church, someone was knocking on the door. Rosie went to answer it and discovered a large basket donated by the church.

"Merry Christmas," chirped the jolly delivery man.

"Look, Mama, we got a basket!" announced Rosie, and everyone ran to inspect it. Inside was a large turkey some apples, some canned vegetables, six sweet potatoes and some fruit. Tucked in the bottom were some small toys.

"Look, toys!" yelled the children as they hurriedly pulled them out. They had a baseball, jacks, a box of chalk, a bag of marbles, a yo-yo, some pencils and about two fists full of candy. The children hovered over the toys and candy, deciding who got what.

Hours later when they could smell the delicious aroma of the turkey baking there was a loud banging on he door.

"Ho, Ho, Merry Christmas!" Jimmy greeted them as he entered the house, carrying a very large sack filled with packages, and all the children came running towards him, nearly knocking him down. There was something for everyone. Fannie and Rosie inspected the little blue velvet matching purses that he bought them.

"Go ahead, open them up!" Jimmy urged.

Fannie excitedly opened her purse to discover a beautiful gold necklace with a heart-shaped locket, a bottle of perfume and two dollar bills. Giggling with delight, she ran up kissed and hugged him, with Rosie following suit.

"Oh, thank yuh, Jimmy, for being our Santa Claus!" they happily shouted. Jimmy's homecoming had made their Christmas complete.

A few days later there was a knock at the door, and Sally rushed to answer it. There stood a tall thin lady with a fluffy hairdo.

"I've come to visit Phyllis," she said.

"Come in," replied Sally.

Everyone was sitting around the kitchen table when Fannie spotted Miss O'Conner.

"It's my teacher," she happily announced. Fannie introduced Miss O'Conner to all the family members, softly giggling as she proudly took Miss O'Conner over to each person.

Giroloma, eager to show her hospitality, said, "Settee," inviting her to sit down. Giroloma had just begun to drain the pasta she was cooking for dinner, so she rapidly ordered Fannie to set the table. Before Miss O'Conner realized it, she had a huge plate of pasta and meatballs before her, and she started to protest, explaining that she did not come over to eat. Then Giroloma stubbornly shook her head and pointed to her plate, saying *"Manga."* Miss O'Conner had no choice but to obey. She had to admit, whatever it was that she was eating was delicious. Everyone smiled at her as she tried to daintily eat the mound of spaghetti which kept slipping off her fork. She then looked around and observed how they were winding and wrapping the long noodles around their forks and neatly putting it into their mouths. Miss O'Conner attempted to do the same, but a long string of noodles made the attempt awkward. Everyone burst out laughing, her along with them.

Giroloma was secretly grateful for the grocery money Jimmy had given her, which enabled them to have breaded veal and homemade bread to go along with the pasta course. Miss O'Conner broke the silence by saying what a wonderful daughter they had in Fannie.

Giroloma(who by now could understand some English) said in broken English mixed with Italian, *"Grazia,* thank you fora buying the coat for my little girl, Fannie, and fora being so kind."

"Your daughter showed how unselfish and generous she was by contributing her best dress for a poor family," explained Miss O'Conner. "I felt that I had to do something nice for her to make up for it. I may be a teacher, but she taught me a lesson that there is kindness in this world. I'm afraid I wasn't a very good teacher to her earlier in the school year, so now I would not only like to be her teacher but her friend as well."

"We know our Fannie isa good girl, even though she is our baby we have tried not to spoil her," said Luigi.

"I hope you will allow me to invite her to visit me tomorrow. I would like to take her to the theater with your permission?" Miss O'Conner asked.

"You hava my permission to taka Fannie to the picture show," Luigi said, smiling at Fannie.

"This is one of the most delicious dinners I've ever eaten," Miss O'Conner said, digging into the veal on her plate.

Giroloma jumped up to serve her some more, but she refused.

"Oh, no thank you, this is more than I've eaten in a week," she responded, laughing.

The next day Fannie happily accompanied Miss O'Conner to her nice apartment for a visit. Miss O'Conner lived in one of the nicer parts of Brooklyn, called Green point, where the well-to-do Irish had settled. As they were walking toward her apartment Fannie noticed some apartment entrances draped in black material. Her curiosity getting the better of her, she asked, "Miss O'Conner, why are these doors draped in black material?"

"Because these people have sons or daughters who married out of their faith, usually to Jewish people. Their relatives consider them dead and they are in mourning. There is a song that describes this called *Abe's Irish Rose.*"

They finally had arrived at Miss O'Conner's apartment. The exterior was white brick with neat little courtyards and a potted plant on each side of every entrance door. Once inside the apartment, Fannie looked around, intrigued. It was decorated in Victorian style furnishings. Every piece of furniture had a hand-crocheted, starched doily on it. What really amazed Fannie the most was her electric sewing machine. She remembered Mama's old pedal machine at home. Miss O'Conner demonstrated how it sewed.

"You have a real nice apartment, Miss O'Conner; do you live here all alone?"

"Yes, I never married; I lived with my parents until they passed away," replied Miss O'Conner sadly. Fannie thought how different it would be to live alone; she never had any privacy, living with her big family. In a way it would be nice, but she couldn't imagine her life without Mama, Papa and all her brothers and sisters. No, she decided, she wouldn't trade places.

Miss O'Conner broke the silence by saying, "I have a very nice day planned; first we will go to the theater, then out to dinner."

Soon they were the subway on the way to B.F.Keith's Greenpoint Theater.

"Someday soonI'll take you to, Radio City in Manhattan," said Miss O'Conner, smiling, "and I guarantee that you will see a show that you will never forget."

After a short walk they arrived at the theater, where the many flickering light bulbs displayed the word: *Vaudeville*.

Fannie had never seen a show like this. She laughed at the comedy and marveled at the dancing and singing of the performers. The tap dancing and bright colored outfits of the performers put her in a humorous mood.

As they left the theater Miss O'Conner asked, "Have you ever had the experience of a delicious Chinese dinner?"

Fannie shook her head, her eyes showing the excitement of going to such a place.

"Well then, I think you should try it. It will be a new adventure for you, something you can tell your family about."

Going to Chinatown from Greenpoint was too far to walk, so they took a subway. Fannie could barely hide her anticipation, wondering what kind of food these strange people ate.

Once inside the beautiful Chinese restaurant, Fannie looked nervous. She remembered her mother telling her that Chinese people were strange and she was never to go around them. They kidnapped little children to cut up and cook in their strange food. Fannie nervously looked around the tables, and there were hardly any Chinese people, mainly American families eating dinner. '*Mama must have been wrong,*' she thought, and she immediately relaxed. Then a strange-looking small Chinese man was at their table, talking with a weird accent and handing them a menu.

"I'll order a variety of different foods, then you can taste them all," said Miss O'Conner. When the strange man came back to the table, Miss O'Conner said, "We'll have the butterfly shrimp with fried rice, sweet and sour pork, egg rolls, and wanton soup and tea to drink." The man kept bowing and finally left. He came back shortly with a tray and placed two little cups without handles and a tea pot on the table. Then in order, two little bowls of soup, two eggs rolls and two tiny little bowls with dark thick sauce were brought.

Fannie looked at the soup, and it looked like it had seaweed in it with chunks of chicken. She tasted the soup, which was rather bland, but after a few sips decided she liked it. Next she tried the egg roll, and Miss O'Conner explained, that the sauce was duck sauce with hot mustard, and the other bowl was plum sauce. After smelling the duck sauce, she decided that it was too pungent, reminding her of Vicks Vapor Rub. So she chose the plum sauce, which was sweet.

Soon the little man was back, picking up the little bowls and serving them three silver, dome-shaped bowls. All the food was delicious, and Fannie excitedly tried it all.

"I never knew this Chinese food could be so delicious, especially the fruit you call pineapple in the food," she said.

After most of the food was eaten, Fannie felt that her stomach would burst if she ate another bite. Then the little man arrived again with some cookies.

"Break these open," said Miss O'Conner, "and you will see a little piece of paper that tells your fortune."

Fannie excitedly broke hers open and it read: "You will have a lasting friendship."

Fannie showed it to Miss O'Conner and she smiled. "We have just begun our friendship. There will be many more days to come. I just can't wait to do all the fun things I have planned for us."

Fannie smiled. It was so wonderful having such a nice teacher and friend. Miss O'Conner smiled back, secretly glad she had made friends with Fannie; her sweet smile and happy giggle would help fill the lonely void in her life.

"Phyllis, I feel that I should explain...I had an illness that caused me to lose my hair. I know you must have heard about it through your sister Rose. Rose had caused me to have a very embarrassing experience, and I wrongfully made you the scapegoat for her prank. I just want you to know I was very wrong to punish you because of that incident." Miss O'Conner thought back to that horrifying day, and her face still burned with shame remembering the laughing students.

Fannie was filled with sympathy at this poor teacher's torment.

"Oh, Miss O'Conner, I'm so sorry that happened. My sister didn't realize how much that must have hurt yuh. She told me that if yuh ever bring the subject up, she wants to apologize. She is ashamed to say it herself, but she doesn't know how to approach yuh, and she certainly doesn't want to cause yuh more pain. You see, our mother has cancer and she lost both of her breasts, so we realize how hard it is for yuh."

Miss O'Conner's eyes stung from fresh tears, and she said, "Tell Rose that you spoke to me and I accept her apology."

All too soon the wonderful day ended with Miss O'Conner bringing Fannie home, but that day was the start of many more days to come. Miss O'Conner couldn't do enough for her new little friend, Fannie. A wonderful friendship that would last for years to come had developed out of the needs of a little girl to be recognized and a lonely spinster teacher. Miss O'Conner, who expressed her kindness, had made Fannie's hardships more tolerable.

Chapter 10—FRANKIE'S DREAMS

"Please, Papa, can I go to the movies?" asked Frankie. Luigi looked at his son Frankie, whose large dark brown eyes were pleading.

"You know that we don't hava any money fora picture shows; besides, you were bad yesterday," he scolded.

"I'm sorry, Papa, I'll never do it again," he promised.

"I think you needa to remember some more ofa what you did wrong. You stay home today and thinka some more," Luigi advised. Frankie reluctantly walked to the back bedroom and sat on the bed. He remembered how he had gotten into Papa's homemade wines the previous day. When Luigi and the whole family were leaving to go visiting, he was asked to come along. He begged off, saying that he had a stomachache. After some misgivings, Luigi reluctantly agreed to leave him home alone.

When Frankie was finally alone, he climbed up on the shelf in the kitchen, where Luigi stored his collection of liquor and wines. Frankie loved the taste of wine and he was curious to taste all the different varieties Luigi had stored. He remembered asking

Luigi earlier if he could taste them. Luigi looked at him sternly and said, "This isa for special occasions. Justa because I give you children *vino* to drink with your meals that isa no reason to think that you can have it all the time; besides, you are only thirteen years old now, and not a man yet. Whena you are eighteen, then you can sit down ana have a drink with me."

'It wouldn't hurt if I sample a little from each bottle,' Frankie thought. Then he gripped the bottles and took a swig from the first one he had. It was a thick, sweet wine, his favorite. He decided he liked it so much that he took another swig. Next he was holding another bottle, and he took another big swig of this. "Ugh!" He made a horrible face. *'This stuff is too sour. Maybe just another swig and it will taste better,'* he thought. Next he held another bottle, and he noticed this bottle was lighter in color than the others, so he took a large swig, and that tasted good.

"It's better than the rest," he giggled, then hiccupped. "I think I'll try some more."

Suddenly the room was spinning and Frankie felt light-headed and strangely happy, so he lay down on the floor, took another large swig from the bottle and started singing.

When the family arrived home, they stared in astonishment at the strange sight on the kitchen floor: Frankie was lying in a pool of wine, sleeping. The bottle of wine that he had held was overturned and wine had spilled out onto the floor. Everyone was in shock. Then finally, the silence was broken as they all reacted at once.

"Waka up, you drunk!" Luigi yelled.

Giroloma started yelling in Italian, "He's going to get it," as she quickly ran to get her broom. All the children started laughing at the comical sight, and couldn't stop for quite some time.. Sally volunteered to drag Frankie to the bedroom so he could sleep it off.

When he woke up the following morning, Luigi gave it to him good with the strap. It was bad enough that his head hurt and his stomach was upset, but he had to hear Mama, Papa and his older brothers yell and lecture him all morning. My hind end hurts, he thought as he rubbed it. I already got a beating earlier this morning so why should Papa punish me again? He wondered, as he lay in bed.

When he heard the door slam as Luigi left for work, Frankie crept out of bed and into the kitchen, thankful no one was around. Wanting some fresh air, he ventured outside, then started walking down an alley, kicking at the trash and debris that had fallen into his path. He spotted a rotten apple and kicked at it. The apple rolled a few inches away when suddenly he discovered that a dime was embedded in the dirt underneath. Feeling elated, he picked up the dirty dime and brushed it off.

'This is just enough money to go to the show,' he thought. Then he saw some kids approaching him, and as they neared, he recognized it was Sally and his friends.

"Hey, blubberhead!" yelled Sally. "Are yuh over your drunk?" He laughed.

"Aw, shut up, Columbus!" Frankie hollered back. It was his name for Sally because he wore his hair long in the back.

"Where are yuh going?" Sally asked.

"I found a dime and I'm going to the show."

"What's playing?" asked Sally.

"The Bowery Boys," Frankie answered.

"Hey, I like watching them," interjected Merc.

"I got an idear," said Sally. "Why don't yuh go in the show and open the back door, so's we all can go in? I'll give yuh five cents."

Frankie thought of the popcorn he could buy with the money, so he said, "It's a deal."

After Frankie entered the show he went to the back door and let in Sally and his gang, then he went over to the candy counter and bought a bag of popcorn and settled down for the show. Sally and his gang of friends joined him when the movie started. The movie was a gangster movie, with a gang of street kids. Sally was enjoying the movie, but when he looked over at Frankie he noticed that he was fast asleep.

After the movie ended, Sally noticed Frankie was still asleep.

'*Well, he'll wake up*,' Sally reasoned, then, before he left, Sally nudged Frankie and Frankie stirred.

"The movie is over," whispered Sally.

Frankie woke up, startled, and said, "I musta missed the movie. I think I'll stay awhile and catch the first feature." Soon after Sally left, Frankie fell back to sleep again.

Sally was outside the tenement house when he heard Luigi's whistle. When he came in, Luigi was counting heads before sitting down to eat. "The white one is here," he said, referring to Sally, "but the black one is missing," meaning Frankie.

"He was in the show when I left, so he must have fallen asleep again," explained Sally.

"Where did you boys getta money for the picture show?"

"Frankie found a dime and let me in the back door."

"I better go ana find him; it's getting dark outa side and I worry—it's a dangerous neighborhood," said Luigi as he put on his hat.

Frankie felt someone nudge him and woke up to see Luigi sitting next to him, then said, "I'm sorry, Papa, for drinking your wine."

Luigi smiled at Frankie and said, "You a good boy, and I thinka you learn your lesson. I know you're the smartest one of the kids; I just wisha I could have money to send you to college to become a newspaper writer like you want. You see, you were born a poor boy and it costs too mucha money to become educated."

The next morning Frankie woke up feeling cramped and uncomfortable. Then he noticed a foot resting against his chin. In anger he gave a hard kick at Sally, who was sleeping at the opposite end of the bed.

"Hey, what the heck is the matter with you, blubber head?" complained Sally.

"Your big feet are stinking me outa this bed," answered Frankie.

"Aw, shut up! I sleep like dis cuz I'm used to it! You should complain about stinking, shit pants." His remark silenced Frankie, as he should have been used to all the teasing by now, but as usual, he was still sensitive about his bowel problem. Sally, fully awake by now, realized how unkind his remark was and said, "Aw, come on Frankie, yuh know I was only just kidding yuh; anyway, sleeping conditions are much better now. Remember how cramped we were with five of us in the bed?"

Frankie, now feeling better by Sally's kindness, asked, "What are yuh going to do today? Do yuh want to go to the barbershop with me and work as a team shining shoes for the gangsters?"

"I dunno; I'll tink about it, but right now I'm going back to sleep for awhile," yawned Sally.

Frankie, feeling fully awake, decided to get up, so he grabbed his pants and snuck past the other double bed in the small bedroom. The three girls who shared the bed were all fast asleep. Frankie had to pass through his parents' bedroom to get to the kitchen in the railroad-style tenement house. He noticed that they were also fast asleep.

Once in the kitchen, Frankie looked in the icebox for something to eat, but the only thing in there was about six eggs. Overcome with hunger, he took out the eggs, then looked in the drawer of the sewing machine that was sitting by a corner wall of the kitchen. There he found a pin and went into the bathroom. Once in the bathroom he stuck a hole in an egg, using the pin, and sucked out all the liquid from the egg. He proceeded to do this until he had every egg drained. Not knowing what to do with the eggshells, he dropped them into the toilet, but in his haste to leave, he forgot to flush the toilet. Since everyone in the house was sleeping, he decided to go back to bed. He knew that someone was going to get blamed for the stolen eggs and he didn't want anyone to realize he was the first one up. As he crept back into the bedroom he noticed Rosie stir in her sleep. Just as he was getting into bed, she opened her eyes and stared right at him. She finally turned over and went back to sleep, so Frankie pulled the covers up over himself, trying to get back to sleep.

As he lay there he began thinking about his school and how proud Papa was of him being the first to graduate from the eighth grade. Frankie was one of the most intelligent kids in the family. He enjoyed school and made straight A's. The field of journalism fascinated him and he fantasized about becoming a great writer in the future. He imagined he would work for a large newspaper someday and become a famous reporter. He would report fascinating news and talk to famous people and travel around the world, with his name becoming a household word. Everyone would forget about his bowel condition because he would be miraculously cured in a foreign land by a healer he was interviewing.

Ever since he could remember he would mess his pants. The ridicule, beatings, and lectures never helped. Nothing seemed to stop this embarrassing problem. He was grateful to his older sister Marian, who would defend him on his problem. When he was younger she would fatefully clean him up, then tell him not to cry because it was not his fault. Giroloma, out of desperation, took him to a doctor, and the doctor could find no physical reason why he lost control of his bowels. As a result Frankie became a loner, not wanting to mingle with Sally's friends. Instead he spent his time studying and going to the show. It was safer this way, he thought, as his condition prompted many fights—when the kids made fun of him he would charge like a bull. He was afraid of no one, and soon acquired the nicknames Blubber head and Lumber head.

One time he was so angry at some kids teasing him that he charged right into a brick wall. After that the kids were afraid to tease him anymore.

Frankie finally drifted off to a deep sleep, when suddenly he was awakened by a loud commotion coming from the kitchen. He sat upright, looking around the bedroom, realizing that he was alone and that everyone had gotten up. As he entered the kitchen he heard loud voices and Luigi yelling, "Who wasa the chicken in the toilet?"

All the kids ran to the bathroom to see what Luigi was yelling about. There was the evidence of the eggshells still floating in the toilet bowl. Frankie scolded himself for his stupidity for forgetting to flush the toilet. All the kids started laughing at this peculiar and hilarious sight. Giroloma, in her anger, grabbed for the broom and swung it at Frankie, missing him as he ran out of the kitchen.

"I know for sure it was you, Frankie; I remember catching you do this before. If I catch you again you're going to get it!" Giroloma yelled. All the kids started laughing at Frankie's quick getaway, including Luigi.

Giroloma made some coffee out of used coffee grounds from the previous day and was busy slicing the stale bread when she started laughing. "Who wasa the chicken in the toilet?" she giggled. "Go tell Frankie, the chicken in the toilet; it's safe to come back into the kitchen now," she said, while trying to suppress a giggle.

Soon Frankie emerged, sheep-faced, as he sat down to eat with the rest of the family.

"You still want to go with me to shine shoes at the barbershop today?" Frankie asked Sally. "Naw, I tink I'll go down to Jew Town with my gang later," answered Sally.

Soon after he ate breakfast, Frankie, carrying his shoeshine box, entered Joe's Barbershop and Joe said, "Hi, Frankie, I'ma glad you could make it today; I'ma expecting a lot of important people here today, so stick around awhile, and you shoulda be able to maka some money."

Joe's Barbershop was more notorious for its undercover meetings among the Mafia. The friendly looking storefront with its red and white-striped pole and green-striped canopy top, framing the large picture window was, in all honesty, a legitimate barbershop. Joe's friendly personality had acquired him a profitable clientele in the neighborhood, but his customers knew what went on in the back room. The backroom was never spoken or referred to in any conversation, out of respect and mostly out of fear. Joe's brother was the Godfather or "Don" of this particular area. Many notorious gangsters had made this place a meeting place, and many decisions, deals and murders were planned in the back room.

It didn't take long before the detectives got word of this little barbershop being used as a meeting place. Detective Pectisino became an undercover cop in the case. He became quite obsessed with arresting the notorious gangsters, so he arranged a set-up with a neighborhood informer. Finally he got word from the informer that the gangsters were at the barbershop.

Frankie was standing outside the barbershop ready to set up his area for shining shoes when he was called into the back room. To his astonishment he was face to face with Al Capone, Lucky Luciano, and Vito Genovese.

"I want yuh to stand outside and be a lookout, and if anyone strange or anyone yuh recognize as an informer or maybe a cop walks into the shop," said the Godfather, "yuh come back here immediately with your shoeshine box." Frankie, dumfounded by their presence, nodded. "Now yuh get back out there and keep a close watch."

Frankie walked back into the barbershop section, then walked outside and took a position in front of the barbershop. After he set up his shoeshine box he started yelling, "Get yuh shoes shined, five cents!" After about twenty minutes he saw a strange man walk into the barbershop, and he watched inconspicuously through the window as the man sat down for a haircut. When the barber's head was turned, he noticed the man put up his hand up as a signal, directed to someone outside the window. Frankie closed his shoeshine box and walked swiftly into the back room of the shop.

"Good boy, come here, now hide these guns in yuh shoeshine box and go home," said the Godfather. "Don't come back until Joe walks outside in front of the shop."

As Frankie was walking out of the front door, he was met by three detectives as they moved quickly, running into the shop.

Frankie made a beeline for home, and as he was coming up the front steps he noticed Giroloma worriedly looking out the window. When he went inside she said in Italian, "Thank God, you are safe; you must not go anywhere until they send a messenger saying that it is safe to go back."

Frankie looked at Giroloma and said, "Mama, how did yuh know what was happening?"

"Papa saw the detectives enter the shop, and he knew what was going on."

Twenty minutes later they saw the detectives leave the shop. Then a few minutes later Joe the Barber walked outside the shop and stared up at their window.

"It's safe to go back now, so you be careful," Luigi warned. When Frankie returned to the shop, Joe motioned for him to go into the back room. The gangsters were still there, laughing.

"They couldn't arrest us with no evidence," Frankie heard one of them say.

"You did a good job," said one of the gangsters as he took the guns out of Frankie's shoeshine box. "Here is some money for your trouble," he said as he handed him some bills.

Frankie was overjoyed! It wasn't just the money that made him happy; it was the importance he felt at working for these famous gangsters.

"Now the next time we come back here, yuh hang around; yuh have proven how useful yuh are by why yuh did for us today," said Al Capone.

When Frankie returned home, he anxiously counted the money. Twenty dollars wasn't bad for a walk across the street, he thought, then said, "I think I should take a dollar and give the rest of it to Mama and Papa."

A few days later Frankie was walking down the street when he encountered a friend of his from school.

"Hey, Frankie, you're just the person I want to see," remarked Mickey. "I....um... sorta got dis here problem...I'm flunking in my math class and if my old man finds out about it, I'll get walloped. Could yuh do my homework for me? I'll pay yuh twenty bucks!"

"Twenty bucks!" exclaimed Frankie. "That's a lot of money; where yuh get that kind of dough?" Frankie asked.

Well...it's not real money, yuh know, but yuh can spend it like real money. Don't say anything. It's counterfeit, and I can't tell yuh where it came from, but yuh could do a lot with twenty bucks."

"Yuh, I don't have to think about it; it's a deal!" exclaimed Frankie, as he was thinking of all the shows he could go to and all the goodies he could eat with the money.

"Meet me in school tomarra and I'll give yuh my homework and pay yuh the twenty bucks. Now yuh have to do my homework until school lets out and figure a way ta pass me the answers on the final exam," Mickey explained.

"No, problem. Leave it to me ta get yuh passed," boasted Frankie.

The next day Frankie met Mickey and they made the transaction. Frankie walked away with a math text book and a counterfeit twenty-dollar bill. Frankie never felt so rich in his life. He spent the whole day pondering what to do with it and how to pass it. Finally a plan emerged.

When Frankie got home, Giroloma was sitting in the kitchen wondering what to cook for dinner. She had some pasta but nothing to go with it for supper tonight.

"Guess what, Mama, I just found twenty cents outside by the alley!" he excitedly exclaimed. "I'm craving chicken for supper, do yuh think yuh could make chicken for supper tonight if I buy it?" Frankie earnestly asked.

Giroloma looked at him as if he was an answer to a prayer. "Son, how did you know that I was craving chicken today too!" She was secretly glad because the extra money he had given her the previous night was already spent on a portion of the rent—which was two months behind—and last night's supper.

Soon Frankie was in the chicken market. The Jewish marketer recognized Frankie when he walked into the market. Since his run-in with Rosie, he knew better then to mess with the Finazzos. That episode cost him a lot of money, and it took awhile before he could open his business again. To show no hard feelings, he even hired a cousin of theirs to work for him.

"Hi Frankie, what can I do for you today?" he asked.

"I need ta buy a chicken," said Frankie. The marketer nodded and went to the back, then emerged with a plump pink chicken with its feathers freshly plucked, and held up the chicken for Frankie's inspection.

"It looks good enough to eat," joked Frankie, as he handed him the twenty dollar bill.

"And a delicious meal at that," commented the marketer, as he handed him back the change. He was surprised that Frankie had handed him so much money.

"My big brudder Jimmy is back in town," commented Frankie, observing the look of surprise on the marketer's face. The marketer instantly relaxed, knowing what a big spender Jimmy was and how he helped the family out when he was home.

On the way home Frankie was pleased how easy it had been. He had all the money jingling in his pocket and trying to make a decision on how to spend it. *'I know what I'll do...after I drop the chicken off home, I'll go to the show.'*

Later Frankie was sitting at the theater enjoying a gangster movie starring James Cagney, and he was already stuffed from the bakery where he had bought a large cream-filled pastry with a plump cherry on top. At the show he filled up on popcorn and candy bars.

When he got home, he was very surprised and relieved to see Jimmy sitting at the table. Even though he was full, he forced himself to eat some of the delicious chicken Mama made, so as not to arouse her suspicions.

A couple of days later, it was rumored in the neighborhood that the chicken market had received a counterfeit twenty-dollar bill, and Frankie was in a cold sweat worrying about all the trouble he was in.

As time went on the chicken marketer accused everyone in the neighborhood of passing that money onto him, but strangely, he never thought of Frankie, who was having the time of his life going to shows and buying delicious food from various venders every day.

One day Frankie spent his last dime on some penny candy before going home, and when he entered the house, he discovered he was just in time for supper. Giroloma had prepared boiled snails. It was considered a very rare delicacy and a very special treat for the family. Frankie loved seafood, and in Brooklyn it was always an ample and stable food supply because they lived near the Atlantic Ocean. It was not unusual to see venders selling freshly cooked fish, shrimp, lobsters, and every variety of seafood on the streets of Brooklyn, but Frankie had never tasted snails. Out of curiosity, Frankie looked into the large pot simmering on the stove, where the snails were being boiled alive. He could see them trying to make an escape by climbing up the sides of the pot, so at supper time he couldn't bring himself to eat them as he watched everyone scoop them out with a toothpick and then ingest them by a sucking motion. He then spied Luigi's leather strap sitting by his plate and he knew he had better eat them or be beaten. He somehow managed to eat, but he felt his stomach lurch each swallow.

Finally after supper Frankie made a beeline for the bathroom, only to discover that Rosie had gotten there first. He started banging on the door as he felt his stomach turn, and it seemed as though his stomach couldn't decide which way to go. Suddenly he felt his bowels move as he stood waiting by the door in embarrassment.

Luigi, who heard the commotion, walked up by Frankie, and yelled, "I smella shit! I'ma going to give it to you good; you justa too lazy to go to the shit pot."

"He can't help what happens!" Marian shouted.

Then Giroloma, full of sympathy for him, spoke up, "How do you think he feels? Marian is right, beating him is not the answer."

"Then whata we gonna do? Something has to be done with him!" Luigi countered.

"I saw Carmellia just the other day; she is in America now, and she has the powers like my mother has, so maybe she can help," said Giroloma.

Luigi was silent for a moment, before he spoke up: "I don't know...some-a-how I don't trust her, but ifa you think she can do something, then let her try."

Later Giroloma walked into the parlor where Frankie sat brooding, and she said, "Son, I know you feel bad about something you can't control, so I'm going to try to do everything I can to help you."

The next day Giroloma took Frankie and went to visit Carmellia. When she answered the door, she was surprised to see Giroloma standing there. "What a pleasant surprise!" she said. "*Venica*, come in, *settee*." Carmellia led them to the kitchen and started heating some coffee on the stove. She then started setting the table with little china coffee cups and saucers, talking in Sicilian all the while as she worked. "How is Luigi doing, and the children?" she asked as she set a large tray of Italian cookies in front of them.

"Everybody isa doing fine," replied Giroloma, lapsing into ancient Sicilian as she talked. "All except for my poor boy here; he has a problem."

By now Carmellia had taken a seat by them so she could give her full attention to her guests. "Tell me what it is that I can do to help and I'll be happy to do what I can?"

Giroloma hesitated before she spoke as she found herself observing Carmellia: '*She is still an attractive woman,*' she thought. ' *I wonder if Luigi still thinks of her.*' Finally Giroloma realized she was staring and suddenly spoke up. "Frankie here has a problem…you see, he has trouble controlling his bowels. I know he doesn't do it on purpose because he is so embarrassed when it happens. I even took him to a doctor and the doctor couldn't find any physical reason why this happens. I just don't know what to do, so I thought you might be able to help him."

Carmellia sat and thought for a few minutes before she asked, "I must ask you, was Frankie the baby you were pregnant with when your husband was killed?"

"Yes," replied Giroloma. "When I saw him shot, my stomach turned, and I felt as if the baby was spinning, then he gave a large kick. Then, when he was a baby, he didn't walk as soon as normal babies. It wasn't until after his third birthday that he walked."

Carmellia thought for a few more minutes and suddenly she said, "That's the trouble; you see, the baby was inside of you when all this happened and he felt all of your shock and sorrow. After he was born, all your emotions were still transferred to him, and his body is still in shock over your husband dying."

Giroloma sat in amazement, as this had never occurred to her before. It still saddened her to think of her dead husband Francesco, whom she loved dearly. "How can you help my boy Frankie?" she finally asked.

"Now that we know the cause, we can work on a cure," replied Carmellia. "I think he has to go into shock again; it must be something from the dead in order to work. You understand, it started from the dead so it must end with the dead."

Frankie began to get frightened. '*What is she planning?*' He wondered.

"I think I know just how to solve this," replied Carmellia. "You bring him over here tomorrow night and I will take care of it."

Giroloma was overcome with her kindness. "You don't know how much this means to me; how can I repay you?" she asked.

"There is nothing I need; I have always been found of the Finazzos and I am only happy to help."

Giroloma's eyes were filled with gratitude. "I know that you and Luigi were spoken for before my husband was killed, and I hope that you can forgive me for marrying him. I didn't want it to be this way, please believe me."

"I don't resent you for a situation that couldn't be helped. It was nobody's fault. Just destiny…God had His reasons," lied Carmellia. "I'm leaving for Detroit, Michigan, next week, where my family has relatives and there is opportunity in the automobile factories over there," said Carmellia, changing the subject.

"Well, I wish you all the luck in the world, and maybe you will even meet your future husband there," said Giroloma.

"I gave up long ago, after that husband of mine ran away. Anyway, I have my parents to look after, so I don't think about marriage anymore."

After drinking the coffee and a few more minutes of conversation, Giroloma excused herself, saying, "I must be going, but I'll see you tomorrow night after supper." Then she and Frankie left.

The next night after supper, Frankie pleaded, "Please, Mama, I don't want to go. That woman is evil, so please don't make me go."

"You should be ashamed to say such things about a woman who only wants to help you. Don't you want to get rid of your problem?" she reminded. "You are going to do everything she asks you to do, understand?" she warned.

When they arrived at Carmellia's house, she greeted them with a big smile. "We must hurry, as I have everything planned. We are going to the home of a young boy about Frankie's age who just died. It is real fortunate that I found these people. I talked with '*The White Ghost*,' the lady who does all the neighborhood healing, and she got in touch with them for us. Now, Frankie, when we get there, please don't ask questions, just do everything I tell you," Carmellia cautioned.

Frankie's fright was obvious by now. '*What crazy thing is she going to make me do?*' he wondered. Frankie tried to catch his mother's eye, and when he did she gave him a warning look. Frankie knew that look; she never had to say a word, just give him that look. Frankie was very desolate, as he knew that something terrifying was in store for him and there was nothing he could do to stop it.

The short walk to the dead boy's house seemed like miles. Frankie glanced over at his mother again to give her a pleading look, when he noticed how she grimaced every time she took a step, and he was suddenly overcome with guilt. *'Here I am,'* he thought, *'worrying about myself when all the while Mama is in such pain. She is doing this for me.'* At that moment Frankie decided whatever she had in store for him he must endure it; after all, he reasoned, it was for his benefit. If Mama was willing to take the time to help him, in all her pain and suffering, then he should be a man instead of a boy and appreciate her sacrifice.

Soon they were entering the front door, and the people who greeted them were nice Italians with grief-stricken faces. Carmellia introduced Giroloma and Frankie and said, "This is the boy I talked to you about helping."

The lady who answered the door said, "My name is Mrs. Mattucci. Please come in."

As they politely entered the parlor, at first glance Frankie could see all the flowers around the room. Then he spotted the casket with a young boy in it. The overpowering aroma of the sweet scent of flowers mingled with the musk odor of death made him nauseous, and all his resolutions left him, in place of the fear that overtook him. He felt his heart pounding like a drum and getting louder every moment. He felt Carmellia's tight squeezing grip on his arm, practically pushing him as she urged him to step closer to the casket. "Don't be afraid, my boy; just walk up to the casket with me," she urged. Frankie was beyond fear as his body felt wooden and his throat felt dry as he gulped for air. Each step he took caused his body the convulse and tremble, and the beating of his heart began getting louder until he felt his ears would burst. The sweet scent of the flowers and the musk scent of death was getting stronger and more pungent as he neared the casket.

Finally they were standing before the corpse of the dead boy. Frankie felt his body turn to stone, as if in a trance, as he stared into the casket. Some unknown force was urging him to stare into the dead boy's face. He could smell death and feel death all around him. *'This is it*, he thought, *they're going to kill me and throw me into the casket with him.'*

"Now don't be afraid; just pull up your shirt," he heard Carmellia order. Frankie slowly pulled up his shirt, wondering what evil thing she had planned for him. Suddenly he felt the ice-cold stiff hand on his bare stomach, and terror filled every fiber of his body. He stood stiff as a board, frightened out of his wits. Suddenly his stomach felt like it was turning and spinning, and he could hear rumbling noises coming from his stomach. Then blackness welcomed him as he felt its merciful relief embrace him.

When he finally woke up, he was surprised to see he was lying down on a couch in a different room. Giroloma was smiling and saying, "You are cured now; all the sorrow and the fear are out of you now."

Frankie felt suddenly refreshed, like something heavy was lifted from him. "Let's go home, Mama!" he finally said.

After all the *'grazias'* were said, they left the house together, and Giroloma held onto her son's arm for support as they made their way home. "Nobody is ever going to hurt you again, my son," she vowed. Frankie was relieved that he was cured and would never have this problem again.

Chapter 11—THE BOXER

The air was heavy, and the smell of chalk dominated the overcrowded classroom in the all-boys school. Sally sat slumped over his desk as he impatiently waited for class to be dismissed. It was the last day of school before summer vacation, and Mister Carney was calling each boy to come up to his desk to receive his eighth grade diploma. It was a slow process, which Mister Carney was enjoying because the class would not be dismissed until each student received his diploma and a final lecture.

Just then the door to the classroom opened and Mister McCormick, the principal, entered. Mister Carney continued with his graduation process. Sally was sure he would graduate. His grades were high on every subject. He knew he was brilliant in spelling. He never missed a word in spelling bees; in fact, there was no one who could compete with him in the whole school.

"Salvatore Finazzo," announced Mister Carney, and Sally walked up to receive his diploma. Then Mister McCormick looked at the short list and said, "Finazzo can't graduate."

Sally was in shock. "Why not?" he asked.

"You are very disobedient and a troublemaker," answered Mister McCormick. Sally knew this was no reason to hold him back, and he felt the anger build up in him. He had a personality conflict with the principal, but that should not of reflected his academic abilities. Suddenly he exploded, letting all his anger out at this unjust prejudiced principal. "You son of a bitch!" he yelled.

Mister McCormick, shocked and flustered at his outburst, yelled, "Get back in your seat or you'll be sorry!"

Sally's arm shot out swiftly, giving Mister McCormick an uppercut and knocking him to the floor. Sally then ran out of the school, angered and upset. He ran past the front door and into the street, never stopping until he was out of breath. The tears of anger stung his eyes. '*That bald headed son-of-a-bitch had no right to hold me back! He fumed. Well they can shove that school up their ass; I'm never going back*,' he thought. Sally continued running until he saw the Jolly Joker's Sporting Club. The old run down building on North Street was his second home. Here he could excel and do what he enjoyed the most—boxing.

Stump McGee saw him run into the gym, and he asked, "Hey Sally, what's up?"

"Aw nuttin; they didn't graduate me at school, and I ain't goin' back next year. And I punched Mister McCormick, so I'm probably in trouble at home, too. I ain't goin back home either, 'cause I don't want to get yelled at."

"Well, maybe the owner of this place will let yuh stay here for a while. For a kid, yuh know, you are one of the best boxers they have in this place."

Stump McGee was one of Sally's boxing friends who hung around the gym. He was born without a left hand and lower arm, with fingers that grew out of the end of his upper arm, but this had not prevented him from actually boxing. He would put both of his boxing gloves on—one on his deformed left arm and the other on his right hand—and swing a mighty punch with his right hand. His deformity had caused him to grow up fighting, giving him a reputation as a tough guy who no one wanted to anger.

Sally still hung around with his gang, but lately his interest in boxing had increased. Sally knew he had talent for boxing. He rarely lost a fight, as his brother Jimmy was an excellent fighter and had taught him many moves and gave him the inspiration to get started.

"Hey, Sally, yuh oughta change your name; yuh know most of the fighters are Irish and they don't take to well with us Italians," Stump advised.

"Yah, you're right, and I've been tinking, how's about cutting my last name to Finn? Sally Finn, how's that sound for my professional name?"

"Yah, I like it, it has a good sound to it, so keep that name and you'll be remembered," said Stump. (Little did they know that Sally Finn would someday be a famous name and he would receive the Golden Gloves Award.)

"I tink I'll get into my trunks and get in some practice by hitting that punching bag," said Sally.

"Yuh know what I was tinking about a little while ago, remember dat fight yuh had with that kid Mario Cherallo? Yuh sure beat the hell outta him," Stump commented.

"If yuh hadn't of jumped in along with Rocco, I would have been beat to a pulp," Sally laughed, remembering how the fight was arranged by Tony Charello. He had a tough son that he was proud of, but he didn't like the fact that Sally had the reputation of being one of the toughest kids in the neighborhood, so he arranged the fight between Sally and his son Mario. Everyone in the neighborhood bet money on the boys. The fight was a good one, with each boy giving equal punches to his opponent. Eventually, Sally got the best of him, and this angered Tony Charello to the point that he had his friends jump in. Sally then was up against three other boys, and he gave a good fight, but in no time they had his arms pinned behind his back and were punching him in the face. Rocco was so furious that he jumped in, along with Stump McGee, and beat the hell out of the boys.

Sally hung around the gym for a couple of days. He did odd jobs for his keep. The owner liked Sally and saw great potential in him. The kid had a talent, and with a lot of practice, in the future he wouldn't be surprised if he became somebody.

Sally felt at home here; whenever life struck him a blow, he would escape to the gym and work off his anger, striking back at life, blow after blow. Sally had a frustration and anger at the humble way he had to live, so his way of coping was punching. The guys at the gym all liked and respected him. This old run-down building was his sanctuary, and here he could fight back at all the unjust circumstances in his life.

Every Saturday night at the club there would be card games and meetings. Many of the men would rent tuxedos and the club would be a meeting place. The men would eventually go to the dance clubs together. One regular club member was nick-named Boohoo (a name he had acquired because every time he lost in a card game he would cry). At first the other guys made fun of him and called him cry baby, but eventually it was changed to Boohoo.

One night all the men had gathered in the back room, dressed in their finest tuxedos except Boohoo, who was wearing a vest. Sally was cleaning up the table where they usually played cards when he spotted three strange men walking into the room. He hurriedly ran into the broom closet, sensing danger. Some of the regular guys at the gym also sensed trouble and they stood in front of an old couch. They nudged each other and emptied their pockets inconspicuously, throwing their dollar bills behind the couch.

Suddenly the strange men pulled out their guns. "This is a stick-up!" said one of the men. "Put your hands up!" Boohoo had watched the other guys throw their dollar bills behind the couch and nervously fumbled in his pants pockets, drawing out his change, then awkwardly threw the change behind the couch. The change made a loud clanging sound, landing near the dollar bills.

"Hey, wise guy, just what do you think you're doing?" challenged one of the robbers. The robber walked over to him and looked behind the couch.

"Well, boys look what we found here...dollar bills, and stupid over here led us right to them." The men picked up all the money behind the couch, laughing, then one of the robbers walked back over to Boohoo, who was sobbing uncontrollably by now.

"I ought to thank yuh, but you're so stupid that I think I'll smarten yuh up instead." He then grabbed him by the shoulders and shook him up and started slapping him. He finally let him go and he fell to a heap on the floor, sobbing. The robber then said, "Alright, I want all yuh men ta take off all your clothes and hurry it up!" The men started undressing quickly. "Now trow all your clothes in a pile, in the middle of the room," added the robber, as the other robbers gathered the clothes up. Then they all swiftly backed out of the room with their guns still pointed at the club members.

Some minutes had passed, before the men started yelling, "Sally come out and help us." Sally emerged from the closet and took in the sorry sight. All the men were looking embarrassed, naked as jaybirds.

"Go see if yuh can find our clothes; they're probably on the lamp post outside," said one of the naked men in an embarrassed voice. Sally ran outside and looked around; sure enough, he spotted the clothes on top of the nearest lamp post. He quickly climbed up the post and gathered all the clothes.

When he arrived back in the room, the men were all arguing. Boohoo was getting slapped around again, this time by them. "It's all your fault, yuh stupid son-of-a-bitch!" they yelled. When they saw Sally arrive with their clothes, they looked relieved. One man said, "Kid, I can't pay yuh today, but when I get some extra money we'll all chip in and pay yuh for yuh trouble."

Sally was at the gym a couple of days later when he saw his three older brothers walk through the door. He knew that he was in trouble for not going home. His first inclination was to run, but where could he run to? Sally wasn't afraid of too many people, but he was no match for his big brothers. After pondering what to do, he decided to stay and face the music. He wondered which brother was going to be the one to wallop him. As they closed in on him he could see their angry faces.

"Hey, Sally, why are yuh worrying Mama like this?" Louie yelled.

"You wanna fight? Well, which one of us do yuh wanna fight?"yelled Jimmy."Well, knucklehead ain't got a chance with us, so how about fighting Frankie? He's the closest to your age," Louie added. "Yah, that's a good idear, fight Frankie," yelled Jimmy.

Sally looked at Frankie, who was almost double his size. Sally was small and skinny, but Frankie, a few years older, was muscular and stocky. Sally knew he had no choice, as one of them was going to beat the hell out of him, so it might as well get it over with.

Frankie put on a pair of gloves and jumped into the ring. After circling each other for a few minutes, Sally took the initiative and swung at Frankie. Frankie had left himself wide open for the punch, and Sally's fist hit his chin, then another one caught his eye. Before he could recuperate, another punch landed in his stomach, doubling him over, and Frankie lost his balance, falling to the floor. The fight was over before he ever had a chance. Jimmy, who was the Light Weight Champion of the Navy, was in shock and then started laughing. "I can't believe yuh just took yuh big brudder, kid. My lessons paid off. You got the same savage punch like me and the rest of the Finazzos. I never would have believed yuh could take Frankie," he added. Frankie, deeply humiliated, ran outside and walked home.

When Frankie got home, Giroloma was in the kitchen, and there was no way to avoid her. One look at his face infuriated her. "Who did this to you? Tell me, was it Jimmy?" she asked in Italian. Finally Frankie had to admit it was Sally, and Giroloma sat in shock, unable to understand how that skinny kid could so savagely mess up his brother's face.

"You let that skinny runt beat you up? You are the oldest and you should let your little brother do this to you?" Giroloma in her fury, grabbed the broom and started swinging it at Frankie. "Now you're going to get it from me!" she raged.

In a few minutes, Luigi came into the kitchen. "Sons-of-a-bitchy, what'sa the commotion? Can't everyone be quiet? My head hurts so bad; I ama sick to my stomach."

Giroloma took a quick look at Luigi and was immediately filled with concern. His face was pale and filled with pain. "I'm sorry, Luigi, I didn't know you were sick, but Sally beat up Frankie, and I got mad," she said.

Luigi sat down on the chair holding his head. "Go getta The White Ghost; maybe she can help me," he said.

Giroloma yelled for Frankie to go fetch her.

After a short time, *The White Ghost* was entering the house, a very fragile old woman with snow white hair and a very long white dress. She was the neighborhood midwife and healer. Her healing powers had made her a saint among the people in the neighborhood. When she saw Luigi, she said in Italian, "Let me see what I can do," while she was gently touching Luigi's head with her small withered hands. "Go get me a small bowl filled with olive oil and a towel," she ordered. Giroloma handed her the bowl filled with oil and the towel. Next she dabbed the oil on his forehead, making the sign of the cross. She uttered a few prayers and rubbed the rest of the oil into his hair, massaging his head. She then wrapped his head in the towel, saying some final prayers. When she was finished she said, "He will be better in a few minutes."

Luigi sat very still for a few minutes, then he relaxed and a slow smile began to emerge from his face. "The pain is gone!" he exclaimed.

"Now you go lay down for a little while, and you will be better when you wake up," instructed *The White Ghost*.

After Luigi left the room to rest, Giroloma lit the burner to heat some coffee, thankful she had a few Italian cookies left over to offer her guest. Giroloma knew better than to offer her money for her favor, as that would be an insult. The old woman believed her powers came from the saints and to take money would be a sin.

"*Settee*," said Giroloma pouring her a cup of coffee and setting a plate of cookies on the table. "My mother in Sicily is also a healer; her name is Phillepa Zanca," said Giroloma. "People used to come from miles around to hear their fortunes or be healed." Giroloma found herself starting to tell the old woman about her mother. As she talked about her home in Castellammare, situated on a high hill overlooking the ocean and mountains. She could almost smell the familiar perfume fragrance of the lilac bush that nestled near the entrance door, and then, as she entered the house, the spicy aroma of the small kitchen where her mother mixed and steamed all her particular ingredients for various spells. On the table sat an old worn-out deck of Italian tarot cards that she often used to tell people's fortunes. She could see her tall, lean mother bending over, working in her garden. People called her garden a witch garden because she grew special herbs and plants for her various spells and incantations. Giroloma talked about her sister Josephina, who remained in Sicily, and her three brothers, John and Tony, who came to America—John eventually owning his own grocery store and about Tony owning a tobacco store—and Guiseppe, who was wounded by the vendettas, who remained in Sicily.

As Giroloma talked, she reminisced how pleasant life had been, especially the tranquility and peacefulness of their small farm, where she was protected from hardships or sorrow. She was the prettiest one of the two daughters, doted on and overprotected. She cherished the memories of the Finazzo homestead in a valley just below her house. She would run to meet Francesco when they were children, and play in the warm sunshine. On special occasions the two families would visit and the gala atmosphere would be filled with much laughter and feasting. Giroloma talked about her mother, who was both respected and feared because of her powers. No one wanted to experience her wrath if they should offend her in any way. The "Evil Eye" and her curses could put the fear into anyone in the town.

Strange as it seemed, her mother would have insight into everyone's future but her own. She was strangely afraid that every time she had the slightest case of sniffles or the smallest scratch, she was going to die. Her phobia continued to grow until she was a hypochondriac. The town undertaker would hide when he saw her coming. No amount of explaining could convince her that she wasn't going to die, and she would finally say, "You come over and pick up my body by tomorrow."

The next day she would be up early, doing the work of a man in the fields!

The old woman laughed at this part of Giroloma's story and Giroloma said, "Even now she is alive and healthy and she is in her nineties!" A look of sorrow passed over Giroloma's face as she sat talking about her mother's warning. One morning when she woke up, her mother was sitting by her bed. Her mother's eyes were very sad, as she said, "Giroloma, I had a vision about your future last night. I saw you on a large ship going to America. PLEASE DON'T GO, I BEG YOU! You see, if you go, your husband will be killed. You will be widowed with many small children to raise, and a baby in your stomach. I see three of your children die; two in infancy and one will be a beautiful young girl. Please promise me that you will not go!"

Not long after the warning, Giroloma fell in love with Francesco. After their marriage, her mother's prediction about one of her infants dying came true when she lost her firstborn baby girl. Then the opportunity came for them to go to America. Giroloma's mother was frightened and she tried to talk her out of going. When Giroloma stubbornly refused to listen, her mother ranted and raged, saying, "If you go to America, I will put a curse on the Finazzo family. Misfortune will befall on them for taking you away." Giroloma thought about her mother's warning, but dismissed it. '*She was wrong about her own future, so she could be wrong about me*,' she reasoned.'

The old woman was intrigued by Giroloma's story, and she took one last sip of her coffee before she said, "The power your mother had is usually passed on in every generation. One of your children could inherit it."

"I already know which one of my children has the gift; it's my daughter Roseria, and I knew this from the moment I laid eyes on her. Sometimes she looks at me as if she can read my mind," answered Giroloma.

"You must tread very carefully with that child, as she is very special to have been chosen to have the gift," cautioned the old woman.

After some more conversation the old woman left, and Giroloma sat deep in thought. ' *Maybe I should write my mother a letter and ask her for advice on how to raise Rosie*,' she thought.'

The next day Sally came home, and he was still upset over not graduating. Giroloma watched him walk into the house, and knowing how upset he was, decided not to comment about his straying away.

After supper Sally decided to take a walk to meet some of his gang. As he was walking he was still feeling low, and staring at the pavement. Suddenly something brown was blowing near his shoe. After a few seconds he realized it was an envelope. He picked it up and started reading the writing on the outside. It was addressed to "Doctor Aalbertsberg," and curious, he opened the envelope. It was filled with money and checks. Then it dawned on him this was a bank deposit that somehow got lost. He instinctively knew that there was a lot of money in this envelope. He never had a conscience when it came to stealing oranges and stuff from the Jewish merchants. Even his everyday scams didn't bother him, but this was something different. This was more money then he had ever seen in his life. He pondered what to do about it. He could hide it somewhere and keep it, or he could bring it home to help his family. It was a big decision. Finally he knew he could never feel right until he at least told his mother. He held the envelope close to him while he was running home, the excitement mounting as reality dawned on him about the change this money could make on their lives.

"Mama, come see what I found!" yelled Sally as he rushed in the house.

Giroloma, startled by his loud sudden outburst, almost dropped the large pot of boiling water she was carrying over to the sink.

"What'sa the emergency?" she yelled angrily.

"Money! I found money, an envelope full of money!" Sally yelled.

Giroloma, thankful the pot of boiling water was safely in the sink, rushed over to Sally to inspect the envelope.

"Read me what it says on the outside," she said.

Sally read out loud, "Doctor Aalbertsberg, 2001 Havemeyer Street Brooklyn, New York."

"*Oh Madre mia*! It's our dentist, and he's such a nice man; he let us come see him on credit when Mariana had a bad toothache, and when Jimmy got his tooth knocked out in that fight," Giroloma exclaimed in Italian.

"Can we keep the money, Mama?" Sally asked hopefully.

"Oh, no, that would be like stealing; besides, I could never do anything like that to him."

Sally already regretted bringing all the money home, and he scolded himself, *'I should have known Mama is too honest to let us keep the money.'* "But Mama, we are so poor, and some of this money will help us at least buy some decent food."

"Oh no, it's not ours. Open up the envelope, let's see how much there is."

Sally unfolded the envelope, taking out all the bills. After counting it three times, he was in shock— twenty-one hundred dollars! He was kicking himself for not taking even some of it. "Mama, it's more money then we have ever seen in our lives! It's twenty-one hundred dollars! Please let's at least keep some of it, and we can return the checks," Sally begged.

"Oh no, we must give it all back," Giroloma said while folding her arms. "You understand, God will reward us in a different way. You know in your heart you wanted to do the right thing by bringing it home to me. In your heart you are a good boy, so don't feel bad."

Sally was upset almost ready to cry, trying to understand his mother's reasoning.

"Go get Papa, I think he is visiting with Joe the Barber. Tell him to come home right away."

As soon as Luigi was home, Giroloma explained the whole story about the money. Luigi was shocked by so much money, but he, without a second thought, agreed wholeheartedly with Giroloma's decision to return it.

"After supper we will walk over to hisa house and giva him hisa money," he said.

The early evening air was cool, which was refreshing after the hot day's sun. Luigi, Giroloma and all the children enjoyed the short walk to the dentist's house. When they arrived in the Jewish section, the neighborhood looked a little more prestigious. They were not in the rich section, but the apartments appeared better taken care of. Doctor Aalbertsberg's apartment house was very neat, with a red brick courtyard and two large pots of flowers by his entrance door.

Luigi spotted Doctor Aalbertsberg sitting outside with his family, and as he approached he waved at Luigi. "What a nice surprise to see you and your family tonight," greeted Doctor Aalbertsberg. '*This is unusual because they never visit me at home*,' he thought.

"I come over to give you some-a-thing you lost," said Luigi, smiling as he handed him the envelope. Doctor Aalbertsberg was flabbergasted when he saw his long-looked-for envelope.

Earlier in the day he walked to the bank to make a deposit, and he remembered he put the envelope in his shirt pocket, but, as he was walking, a gust of wind suddenly came up, and he was holding his straw hat when he bumped into another man on the street, almost causing him to lose his balance. Shortly after the incident he reached the bank, and once inside he reached into his pocket, but, to his dismay, the envelope was missing. In a panic he ran outside and tried to backtrack his journey. He noticed that the wind had picked up blowing papers on the street. Now he was really upset, and he spent over an hour looking in every crook and cranny trying to locate his envelope. He finally saw the neighborhood policeman walking his beat, and after explaining his plight, the policeman walked over the complete area with him, also to no avail. Finally even the policeman had to give up his search, explaining that someone must have found it by now.

Doctor Albertsberg had scrimped and saved that money for several months as his payments on his dentist practice were enormous, and without this money he didn't know how he was going to pay for the new dental equipment for his office. Not to mention the other expenses he had with a large family.

"It's like a Godsend, and I am lost for words! I don't know how to thank you or repay you!" he explained in a choked-up voice.

"It wasa my son Sally who found the money and brought it home," said Luigi, as he proudly pointed to Sally.

"You should be proud of such a fine honest son; we don't see to much of that these days," said Doctor Aalbertsberg, while wiping his eyes.

"You were very good to us whena we needed our teeth fixed. We never forgot ana we still gonna pay you," said Luigi.

"You can't imagine how much I am in your gratitude. You don't owe me anything; in fact, I promise that I will be in debt to you for life. You will have my free dental services for your entire family for as long as I live," Doctor Aalbertsberg declared.

"It'sa not necessary to do that. Even if you are a stranger we would have donna the sama thing. You see, our family believes in God and we live by hisa teachings," said Luigi proudly.

"Even though we are a different religion than you, we believe the same thing, and God sent that lost money to you, knowing that I would get it back. Now it is my turn to help you. I want to see all of you in my office starting tomorrow and I will work on your teeth," said Doctor Aalbertsberg.

"I can't argue, but I am grateful. Crazy thing, all of the Finazzos were blessed witha beautiful teeth. We taka pride in that. We don't want them to go bad. Thanka you very much for your offer," said Luigi, smiling, and displaying his beautiful white teeth.

The next day Luigi brought four of his children in to the doctor's dental office. On the first visit each family member would receive a thorough check-up. After this visit, Doctor Aalbertsberg explained that he would schedule a certain day of the week to do the rest of the family members, alternating two days each week to do the actual dental work that was needed for each person.

Rosie had never been to a dentist, so she had nothing to fear, but from the moment they walked into the office, the particular smell of medicines, mixed with the sharp acid odor of antiseptics, made her nauseous. Her large round eyes grew wider as each person was called to enter the room where the dentist did the actual dental exam. When they first entered, the office was empty, but, after Luigi and the boys returned from their exams, the office began to fill, and she knew she was getting closer to being called. Suddenly she heard her name being called by the lady assistant in a white uniform, so she nudged Fannie, and said, "It's really your turn. You go in foist, cuz I got to go to the bathroom."

Fannie, happy to oblige and having no fear, skipped into the room. Then Rosie noticed a chubby boy sitting next to her.

"Boy, I'm glad it's her turn," he whispered.

Rosie, who could easily talk to anyone, asked, "Why? He seems nice, and everyone gets a new toothbrush when they come out of his office."

"Yah, that's just ta shut them up so's dey don't talk about his big pliers and pointy needles," he boasted, trying hard to hide the snicker that almost escaped . 'The game of scaring her is going to be fun,' he thought.

"You're lying; yuh look like yuh never been here, cuz of all your rotten teeth," Rosie commented, but she was getting more frightened by the minute. The chubby boy was really enjoying the way her round eyes got bigger and the way her hands were gripping the seat.

"Oh yah, well yuh know what else—if he don't like yuh he ties yuh to the chair with big straps so's yuh don't run away. Then he ties yuh neck real hard, so's yuh eyeballs pop out and your mouth opens. Then he gets a long pointy needle and gives yuh a shot in yuh tongue. He's got a big drill that goes, rat-tat-tat-rata-tat-tat, while he's sawing your teeth in half and then yuh spit out yellow powder. Then he stuffs yuh mouth with cotton and ties a big bandage around yuh face, so's yuh look like a chipmunk," whispered the chubby boy, holding his stomach to keep from laughing.

"You're lying, cuz you're fat and you got rotten teeth," Rosie countered angrily. She decided she had enough of this ignorant fat kid and started to get up to move.

Suddenly she saw Fannie coming out and her name was being called. She looked around and noticed the room had filled up with people. She didn't want the chubby boy to think she was scared, so she had no choice but to go in. She got up to walk and the room spun slightly; she felt light-headed. When she entered the little room, she could hear the loud beating of her heart. Then she spotted the chair.

"Have a seat, the doctor will be right in," said the lady in white. Rosie stood in fright, looking at a huge obnoxious green chair that was at a reclining position. She tried to look for straps. 'They must be underneath,' she thought. She stared at a huge machine that looked like it was hanging from a wall Then she spotted a small tray with instruments. The instruments looked threatening, with all their little sharp edges, and on the tray she spotted a jar of cotton. She was about to run, but realized it was too late when the door opened and the dentist entered the room.

"Please sit in the chair, dear, so I can have a look at your teeth," said the dentist, smiling. Rosie obeyed his orders, too frightened to do otherwise. The leather chair was cold and uninviting. She felt a shiver of cold sweat wave though her trembling body. She gripped the armrests, making her little hands resemble claws as she clutched the ends. She could hear the loud thumping of her heart getting louder.

"Now open your mouth real wide so I can look inside,"said the dentist. Rosie opened her mouth, fearfully watching out of the sides of her wide-opened eyes as the dentist took a sharp pointy instrument off the little tray. By this time she was frightened out of her wits. As the dentist neared, she could feel his breath. She felt a cold instrument touch the gum inside of her mouth AAGHAAAAAAAGHAAAAAAAGHAAAAGH AAAAAGHAAGH!"

Suddenly her small, piercing scream penetrated the room. The people sitting in the waiting room heard the loud earth-shattering scream, and they looked around nervously, then some of them got up ready to leave. The chubby boy was laughing so hard he fell off of his chair. Luigi had immediately jumped out of his chair, ready to run into the room. Doctor Aalbertsberg was in shock; he never had seen a patient so frightened. He ran into the waiting room to reassure his patients.

"I NEVER TOUCHED HER!" he yelled.

Luigi ran into the room and gathered Rosie in his arms. She was sobbing so hard her little body shook with each labored breath.

"It's okay, honey, we can go home now. You don't have to see the dentist anymore," he said sympathetically.

Sally was standing on the street corner with his gang. Now that school was out, he wanted some time to enjoy hanging out with his gang of friends before becoming a full-time shoeshine boy.

"What'll we do today?" asked Spike.

"I dunno. Maybe we could sell some of dose newspapers to the junkyard," answered Sally.

"Yah, good idear, and I got a good plan for dat," said Merc.

After walking a couple of blocks they came to Havemeyer Street and Metropolitan Avenue. A few more blocks and they were at the junkyard. They could see there was a long wait, about three blocks of people standing in line waiting to cash in anything of value for the small amount of money they hoped they could get.

"Let's duck outta here; follow me," Merc ordered. The boys quickly followed Merc into the junkyard and he led them between two wagons where the newspapers were stored. Then Merc looked around, relieved the junkman was nowhere insight.

"Now see the scale on the wagon; dat's where the Jew is goin' ta measure how much the stack of newspapers we brought weighs," explained Merc.

"Oh, I get it, we can grab a few stacks of his newspapers on the wagon, right," said Spike.

"You're gettin' smarter every day, wise guy," laughed Merc, thumping him on the head. "Now dis is da plan...we don't take too much or da Jew will notice them missing." Sally grabbed a stack of newspapers and the other boys followed suit. Soon the junkman was walking toward them.

"Here comes da Jew now, so hurry up and sit on your stacks," explained Merc.

"Hi, Moe, we brought some newspapers for yuh," said Sally. The junkman just nodded his head.

"Let's weigh them and see what yuh get," he said. Then he put each bundle of papers on the scale, weighing them, one by one. The scale total weighed in at two-hundred and fifty pounds.

"A total of one dollar and fifty cents is what yuh boys get," he remarked.

"What? Is dat all we get for all dese papers? Dat don't seem hardly fair!" complained Merc.

"Take it or leave it; it's the going price and it's all yuh going to get," the junkman grumbled. He knew he was cheating these kids out of a couple of bucks, and he laughed to himself. '*They'll take it.*'

"Well, I still tink yuh can give us more; could yuh give us at least fifty cents more and we'll bring yuh more next week?"

"It's a deal. Yuh keep them papers coming to me every week and I'll give yuh more money," said the junkman, handing them the money.

The boys walked away, grumbling, and as they left the junkyard, Merc was still grumbling.

"How yuh figure we got gypped when dey didn't cost us nuttin' in the foist place?" asked Sonny.

"We should of got a lot more money, dat's why, stupid," answered Merc.

Sally, siding with Sonny, said, "Yah, yuh figured it wrong; how can yuh get gypped if yuh screwed him in the foist place?"

Merc, getting mad put up his fists and said, "Who's da brains and leader of dis gang anyway? It was my idear in the foist place."

"Yuh don't ak like yuh got brains when yuh puts up yuh dukes ta me. This is the stoipidest argument we ever had, asshole!" Sally yelled.

The boys walked several blocks in silence when a push cart interrupted their thoughts. Soon they saw a vendor coming down the street yelling, "Meatball sandwiches, come get them while they're hot!"

Sally's sudden hunger overcame his anger. "Hey, over here; I'll take one!" he yelled. The rest of the boys joined in as the delicious aroma filled the street. Sally paid the vender fifteen cents and received a hot sandwich wrapped in a paper napkin. The plump meatballs were drowned in the rich red sauce and layered between two thick slices of fresh Italian bread.

The boys then started walking back to Roebling Street in silence, enjoying the sandwiches.

Sally spotted The Jolly Joker's Sporting Club and said, "Let's divide up the money now, as I'm goin' ta go ta the gym and box for awhile."

Merc counted the money out, giving each boy his share. As he handed Sally his money, he said, "See yuh tomarra."

When Sally walked into the gym, he heard his friend Stump McGee announce, "Here he is, Sally Finn the Champ."

Chapter 12—JIMMY VALENTINE

Sands Street was alive with action, and the prostitutes were busy getting dressed in their prettiest dresses, as they just got word that a navy ship was about to pull into port. This should be a profitable night because the sailors were always ready for a good time. They would be loaded with money from their ship's pay and looking for excitement, anxious to spend it freely after their long, uneventful trip.

The excitement was evident among the many shop owners, too, in the pawn shops, taverns and whorehouses that lined the street adjoining the Brooklyn Navy Yard.

Elsie stood on the dock watching the enormous navy ship enter port. The soft breeze from the ocean made her flaming red hair blow softly back and her dress adhere to her long legs, exposing the curvy shape of her slender body. Elsie had mixed feelings over the coming arrival of Jimmy. She felt the anticipation of seeing him again, along with the dread of what she knew would happen when he looked at her.

Elsie stood, biting her lip, and pondering what to say to calm Jimmy's quick temper when she noticed the ship unloading. All too soon she recognized the small form walking with a swagger. It was too late; she couldn't turn and run, as he already had spotted her. She then saw him wave and throw up his hat, then come running. The next thing she knew he was hugging her and holding her up high.

"Baby, I missed you, and I spotted yuh a mile away with yuh red hair flying in the wind!" Jimmy exclaimed. "We'll hit the town and paint it as red as yuh hair, but first I want yuh all to myself. Did yuh get our room ready?" It was then that he sensed her silence.

"Hey, baby, why ain't yuh talking?" Jimmy took a closer look, his expression changing from shock and astonishment into fury.

"Who did this ta yuh? I'll kill that son-of-a-bitch!" he screamed. "Please, Jimmy, it was my fault; yuh know my temper, so please calm down," Elsie pleaded.

"Who have you been messing around with when I was gone? Who is the son-of-a-bitch, tell me!" Jimmy demanded in a rage, shaking her shoulders.

"It…. was……….. Casey O'Malley, but please understand…I ran out of money, and had to send my Ma some money, as she was sick. Casey got sore because I wouldn't sleep with him after her made me do it with a creep, so he started beating me," she cried.

Jimmy looked at her swollen eye and the purple bruise that extended down to her cheek, then said, "That son-of-a-bitch should know better than to mess with my woman! Come along; I'm walking you back to yuh room and then I'm goin' lookin' for him." Elsie knew it would be useless to try to talk him out of it, as he took her arm and led her past the crowded dock.

As soon as they were in her room at the dingy hotel, he gently sat her on the lumpy bed and said, "You stay here until I come back, and I'll guarantee yuh nobody will ever mess with you again."

Jimmy left quickly knowing where to locate his opponent. He felt his anger rise with each step as he walked down the street, past all of the familiar whorehouses and taverns.

Suddenly he heard a voice call out, "Hey, sailor, yuh want to have some fun?" A pretty blonde woman with a low-cut dress was standing on the street corner.

Jimmy was surprised he didn't know her, as everybody on this street knew Jimmy Valentine. He shrugged her off, thinking she must be new around here. "Later, doll, I got some business to tend ta first."

Soon Jimmy was in front of the Anchor Inn Saloon, then he swaggered in and looked around the overly crowed, smoky room. He finally spotted Casey O'Molly standing by the bar, talking to a prostitute.

"Hey, Jimmy, how was yuh trip?" greeted Casey. He was suddenly silenced as Jimmy's quick fist shot out, hitting him so hard he lost his balance and stumbled, knocking over his drink on the bar. Before he had a chance to recover, Jimmy's fists were slamming into him with a brutal forcefulness, each blow deliberately aimed at his face, with the final blow ramming him in the stomach and causing him to groan as he fell to the floor in a stupor.

"You just don't learn your lesson! Yuh should know better by now to mess with my woman," Jimmy growled.

"Why are you so mad? Elise's just a whore," said Casey, panting as he attempted to get back on his feet. That remark just angered Jimmy again and his fist shot out, slamming into Casey's face, causing him to crash back on the floor.

"You stupid son-of-a-bitch, she's my whore! She's not the only one you hurt. I hear any more stories about you beating up women, and I'm comin' back after yuh and next time yuh won't get off so easy."

The noisy room was suddenly silenced as recognition passed over the faces of the crowd. Everybody knew, respected and feared Jimmy Valentine. His reputation as a fighter was notorious; he held the title of Light Weight Champion of the Pacific Fleet. Jimmy would protect anyone who needed protection, especially the prostitutes who fought over him when his ship was in dock. They knew that for a couple of days they would have the time of their lives. Jimmy would take them all over town, dining in the finest restaurants, and would empty his pockets, buying them anything their hearts desired. Jimmy had an enormous heart that was filled with generosity. He was always very empathetic toward people and a sucker for anyone's hard luck story.

The only time he could honestly say he didn't show a woman a good time was once when he picked up this blond from the bar. She looked young and beautiful; her profile was perfect, with delicate features and a cleft in her chin. She was wearing a white silky dress which was cut low enough in the front to expose her ample breasts. He could tell she was braless by the way her nipples were outlined, almost peeking through the thin, silky material of her dress.

"What's your name, cutie? he asked.

"Madeline is my name, and I know who you are," she answered. "Jimmy Valentine the boxer." After a few more drinks and a dance on the dance floor, Jimmy whispered in her ear, "How about us dumping this joint and finding a more cozy place."

She tilted her head, allowing a short blonde ringlet to fall over her eye, and said, "Now the party begins."

It wasn't long before Jimmy was in bed with Madeline. They had ended up in her apartment and Jimmy awakened with a start. At first he looked around the unfamiliar room, unable to focus on where he was. Then it slowly came back to him. He remembered leaving with the blonde, ripping off that sleazy dress she wore and then savage love-making.

'I must have passed out after that,' he thought. He lifted up his head to look at her and was overcome with the pain of a throbbing headache. It felt as if a sledge hammer was banging him on the head. The blinding sun that was escaping through the curtains made his eyes squint. A beam of light was shining on her brassy-colored hair. He then turned toward the blonde, but she was passed out. His passion spent, he had no desire to pursue her. She was just another broad and an easy lay. She lay facing him, her mouth partly open, exposing a stream of spittle. Jimmy examined her face, and the hard lines showed her to be much older than she appeared last night. She smacked her lips and softly and moaned, and, in doing so, a foul odor escaped from her breath. Jimmy was overcome with disgust. He felt the bitter taste of bile rising in his throat, and not being able to swallow it, he belched. Suddenly his stomach lurched, emptying its contents. The vomit exploded from his mouth like a waterfall, splashing on her chest and face. She woke up with a start from the shock of the wet, warm liquid, gasping and then screaming as she realized she was covered with vomit.

*"YOU BASTARD! YOU PIG! GET OUT! GET
OUT! GET OUT!"*

Jimmy reached for his pants to get away from
her. As he slammed the door behind him, he could
still hear her screaming.

After three days of enjoying Elise's company,
Jimmy decided it was time to go home to visit his
family, so he checked his pockets and discovered he
had several hundred left from his pay.

On the way to the subway he passed a dress shop
with a pretty flowered dress on the mannequin.
When he entered the shop he greeted the pretty
saleslady, "Hi, gorgeous, give me two of those dresses
yuh have in the window," he ordered, giving her a
wink.

"What dress sizes do you need?" she asked
flirtatiously.

"They're for my two little sisters, and they got
cute little figures like you do, doll, only they're just a
little bit smaller." Jimmy held out his hands,
demonstrating a curvy silhouette, then, after paying
the saleslady, he left to go look for a jewelry store
where he could buy a brooch for Giroloma. Finally
he was on the subway, loaded with presents for his
family and heading home.

Rosie and Frankie were sitting on the stoop
when they spotted Jimmy coming up the street.
Happy at the sight of him, they ran to greet him.
Jimmy was their Santa Claus, always bringing them
presents.

"What do yuh have in those boxes, Jimmy?"
asked Rosie in an excited voice.

"When we get in the house, you can see," replied
Jimmy. "Have yuh been behaving?" he teased,

remembering all the mischief Rosie easily could get into.

Rosie's large round eyes took on an innocent expression as she answered, "I've been good, honest."

"Yah, I know yuh wouldn't tell me the truth," said Jimmy, laughing.

As soon as they were inside their tenement house, Jimmy handed Rosie and Fannie a large box before everyone came running up to him. The house was filled with excitement as he passed out gifts to all the kids.

"Look at the pretty dress, Mama, and Fannie has one just like mine," Rosie gushed. "Oh thank yuh, Jimmy," she added as she rushed up and hugged him.

"Hey, give me some air," said Jimmy, laughing as he was being hugged and kissed by Rosie and Fannie. Jimmy's eyes met Giroloma's, who was sitting quietly, waiting for all the excitement to die down before she could talk to him.

"Mama, I got something special for yuh," he said as he handed her a little box.

"Vincenzo, you shouldn't spend all your money on us," she said, with smiling eyes.

"Why not? Who else do I have to spend it on besides my family?" Jimmy quipped.

Giroloma's eyes were wide as she lifted the top off the little box and saw the expensive cameo brooch.

"Oh, this is so beautiful!" she exclaimed in Italian. "But where will I wear it?"

"You can wear it every day and remember me when I'm gone, Mama," Jimmy replied before he was interrupted by Rosie and Fannie wearing their new dresses.

"Look, Jimmy, they're a little big on us, but we need ta grow yuh know where before we can fit into these dresses right." Everyone laughed at the sight of Rosie and Fannie parading around in the dresses, their flat chests obvious, making the dresses pucker where their breasts should be.

After supper everyone was anxious for Jimmy to tell another one of his stories. He usually talked about all the adventures he had in foreign countries or entertained the boys with stories about his boxing career.

"Tell us about China," Rosie requested.

"No, tell us about Hollywood," piped Fannie. "Did yuh really meet Gloria Sweeney?"

"I not only met her, I laid her," he joked as Giroloma shot him a dirty look.

"You watch what you say around the children," she warned.

"Okay, I'll tell yuh the story about when I played in the movie *Twenty Thousand Years in Sing Sing*. You see, I was just an extra, but the director of that movie noticed that I resembled Edward G. Robinson. I don't mean that I actually look like him, but I'm small like him. The next thing I remember is, he asks me to double for him in the movie, so I ended up being his stunt man."

"Did yuh ever go to any of those Hollywood parties?" asked Rosie.

"Yah, I had my fill of those stuffy doings, except one party I'll never forget. It was at some movie star's house—I can't even remember her name. Anyway, the party started getting wild, the booze was flowing freely and all the expensive o'derves were being served. I was making it with this broad who was up for an audition the next day for a movie, and she was a real beauty with wavy blonde hair and a figure to knock your eyes out. All the Hollywood bigwigs were there and she was trying to get noticed, when suddenly this other broad made a grand entrance looking like a million dollars with this long white mink coat draped over her shoulders. She was the center of attention, a well-known movie star, and her escort was a mean-looking bodyguard who acted like he owned her. Anyway, this broad spots my date and starts right in giving her insults. Meanwhile, she takes off this long mink coat and drapes it over a chair near the pool. She was wearing a skimpy dress underneath and strutting around enjoying all the attention. Then she looks at my broad and says, "Too bad about the part that you're auditioning for tommara; you'll never stand a chance against me." Then her bodyguard comes up to me and starts yapping off his big mouth, calling me a pipsqueak. We was standing close to the pool when I lost my temper. I jumped up, ready to attack this huge man, when suddenly he takes a step backward and falls into the pool. My broad gets into the action and pushes the movie star into the pool, yelling, "Here yuh wet movie star bitch, yuh forgot this!" as she trew the mink in after her.

"Next thing I know, my broad gets pushed into the pool, then somebody from behind me pushes me into the pool. Pretty soon the whole party ends up in the pool. Everybody was laughing, having a ball floating around in the pool with all their expensive clothes on. I swims over to the bodyguard and start punching him and dragging him out of the pool. Anyway, it ended up to be one of the best parties I ever went to. My broad got the part the next day and has been famous ever since."

"What ever happened to the movie star?" asked Rosie.

"Oh, that old broad was too embarrassed after she was thrown into the pool, and her skimpy dress practically disintegrated, exposing her flabby breasts. She finally got out of the pool and took off running, leaving her mink coat floating in the pool. Later on I grabbed the mink and gave it to my broad—it looked more like a dead rat by then, but I never found out if she could get it repaired."

Everybody laughed, enjoying Jimmy's story. Then Sally spoke up, "Jimmy, can yuh tell us about your boxing career?"

"Well, I remember once when I was supposed ta fight at Madison Square Garden—that's where they hold fights for the championship boxers—Frankie Carbo was the man who was in charge of setting up the fights, and I was supposed ta fight Tony Canzoneri, who was a well-known champion fighter. Well, Frankie says to me to trow the fight and he was going ta pay me tree or four hundred dollars. I flatly refused. I don't mind honestly losing a fight, now and then, but never will I intentionally lose a fight. There is a sort of moral thing here and I may be a lot of things, but nobody can ever say I'm dishonest. Ta me a fight ain't woith it if yuh do it dishonestly."

"Did yuh ever get ta fight at Madison Square Garden after that?" asked Sally.

"Oh, yuh, many times, and many times I won, and a few times I lost, but never intentionally."

After Jimmy told a few more stories, he yawned and said, "That's it for tonight."

Giroloma started clearing up the table, saying, "You are our best entertainment since the radio broke."

"Well, I can't always be around, so here's some money for a new one," Jimmy said, reaching into his pocket.

"Now Vincenzo, you don't have to do this, always bringing us gifts. You are a gift, just making us laugh with your stories," replied Giroloma.

"Mama, yuh don't look so good, and I worry about yuh. Have yuh seen a doctor lately?" asked Jimmy.

"I'm alright...just a little tired, that's all," lied Giroloma. "Well, I'm giving yuh some money ta see one anyway and I ain't taking no for an answer," he ordered.

Soon Marian stopped in carrying her two baby boys.

"I need Rosie and Fannie to baby-sit tonight. Joe's taking me out dancing," she said.

Marian, the oldest daughter, was big but beautiful. She was at least six feet tall in her high heels that she always wore, and she looked more like a Greek than an Italian. Her coal black, natural curly hair framed her face and set off her hazel eyes and fine features, focusing on her perfectly sculptured nose. Marian resembled a very large Grecian statue, a perfect work of art. Marian had married Joe Grecco and had an apartment upstairs. She had long broken her relationship with Paul Caruso after she met Joe. It was against the family's wishes, even though they didn't have anything against Joe, but they knew how Marion liked to enjoy life and liked the finer things in life. Paul was a doctor and Marian would be very well provided for and respected in the community as a doctor's wife if she married Paul. After much pleading they finally consented to Joe courting her, hoping she would tire of him and return to Paul. Marian fell head over heels in love with Joe. Joe had the good looks of a movie star and was exciting to be with. Soon they wanted to marry but knowing how her parents felt about him, they decided to elope. When they returned from their elopement in Niagara Falls, they rented a small apartment upstairs. Before long they began their family and Marian had a beautiful baby boy she named Frankie, and she got pregnant again and had her second son, another beautiful boy she named Joseph. Rosie and Fannie adored them and felt they were the dolls they never had. Rosie claimed little Joey to be her doll, while Fannie claimed little Frankie to be hers. They played for hours, acting like little mothers to the boys.

After everyone settled down in bed, Jimmy lay awake on the sofa in the parlor. For some reason he couldn't sleep, so he stared at all the old photographs hanging on the wall. '*All of these people are my relatives*, he *thought, yet I've never met any of them and they all look so stern...not even a smile. Well, I guess they had nothing to smile about, with all of their loved ones getting shot or going to prison*'. Jimmy remembered where he had read that at least eighty percent of the male population went to prison in Castellammare, Sicily. Jimmy suppressed a yawn, thankful he was in America. He truly loved his country and was very patriotic. He could remember having these same feelings as a small boy. Even when he was young he could remember admiring the military.

Jimmy lay on the lumpy sofa, staring at the small sparse room and letting his mind go back to the days when he was young. He remembered when he was fourteen years old, shining shoes by the Williamsburg Bridge in front of a hat parlor. He became friends with the woman who owned the shop. He was a tough kid and was streetwise, always having his hand in some sort of con game. Jimmy was small but mean and learned early how to box. He was always in some sort of street fight and soon made a name for himself.

One day Mrs. Zimmerman, the Jewish lady from the hat parlor, came outside and said, "Jimmy, you have to hide or you'll go to jail. Some cops were around here asking questions, and they said you broke into a jewelry store and stole some watches. They are looking for you and they found out where you live. Now I've taken a liking to you and I can help you. Here's five dollars, so go to the navy recruiting office and join the navy. I'll come by later and say you are my son and sign for you since you are underage. Also I'll have a birth certificate made up for you for identification. It's fortunate that I have connections with someone who will make up these papers for you, so hurry, go now and I'll meet you there in an hour!"

Jimmy knew that he was innocent of actually breaking into the jewelry store, but he did make a deal with the kid who did it, by selling the watches and splitting the profits. *'Some informer in the neighborhood must have ratted on me,'* he thought.

Jimmy remembered running to the navy office and lying about his age. He remembered seeing Mrs. Zimmerman and hearing her say he was her son and taking care of all the particular details. Next thing he remembered he was being sworn into the navy.

Everything happened fast after that. He could remember the first time he was on the huge ship. It didn't take him long to adjust to navy life, and after a while, he discovered he liked it. At first he didn't write home because he was afraid that Mama would somehow make arrangements for him come home. Then, as time progressed, he knew he must have hurt Mama deeply and was ashamed to write. Finally his guilt made him write home, letting everyone know that he was in the navy.

As the years passed, Jimmy enjoyed traveling all over the world, seeing many different countries and meeting people of every nationality. Jimmy's boxing career developed while he was in the navy, and he fought professionally, changing his name to Jimmy Valentine.

Then came the day when he received the title of Light Weight Champion of the Pacific Fleet. Jimmy's life revolved around his boxing career and his navy career. He enjoyed the excitement of travel, wild women and drinking. Although he loved his family dearly, he became depressed when he was around them, especially seeing his mother suffer from cancer. And it depressed him to see the struggle his family had with the Depression, so he eased his conscience by trying to help out whenever he could. Jimmy knew he would stay around a couple of days and be gone, but he couldn't stay for too long, so he was already itching to move on. He finally fell into a deep sleep where he had the dream that always haunted him: Giroloma was calling for him. "Has anybody seen my boy Vincenzo?" she was crying.

The next day Giroloma sat at the table cutting vegetables after Jimmy had left with all the kids on a mission to buy a new radio and some groceries. She thought how happy everyone seemed to be when Jimmy was around. She felt like a lost lamb had returned to the flock when Jimmy was home. She could never depend on how long he would stay, or how long it would be before she would see him again; it could be in a few weeks or a few years.

She remembered the day he left the first time. The day had begun, as usual, with Jimmy leaving with his shoeshine box in the morning. At suppertime Jimmy had not arrived home, so she sent Rocco looking for him. Then two policemen came to the house looking for Jimmy, explaining that he was wanted for questioning because of a robbery of a jewelry store. When Giroloma explained that he had been missing, they took down all the information and his description. Later when Rocco returned alone, he explained that he had looked everywhere and no one had seen him. Soon it was pitch dark outside and still Jimmy had not returned. Giroloma sat up all night waiting for him to return, and by morning Giroloma was inconsolable, as she knew something dreadful must have happened to her boy. Luigi talked her into seeing the neighborhood Godfather, who said he would use all his resources to try and locate her boy.

In the many days that passed she never stopped hoping Jimmy would somehow be found. At first it was thought that he was just hiding out from the police, but as time passed even that theory proved wrong. The assumption that he must be dead by now or he would have come home or at least given word that he was alive was clear to everyone by now, except Giroloma, who would not accept the fact that he was dead. She went to church every day and lit a candle then prayed for her son's return, but soon the days turned into months. Life resumed its normalcy, but Giroloma never stopped crying for her boy. Then the months turned into a year, then another year and still no word of Jimmy's whereabouts. Luigi tried to talk to her, saying she must accept the fact Jimmy must be dead. She would shake her head and say, "Never will I accept that he is not alive."

Then came the day she had prayed for. The postman knocked on the door, holding the precious letter. "Mrs. Finazzo, I kept my promise to deliver any news concerning your son to you personally. Well, today is a very happy day. Here is a letter from Spain, addressed to you from Jimmy Finazzo."

Giroloma was in shock; she suddenly felt faint. "Vincenzo's alive!" Giroloma screamed. "My boy's alive, go get Luigi and gather all the kids, hurry!" she ordered Louie, who was the only one home at the time. Soon the house was in chaos. Family, friends and neighbors all gathered in a matter of minutes, all talking at once, the excitement mounting.

"Vincenzo's alive!" Giroloma shouted with happy tears running down her cheeks. "Please read the letter now!" she nervously asked the postman. The postman cleared his throat and the noisy room became suddenly silent.

August 9, 1930
Dear Mama and family,

I'm sorry to have worried you but some thing happened to me that last day I was shining shoes. I found out the cops were after me for selling some stolen watches, so this nice old lady helped me by signing for me to join the navy. I didn't write you at first because I was afraid that you would make me come back home. As time went on it became harder to write because of the pain I must have caused you. Please forgive me for hurting you, Mama, because I doubt if I will ever forgive myself.

I really love the navy and I know that I've found my niche in life. I love traveling to all the different parts of the world and meeting people of different nationalities. In a couple of weeks I'll be coming home. Mama, I love you—Please forgive me!"

Your Loving Son, Jimmy

After the letter was read, Giroloma had tears streaming down her cheeks. "I told you he was alive, and this is the happiest day of my life! I can't wait to see my little boy, and the first thing I'm going to do is hug him, then he's going to get the biggest slap across the face from me to remember how much he hurt me," Giroloma sobbed.

Soon the kitchen door was opened, interrupting Giroloma's daydream, and the house was filled with happy voices as Jimmy and all the children came running in.

"Look at the radio Jimmy bought us, Mama!" Sally sang out happily.

Jimmy walked up to Giroloma to hug her, then noticed tears in her eyes.

"Mama, what's the matter?" he inquired.

"Nothing; I was just thinking," was her reply. Jimmy instantly knew she must have been thinking about the time he had disappeared, and he felt a stab of guilt, the guilt that would always haunt him whenever he looked into Giroloma's eyes.

A few days later Jimmy was back on his ship, heading for Germany, life once again at the Finazzo household resumed its normalcy.

One day several months later, a strange sailor showed up at their door saying he was Jimmy's friend. He went on to explain that somehow he and Jimmy had gotten separated while they were hobo-riding the box cars of a train, and they made a pact that if they got separated, they would meet at Jimmy's family home in Brooklyn. The strange sailor said his name was Billy, but most people called him

Crazy Billy because he was always doing something crazy. The sailor stayed with the family a week, as Giroloma, being a gracious hostess, said, "Any friend of my son Vincenzo is always welcome in our home." Billy was treated like a king; Giroloma couldn't do enough for him." It's almost as good as having my Vincenzo back home, as you tell all those funny stories and keep us laughing just like he does," she happily remarked.

Frankie sat outside on the stoop watching for Jimmy every day. Finally one day he joined some kids playing kickball, when he glanced down the street and he noticed a small man walking with what was referred to as the sailor's walk, with a slight sway to his body. As the man neared Frankie recognized it was Jimmy.

"Hey, Chico!" yelled Jimmy, his pet name for Frankie.

Frankie ran up to meet him, then he suddenly noticed that Jimmy's hands were bleeding. "What happened to your hands, Jimmy?" Frankie asked, his large brown eyes expressing his concern.

"It's nothing; I rode in from the West Coast on the rails of the train, and hobo-riding can be a little rough on your hands," Jimmy explained. Frankie took his small hands and turned them palms up to examine them. His hands were cut and bleeding profusely. Frankie looked at his hero and started crying.

"You mean yuh rode all the way from the West Coast holding on to the rails?" Jimmy just nodded. "Why did yuh do that to yourself when yuh could have paid for the ride?"

"Don't say anything ta anybody, but I got paid about three hundred bucks when I landed and got drunk. Next thing I knew I shacked up with this broad. The next day, all my money in my wallet was gone. Luckily, I still had two hundred left in my sock, my secret hiding place for when things get rough. That wasn't enough money ta pay for my fare and have enough left over for the family, so I hobo-rode. Now I got enough money left over to show everyone a good time."

Soon they were in the tenement house, with the family gathered around Jimmy. After greeting his friend Billy, Jimmy announced, "I've got a special surprise for everyone tonight...I'm taking yuh all out ta dinner." "Not until I bandage up your hands!" exclaimed Giroloma.

After Jimmy cleaned up and let Giroloma bandage his hands, he looked at her and said, "Now where do yuh prefer ta eat tonight? Chinatown, or could yuh go for some seafood?"

"No, Vincenzo, you don't have much money on you this time, so we can eat at home; besides, I don't trust Chinese food," Giroloma replied.

"Do yuh still think that they cut up little children to put into their food?" Jimmy laughed. "Okay, I could go for some seafood anyway. I know a nice place called Joe's Seafood Inn at Shepphead Bay. We will go in real style and call a cab."

"Jimmy that is too much money. I can't let you do that," protested Giroloma.

"When was the last time yuh ate out, Mama? I'll bet it's been years, and yuh deserve ta have some fun; anyway, I blow my money on less important things like broads and saloons, so I might as well spend it on my family once in a while."

Giroloma understandably could not argue with Jimmy's philosophy, so she had remained silent and soon got caught up in all the excitement of the event.

"After dinner, we will all go to Broadway ta see a hit play, so hurry up, everyone, let's get ready," Jimmy went on.

The house suddenly was filled with chaos as everyone hurried to get ready for the time of their lives. Rosie and Fannie made a mad dash to put on the dresses that Jimmy had brought them on his last visit home. Rosie was happy that Marian had tailored them so they now fit them perfectly. Giroloma put on her best black dress and called Rosie and Fannie to help her pad her breasts with tissue paper. This one time she promised herself that she wouldn't cry when she looked into the mirror to see the flat area where her ample breasts were supposed to be.

At last everyone was ready, dressed in their Sunday best and presenting an acceptable picture of a well-dressed family. Fannie giggled with excitement as they sped off in the rented cab, ready for her night's adventure.

Soon they pulled up in front of the well-known restaurant, and Jimmy helped Giroloma out of the cab, tipping the driver. Inside the restaurant the waiter escorted them to a large round table. Since everyone was hesitant, Jimmy did all the ordering. "Give us a family-sized order of jumbo fried shrimp, and lobster, plenty of salad and all the fancy foods yuh have ta go with the dinners. Give us adults some coffee and all the kids a large Coke."

Rosie's large, round eyes widened at the thought of having a soda, as she remembered once, when she was nine years old, Jimmy had bought her a Coke. It was the first time she ever had tasted soda, so this was a rare treat indeed. When the soda was placed before her, she took a very small sip, savoring the wonderful taste.

Finally dinner was served, the waiter returning with a large tray filled with food. The tantalizing aroma overwhelmed everyone as the food was placed on the table. Frankie couldn't remember when he had had such a delicious meal, so he stuffed himself with second helpings on everything. Finally, when everyone thought they could eat no more, three large pies were delivered to the table. Rosie decided she liked the cherry pie the best, after sampling the blueberry and lemon meringue. Fannie giggled with delight at her large piece of blueberry pie. Everyone laughed at how much they all had consumed. None of the food was wasted. The happy chatter that continued throughout the delicious dinner had not impaired their ability to consume more than their stomachs could handle.

After they left the restaurant, a cab was waiting for them, and the long drive only added to their excitement at seeing a Broadway play. Soon the theater was insight, with all its welcoming flashing lights. Rosie and Fannie were excited taking in all the marvelous sights.

Inside the historical theater with all the plush red carpeting and elaborate sculptured railings, the air was filled with the aroma of freshly buttered popcorn and chocolate candy. Rosie looked up to see two balconies behind her and small little boxes of balconies lining the wall. The elaborate red velvet draperies then opened, exposing a large cast of dancers dressed intricate costumes. The opening song was called 'New York, New York' with everyone on stage singing. Rosie took a bite of the popcorn that was handed down to her without taking her large round eyes off the stage. It was the most fascinating experience she ever had encountered.

All too soon the show ended and they were back in the cab heading for home. Once home they couldn't stop talking about the great time they had.

Even Giroloma was flushed with happiness at the wonderful adventure. She was fascinated with the theater, and vowed if she was rich she would go there every day.

For one day in their lives they had experienced a day filled with all the food they could eat, and the adventure of a world they had never known, a world without worries and hunger, a world filled with entertainment and happiness. They knew that this night would be the topic of conversation for many years to come.

A few days later Frankie sadly waved good-bye to Jimmy as he watched him walk down the dock in his crisp navy uniform, carrying his large sack behind him. Frankie had come to the Brooklyn Navy yard with Jimmy to see him off, and he wondered when he would see his big brother again.

"Will it be a month, a year, or longer? No one ever really knows for sure," Frankie said aloud. One thing he knew for sure: when Jimmy was home, it was like Christmas, as Jimmy was his hero, his Santa Claus—only this Santa Claus wore a white navy uniform and carried a navy sack.

Chapter 13—THE BLACK DRESS

Giroloma was getting very sick. Her cancer was at an advanced stage. She had started out having breast cancer and having one breast removed, then it spread and she had the other breast removed; now it had spread throughout her body, and she was having a difficult time hiding her pain. She knew she was going to die soon. Most of her children were grown. Marian was married with two small baby boys. Poor Mary had died. Frankie and Sally were still at home, but she didn't worry about them too much, as they were boys, almost men. It was her last two children that worried her the most, her two little girls, Rosie and Fannie. They were still young. Rosie was only twelve and Fannie, the baby, was only nine. She didn't want to leave this world. She didn't want to leave her husband, Luigi. She knew that their marriage, at first, was not a union of love—it was a union of respect—but almost twenty years and four children later that respect had developed into a deep love. Now she must leave them all. She knew her end was near.

Rosie was coming up the steps to the tenement house home from school, and when she entered their apartment while Giroloma was lying in bed, so she cheerfully said, "Hi, Mama."

Giroloma forced a smile to hide her discomfort.

"How's my beautiful Rose?"

"Can I get you something, Mama?" Rosie asked while fluffing up the pillows to make her more comfortable. Rosie noticed how Mama had aged. The lines in her face grew deeper as she grimaced with pain. Her once bright gray-hazel eyes were filled with suffering and worry. Her voice, which once was strong and forceful, had developed into a whisper, except when she screamed. Then it would lapse into a whisper again, as if it had drained all the energy her poor emaciated body could endure.

"Is Fannie home?" Rosie heard her frail voice whisper.
"Yes, Mama," Rosie answered.

"Call her in here…it's time for our prayers," whispered Giroloma. Pretty soon Fannie was in the room "Get down on your knees," whispered Giroloma. After the prayers, Our Father and Hail Mary, were said, then Giroloma whispered, "Dear God, if you have to take me, please take my little girls, too. I don't want to die without them. They are too young to be without me."

The next day after school, when Rosie entered the tenement house she sensed something was wrong, so she walked into the bedroom and Mama wasn't there.

"Where's Mama?" Rosie asked, afraid of the answer. Just then the door opened and Fannie entered the house.

"Girls, Mama went to the hospital today," Marian said, weeping. Rosie knew what that meant. When you go to the hospital you go there to die.

Everyday after this, Rosie and Fannie would walk to the hospital to visit Mama, and everyday their mama would make them eat her food.

"I don't know this kind of food. This American food I cannot eat," Giroloma scoffed, looking at the mashed potatoes. Rosie, you are so skinny, *manga*, eat." Rosie knew it was an excuse, that Mama had no appetite. It was true she worried about Rosie's undernourished body, so, to make sure she ate, she would expect her there everyday at supper time. After Rosie would eat, Giroloma would whisper, "Now it's time for prayers." Rosie and Fannie would get on their knees to pray, and the Our Father and Hail Mary prayers would always be followed by her urgent plea: "Please God, take my two little girls with me when I die." Everyday the family would visit Giroloma, watching her deteriorate and praying that somehow she would miraculously recover.

Giroloma had acknowledged their presence, but someone was missing. It was her son Rocco, so she whispered, "Please bring Rocco to see me."

Luigi had contacted Danamora Penitentiary, but there was a lot of red tape involved. One day Annette, the pretty actress, came to visit Giroloma, and through her pain-filled eyes Giroloma expressed recognition. She lifted her head up off the pillow, pleading, "Please, I must see my son Rocco before I die. You can fix it…like you did before."

Annette knew she was referring to the time she pulled strings to prevent Rocco from being deported. Annette looked at Giroloma and said, "I promise I will do everything in my power to bring him here."

Giroloma's face took on a contented look and she dropped her head back on the pillow. She now had faith that Annette would somehow manage the chore, and she vowed to hang on and fight death until she saw her beloved son again.

Annette knew powerful people, and she made the right connections to have Rocco released for a visit to his mother the next day.

Meanwhile, word had gotten back to Detective Caroselli who knew that the Finazzo family was acquainted with the underworld, and he knew that Giroloma was greatly respected among the gangsters in the area. In his pursuit to catch these men, he set up undercover police to surround the hospital—they wore plain clothes and carried shopping bags filled with guns.

Rocco walked into Giroloma's room slowly, two uniformed policemen followed behind him. When he awkwardly bent to kiss her, she noticed the handcuffs on him, and tears rolled down her cheeks at the sight.

"Please...take the chains off my boy. I don't want to die...seeing him like this," her weak voice whispered.

The police officers looked at each other, lost for words, knowing that this request they couldn't grant.

"Do you think that he is going to run...instead of seeing his mother for the last...time?" she whispered with tears running down her face.

The police officers' eyes were tearing up, and they looked at each other again, both choked up and wiping their eyes. *'How can I deny this poor woman her last dying request?'* one officer thought. "Let him loose," he ordered.

The other police officer took out a key in his pocket and soon the sound of the chain hitting the floor was the only sound in the silent room. Giroloma managed to gather the strength to open her arms to embrace her son.

"Rocco my boy...how...... I have missed...you. Please...be good and stay...out of trouble," Giroloma whispered.

"Mama, don't die! I can't let you go," Rocco cried.

"God is calling...now that you're here...I can die...in piece."

"NOOO!" sobbed Rocco.

Giroloma's face took on a radiant smile, and suddenly, as if in a dim, shallow light, Francesco appeared to her carrying a small baby girl. Standing next to him was Mary, holding a newborn infant. The light was getting brighter, illuminating the room, and she whispered so low it was barely audible: "They're here...to take me...Francesco, Mary...my babies." Giroloma's head fell backwards then and she was still forever, but her radiant smile remained on her face.

The silence in the room suddenly erupted into sobs and screaming as everyone suddenly realized she was gone.

The doctors and nun (who was the nurse) tried to look professional at first, but couldn't control their emotions, with their eyes misting up with tears. The very strong family devotion and pain was just too overpowering. They watched the dramatic scene unravel before them, sensing the loss as if they, too, had been a part of it.

Finally the doctor walked over to Giroloma's bed and examined her, saying with tears blinding his eyes, "She is gone."

The sympatric nurse wrote carefully in her chart: " Patients Name, Giroloma Finazzo; Date of death, September Twentieth, Nineteen thirty-five; Age, fifty-three; Cause of death, Cancer."

Annette, being a very talented, sensitive and creative actress, could not dismiss the scene of Giroloma dying from her mind. In all her years of playing a dramatic actress and singer, she had never come across a scene so moving. *'True life is indeed more traumatic then fiction could ever hope to be,'* she thought. She tried for months to forget the hardships and tragedies of the Finazzo family, but finally she realized she would never be at peace until she could somehow re-enact the trauma of the sad death of Giroloma. She was captivated by the Finazzo family, as they had such an unusual quality about them. Out of loyalty and respect for them she wanted to make a play about them. She had that strong urge similar to an artist in capturing his portrait and displaying his own unique impression of his subject. This poor immigrant family who had come to America to fulfill their dream had to undergo all the extraordinary hardships that life could possibly bestow upon all of them. Yet they survived blow after blow, each challenge as it came. Feeling truly inspired, Annette discussed this family with her theater manager.

The rows of flashing light bulbs at the R.K.O. Theater surrounded the lighted sign that read: *The White Nun*. The people were lined up, anxious to see the latest play. Finally the commotion settled down as the maroon curtains parted, and the scene before them was an opera sung in Italian by Annette. She played the nun who was a nurse at the hospital where Giroloma lay dying. The story unfolded Giroloma's tragic life, from the time her husband was killed, up to the present time where she lay in her hospital bed. The big dramatic scene that captivated the audience was when the actor who portrayed Rocco entered onto the stage wearing handcuffs, followed by two policemen. The audience could barely contain their emotion when the famous line was repeated by Giroloma: "Please...take the chains off my boy. Do you think he is going to...run, instead of seeing his mother for the last...time?"

The audience was inconsolable, with people sobbing loudly and blowing their noses into their handkerchiefs. Every person there felt the emotional impact of the tragic scene, and when the curtains closed, the audience went wild, clapping and yelling! Annette knew she had given the best performance of her life—the show was a smashing hit! The show went on for months, filling the theater to its capacity. An Italian radio show got word of the successful play, and soon a soap opera was played every night on the radio. The name of the show was *The Finazzo Family*.

Life for Rosie, after her mother's death, was unsuccessful at resuming its normalcy. It had been a year since her mother's death, and she dreaded having to go back to school this year, especially since she found out she had Miss McGuire again. Miss McGuire was a stern teacher. She resented the traditions of the ethnic backgrounds of many of her students. She felt that many of these old country traditions made people backward and ignorant. These traditions to her were senseless and should not be practiced. She was proud that her own nationality was of a mixed English and Irish decent; it made her feel more civilized than her Italian students.

Rosie sat at her desk, scribbling in her notebook, and she felt that Miss McGuire had a dislike for her, no matter how hard she tried to win her over. Rosie was all A's in academics and all E's in conduct. She was a very intelligent girl and sensed the disapproval of her teacher. After a while she lost interest in trying to gain her approval, and instead rebelled. It was really a shame because she had an avid appetite for knowledge.

Suddenly her name being called jolted her back to the present. The next thing she noticed was the ruler tapping impatiently on her desk. When she looked up she saw the tapered end of Miss McGuire's long, narrow nose. She had a triumphant gleam in her piercing green eyes. Rosie felt this was her entertainment. She had a victim now to unleash all her own life's frustrations on. "Stand up and recite the last chapter," she said.

Rosie stood and started stumbling through the lesson, when suddenly Miss McGuire pointed her ruler at Rosie's dress.

"What did I tell you about wearing that black dress? You have worn that same dress for a year now and I forbid it in my class!" Rosie started an explanation, but was interrupted. Miss McGuire, shoving her, said, "Go stand in the corner. You Italians try to keep people in the dark ages. We are not in the old country, we are in America. Remember when you come back to class tomorrow. I expect to see you dressed in another color."

Rosie was embarrassed and deeply humiliated. The teacher had taken all her self-esteem away. She made her feel dirty and not worthy to be in her class. Rosie stood in the corner and stuck her nose close to the wall, so no one could see her crying. This incident

274

ignited all the pain and grief that she had hidden in her heart. It was like a flood of emotion, like the reality of losing her mother. There was no one there to protect her and understand her anymore. She didn't know what to do about the teacher. It was a strict Italian tradition to wear black to show she was in mourning. Miss McGuire watched Rosie's form standing in the corner, and she was secretly gloating; she had a loathing for that Italian girl that she could not suppress.

When Rosie came home from school Marian was in the kitchen cooking supper. Marian had come over every day to cook supper and stay with the younger children until Luigi would come home from work, temporarily taking over Giroloma's role as mother of the younger kids. Marian's large and perfectly proportioned body stood over the stove, and she looked up to see Rosie's red eyes.

"What's wrong Rosie? What happened in school today?"

Rosie tried to avoid the subject for a few minutes, fighting to gain control over the flood of tears that she was holding back. She bent down and picked up a fat baby whose head was crowned in tight tiny ringlets. Her voice sounded small and shaky as she explained, "The teacher said that I can't wear this black dress again to school."

"Tell hah to go to hell! It would be the biggest insult ever to Mama's memory if yuh didn't wear a black dress. Besides, we can't afford material for another dress," Marian continued.

Marian was a dressmaker at the garment factory where she worked and she made all of the family's clothes. Marian had a special talent for sewing and this job enabled her to purchase the accessories that matched all her homemade clothes. Her talent for sewing attributed to her expensive-looking wardrobe.

She would window shop at the finest stores and examine the latest fashions, then purchase the material. Marian's strict dress code included a dress with a matching hat, purse and shoes.

Since Giroloma had died, Marian had to forget her fashion sense and stick to the old Sicilian custom of wearing a black dress for a year. This she did proudly showing her sorrow and respect for her dead mother. She carefully sewed dresses for her younger sisters and herself trying to make them as attractive and stylish as possible.

The next day Rosie dreaded going to school, then she remembered to take pride in her family and show the love she had for her mother by wearing the black dress. As soon as she entered the classroom the teacher approached her. "Didn't I tell you not to wear a black dress today?" Miss McGuire said sternly.

"My sister told me to wear it; we have no money for another dress," Rosie replied. "I have to wear this dress because my mother died and it is our way of showing our love and respect for her."

"This is my classroom and not your sister's. Go stand in the corner. Tomorrow, I had better not see you in black." Rosie went into the corner, feeling like she was her victim again. It seemed like she was standing forever. She kept adjusting her weight on each foot to gain a little comfort from the stiff position of standing all day. She seemed defeated; since her mother died, the fight had gone out of her. The wave of depression had overcome her again.

Finally the bell rang and school was out for the day. Rosie scuffed her shoes against the pavement as she slowly walked home.

Marian was in the house cooking again when Rosie got home. One look and Marian could see her red, swollen eyes. Marian had noticed the change in her. Her big round eyes had a hollow look of defeat. That spit-fire flicker of mischief was missing.

"What happened with the teacher?" Marian inquired.

"She made fun of me and made me stand in the corner again all day," Rosie said in a small voice.

"Did yah tell huh what I said?" Marian's voice rose in anger.

"She told me it's hah classroom, not yours. If I wear that black dress again tomorra I'll really be in trouble," Rosie added.

"Oh, did she? Well, we'll see about that," Marian said, folding her arms.

Fannie overheard the conversation, and she breathed a sigh of relief that she had such a nice and understanding teacher in Miss O'Conner. Fannie still played school at the worn-out old pedal sewing machine in the kitchen.

It was one of the few places in the house where she could sit. The sewing machine was her special retreat. It was her special spot to daydream and hope. It was her sanctuary, her world to escape from when the cruelty of life seemed to stressful to endure. She would sit for hours, pretending that she was a teacher. Miss O'Conner had been wonderful to her, giving her boxes of clothing, even though she understood that she couldn't wear them until the period of mourning was over. Miss O'Conner ignored Fannie's black dress, as did all the other students in her class. They all had grown to like and respect Fannie. Miss O'Conner had become Fannie's closest friend, almost like a surrogate mother to her since her mother's death. She remembered how she cried in her arms over the loss of her mother. They had spent many days together, seeing all the wondrous sites of New York. Miss O'Conner couldn't do enough for her, taking her to special places and she even made special arrangements to teach a higher grade to enable Fannie to be in her classroom again this year.

Today Fannie could barely contain her excitement as she impatiently waited for the school term to end. She wished it was the day of her sixth grade graduation party. Miss O'Conner had spent days with her, arranging all the details, including all the pretty little graduation invitations with her name engraved on them. Miss O'Conner wanted this party to be very special, a wonderful memory to cherish the rest of her life. The party was to be held at Miss O'Conner's house. They had a long discussion after school concerning the refreshments that were going to be served, and they had decided on ordering a special cake in honor of the occasion. Fannie's mouth watered, thinking about the fresh strawberries that were going to adorn the cake.

Suddenly she was abruptly awakened from her daydream when she heard Marian say, "Fannie, are you going to sit there all day? Supper is ready."

Marian then turned to Rosie and said, "Yuh would think she'd outgrown huh playing by the sewing machine by now."

The next day Rosie went to school wearing the black dress, and when she walked in the classroom, it was about fifteen minutes early and none of the students had arrived yet. Miss McGuire was busy checking papers on her desk, but when she looked up she was staring into Rosie's face. Then her face turned an angry red as she realized Rosie had on that damned obnoxious black dress again. "You dirty little Italian, how dare you defy me by wearing that ugly black dress again?"

"My sister told me to tell yuh to go to hell!" Rosie snapped defiantly, the sparkle returning back to her eyes again.

"How dare you talk to me like this! I'll teach you a lesson you'll never forget!" she screamed. Losing control of her composure, she grabbed Rosie and started shaking her and striking her with her ruler.

Suddenly the classroom door flew open with a loud earth-shattering noise, and there stood this huge Amazon woman wearing a very large black dress. Miss McGuire's eyes opened wide. She was trembling with fear. She had never seen a woman so large. Before she had a chance to speak, she heard a loud angry voice: "I'll teach yuh a lesson that yuh will NEVER FORGET, TEACHER!"

Miss McGuire was no match for this big woman. Marian doubled up her large fist, and WHAM! Miss McGuire's face felt like putty under her powerful fist. The impact had landed Miss McGuire on the floor, her thin body sliding under her desk.

"Yah had better like seeing BLACK DRESSES because my sister will be wearing hahs in this class! And yuh better treat my little sister with respect, or I'll be BACK!" Marian warned, grabbing Rosie's hand. "Come on, Rosie, yuh can come home today. Maybe tomarra, your teacher will regain hah senses."

The next day Rosie wore her black dress to school, and she noticed that Miss McGuire had a bruised swelling on the side of her face. The teacher stared at her, narrowing her eyes, but she didn't say a word.

Luigi sat at the kitchen table, and he couldn't believe his eyes; he was looking at a letter from Carmellia. It had been over twenty-five years since he last had seen her. He had heard from the grapevine that she had come to America with her relatives. He remembered that she stayed in New York for while, but that was many years ago and he hadn't given her much thought. Now he had this letter from her. He hurriedly opened the envelope and started reading:

Sept 12,1936

Dear Luigi,

I have been in America since 1925, coming over with my brother's family. We were in New York for awhile, then we settled in Detroit, Michigan. My brother had been promised a job at Ford Motor Company. It is such a coincidence because my brother works with a man named Sam Bruccellato. When they were talking the other day, Sam mentioned the Finazzo family in New York. Sam said that he was a cousin. It sure is a small world. Sam gave my brother your address. I heard the sad news about your wife passing away, and I want to extend my fullest sympathy to you and your family.

Since I have come to Detroit, I have been working in a garment factory. I took care of my mother for many years and she passed away a few years ago, leaving me the house. Luigi, I think of you often, with very found memories of our childhood days back in Castellammare, Sicily. Please write me back. I am very anxious to hear from you.
P.S. Please send me some pictures.

Your Friend,
Camellia

Luigi sat in thought as he read the letter and reread the letter several times, then he let his thoughts go back...back in time to his childhood. Some of his first memories were of Castellammare, a paradise where the mountains fell into the sea. Where the aroma of fresh air was filled with the vegetation, fruits and wild flowers that grew in abundance everywhere. Where he could see every living creature as small as the pill bugs. He laughed as he remembered the aggravation of the dragonflies that would somehow end up in his salad. They would be saturated with olive oil. He wondered how many he had mistakenly eaten as he scooped them out with his fingers. He thought about the paradise where the field of wild oats would gleam in the sunset. The olive trees that grew on the mountain side. The Italian squash called *cuzuzzata* he ate in a variety of ways that made up the majority of their summer diet. The first harvest of oregano that hung in his kitchen from the rafters in the *patmento* which filled the room with its peppery perfumed aroma. The sweet thick aroma of the figs, grapes, cherries, and orange blossoms. Then, for a brief moment, he allowed the vision of Carmellia with her delicate angel face and slim dainty body. Her wavy hair with the golden highlights entered his mind. Her soft laughter as they ran barefoot through the golden fields.

The sudden screaming of a kid outside abruptly dissolved his daydream, and Luigi immediately felt a stab of guilt overcome him—remembering his grief for his wife, remembering his vow to bring the light back to her gray hazel eyes. He may have succeeded if there weren't so many heartaches, tragedies, and disappointments in her life. First it was her baby dying when she was in Sicily. Then her husband getting murdered. Then poor Mary dying, for which he would carry the blame the rest of his life. Then her sickness and pain with the cancer. She had suffered through too many hardships. There were some good times when he would almost see her happy, but the curtain would come down over her eyes, so as not to

281

let the brightness back in. Luigi searched his soul. It was true he didn't love Giroloma when he married her, but he grew in love with her through their friendship and respect for each other. After being together for so many years, he realized he truly loved her. He wondered if she were with his brother now. He hoped that now her eyes would be bright again.

The screaming kid in the street brought him back to the living. He looked out of the window onto the street, and some other kids were beating him up. *'Just an everyday occurrence on the streets of in Brooklyn.'* He thought. Then he remembered his wonderful childhood in Castellammare and it was a paradise compared to this place. He looked at the street with disgust. Here the children's playground was the streets.

He then caught a glimpse of a small girl in a black dress walking across the street. The girl was being teased by a group of kids. She started fighting with one of them, putting up her fists and dancing around. Then a blond boy had jumped in, as if to defend her. His second glance made him suddenly realize that they were his children.

Now Luigi turned his attention to the letter on the kitchen table, and he felt a sudden rush of loneliness. He consoled himself that it wouldn't hurt to have a friend, and he sat back down to answer Carmellia's letter.

About week later another letter arrived from Carmellia, and Luigi hurriedly opened it.

Sept 20,1936

Dear Luigi,

I received your letter and was excited to hear from you. It must be wonderful to have such a big family. I envy you. I always wanted children, but my life was devoted to taking care of my parents, which left me little opportunity to marry early in life, and when I did it was a sad mistake. My close friend and cousin, Tavita, along with her two children and husband, live upstairs in my two-family flat. They have grown to be a second family to me. I have become very fond of her children through the years.

I received the pictures you sent of you and your children. You are still a very handsome man and your children are beautiful. I would give anything to have such a nice family. It would be nice if you and your family could move to Detroit. My brother says he can get you in at Ford Motor Company if you decide to come here. I'll close this letter thinking of you with fond memories. Please write me back soon. Hearing from you brightens my day. You mentioned how lonely you were; you can't imagine how lonely my life is. I am so glad that I found you again. Receiving your letters gives me something to look forward to.

Yours Truly,

Carmellia

The rapid correspondence between Luigi and Carmellia went on for almost a year, at first a renewed friendship which involved friendly letters and their trivial incidences and events that happened each day, but, as time went on, their letters grew more serious. Luigi poured his heart out over all his many problems. Carmellia's recent letter again had mentioned that there was an opening at Ford Motor Company and Sam had spoken to the Personnel Department Manager, and if he wanted to come to Detroit he would be guaranteed a job. This last letter had solved the problem that was on Luigi's mind for quite some time. Luigi had grown lonesome and he needed someone in his life. His children needed a mother; they had gotten out of control lately. Sally was hanging around the pool halls and gym, boxing. He had gotten in with a tough gang of kids. Luigi also worried about his girls, Rosie and Fannie, without a mother's guidance. He couldn't depend on Marian to help with the girls, as she was already having marital problems and had enough troubles of her own. She had matured since Giroloma's death and had tried to help out raising the girls as much as she could. Her job at a garment factory and her two little boys took up most of her time. What time she had left over was divided between trying to cope with her failing marriage and trying to help with the girls. She was still determined to make her marriage work, but she was exhausted mentally and physically and couldn't give the girls as much time and attention as she wanted.

Luigi thought about the older boys. '*Well, they are men now and my job is done.*' Louie was married and settled down. Frankie had a job now so he was doing alright. Luigi felt he had given all of them his life, his youth, his blood, and they were all adults now, so it was time he thought of himself. Luigi was tired of the rat-race. He was afraid of his younger children turning out bad; this New York was not a place to raise children. Gangsters, racketeers, and Mafia—he had his fill of it all.

Luigi thought he was still young enough to make the transition, and he still had his good looks and health; he wanted the best for his children, a better life than they could have in Brooklyn. He thought of the stories he'd heard about Detroit, the clean air and nice neighborhoods. He was tired of the smell of garbage, musty old buildings, cockroaches, rats and contaminated air. It was time to clean up his life before it was too late, so he sat down to write a letter to Carmellia:

Feb 2, 1937

Dear Carmellia,

Through our letters I feel as though we have been together for years. I feel I can tell you now that all these years I have thought of you. First as a childhood friend, then as a young boy's sweetheart and now in my mature years as a partner for life. Will you marry me? I know I may not be worthy of you, since I have nothing to offer you except my respect, love and devotion to life. Please be sure before you say yes. It is a big step and I still have four children to raise. Maybe I am being selfish in asking you. I need the love and companionship of a wife, and my children need a mother. If your answer is yes, we can make arrangements after my arrival by bus to Detroit. I am anxiously waiting for your reply.

Love Always,

Luigi
P.S. If your answer is yes, I'll take that job at Ford Motor Company.

Rosie was walking to school thinking about what Pa had said the previous night. He had called a family meeting, and he looked excited and happy as he explained all the new plans. He announced that he was getting married to the lady he had been writing to all this time. She had never seen her Pa look so glowing; he looked so much younger, and it was like he had shed ten years of age. Pa explained that they would be moving to Detroit. This lady had a nice house in a nice neighborhood. She never had any children and she wanted to be a mother to them. Pa went on and on about all the advantages they could have in Detroit. He would have a new job in an automobile factory, which would pay him over twice the amount he was making now. Rosie was perplexed. She didn't know if she should be overjoyed or afraid.

Her life was in for a drastic change, she hoped for the better. The only thing that bothered her was that Frankie did not want to come. She wished he would reconsider. After some considerable thought, Rosie decided to be caught up in Pa's happiness.

"I proposed marriage and Carmellia accepted," he said. A big smile appeared on his face, showing his beautiful white teeth.

At last the school steps appeared. Rosie's class was three flights up. The heavy pungent odor of strong disinfectant, used to clean the floors, filled the air as she climbed the steps. Miss McGuire had on her usual sour face. When she saw Rosie it seemed to sour even more.

"Good morning, *Miss McGuire*," said Rosie sarcastically.

She was answered with a loud grunt, so Rosie thought, '*I wish she would take a crap and get it over with.*' Things hadn't really improved in their personality conflict. Rosie stopped having to wear those homemade black dresses; but Miss McGuire never acknowledged it. Rosie was still picked on in little aggravating ways. Miss McGuire knew how far to go with discipline for Rosie. She still had nightmares about the attack of the big Amazon woman. She had considered telling the authorities or the school principal, but decided against it. For one thing, she was afraid of the Mafia. This Finazzo clan was a rough bunch.

It had gotten to the point she couldn't tolerate this horrible child, but she knew she couldn't do anything drastic except to torment her in little ways. No matter how hard Rosie tried, Miss McGuire would humiliate her. If Miss McGuire would have shown her just one ounce of kindness, one good word, one gesture of humanity, Rosie, who was always hungry for love, would have forgotten and forgiven her cruelty. Rosie could sense the hate that this mentally deranged woman would feel for her. Rosie decided that she was evil and shouldn't be a teacher. '*Anyway*,' thought Rosie, '*Today is the last day of school before I move to Detroit, and it is also my day to deal with Miss McGuire*'.

On this particular day of school, since it was the last day of school before the spring break, the class had a special program in the auditorium to attend, so upon leaving their classroom they had to form a single file line on the marble stairway extending down the long flight of stairs. Miss McGuire was at the head of the line, at the top of the stairs. A girl had asked her a question, and she had leaned over slightly, leaning into Rosie.
Rosie stuck her foot far out, and when Miss McGuire leaned back, Rosie's foot gave a little shove at the back of her heel. Miss McGuire lost her balance and fell forward. Down she went, down the flight of stairs, hitting the marble slabs of the steps each time, with a sickening thud as she finally hit the bottom. All the terrified girls were yelling, screaming and crying, "Oh, Miss McGuire!" In sympathy for her unfortunate flight, Rosie joined in: "Oh, Miss McGuire," she screamed. Then she covered her mouth with her hand as she mumbled under her breath, "Goodbye, Miss McGuire!"

Chapter 14—ARRIVAL DETROIT

It was March 3, 1937 when Luigi and the kids left Brooklyn. A thunderstorm had developed by the time they reached the underground subway. They had noticed a slight mist when they started out on their journey, each one carrying a small suitcase except Sally, who carried a cardboard box. Luigi was walking with his pronounced unique style, almost marching ahead of the three teenagers, who were trying to keep up with his stance. A light wind blew Fannie's wide-brimmed hat into the air, sending it gently dancing until it hit the pavement. In her pursuit, she had lapsed behind the group.

"Hey wait for me!" she yelled as she tried to catch up, awkwardly holding onto her hat with one hand on the top of her head and dragging the suitcase with her other hand. Then the slight mist had decided to turn into a full shower, but luckily they reached their destination before they were drenched. A load roar of thunder and a sudden flash of lightning hit just before they entered the underground subway.

As they entered the subway car, Luigi thought he had heard someone screaming. He tried to turn around, but was packed in with a crowd of people, anxious to board the subway.

Frankie stood crying while watching the subway descend down the tracks; he had given up his chase running alongside of the subway when he realized it was a futile attempt. He was drenched to the skin, and his suitcase was open, showing the few clothes that remained from his chase scattered out onto the pavement. The tears mingled with rain and ran rapidly down his cheeks, and he was still yelling and crying, "Pa ,Pa, don't leave me!" He had reached the station just in time to see a glimpse of Luigi and the three kids boarding the subway, and then just as he approached, the doors shut and the subway went speeding off.

When the subway came to their destination, Luigi and the kids got off and walked the remaining block to the Greyhound bus terminal. The storm had let up and had been reduced to a slight sprinkle. They were glad the sudden storm didn't leave too much damage on their immaculate appearances. Luigi was shaking out his new hat when his glance fell on a dark young man. He had to look twice because the resemblance was astonishing; he looked so much like Frankie. Luigi wished it was. He felt a sudden stab of remorse that he had left Frankie behind, but he was tired of having all the responsibilities all these years and feeling unappreciated for all his sacrifices. All he cared about doing now was taking his kids and going to Detroit. In a fit of anger he had told Louie that Frankie was eighteen now, and it was his job to look out for him. Now he felt that some part of him was missing.' *It isn't Frankie's fault that he is the youngest of my brother's children; Frankie is more my son since he knew no other father,'* he thought with a stab of guilt. Then he' *reasoned, Frankie has a new job and he seems content to stay in New York…well, when we get settled I'll send for him, if he wants to come.'*

Sally's yell then disrupted his thoughts: "Come on, Pa, the bus is getting ready to leave!"

"Do you hava the box?" he asked Sally.

"Yah Pa, it's already on the bus by the girls," answered Sally. The stuffed cardboard box and a few suitcases where all they had. The box contained a few treasured knickknacks, important papers, clothes and pictures. The most precious item in the box was Luigi's Philco radio. Jimmy had bought it for them a few years before. Luigi and Giroloma spent hours listening to the little wooden radio, especially every night to the Italian Hour. '*The little radio had a lot of happy memories, with Giroloma singing along to all the Italian tunes,*' thought Luigi as he entered the bus.

The long ride was uneventful except for Rosie, who developed motion sickness and vomited all the way. Luigi wanted everything to be perfect. He had taken his savings and, for once in his life, decided to be extravagant. He bought a new suit, hat and shoes for himself. Next he outfitted Sally with a new shirt and dress pants to match, a spring jacket, and new shoes. Finally it was the girls turn. They tried on every dress in the store until they finally made their decisions: matching cotton spring dresses with shoes and purses to match. After some persuasion from them, he set off their outfits with wide brimmed straw hats that had a ribbon to match their dresses, white gloves, and new spring coats. The girls were elated, showing off their new pretty clothes as they left the tenement house for the last time.

"Were moving to Detroit," they bragged to all the neighborhood kids. Luigi was very proud of his family when he saw his children dressed up in the new clothes he bought them. He wanted to make a good impression on Carmellia when they arrived in Detroit.' *It was worth the money,* he thought. 'This *is how it's going to be from now on. Our lives are going to change. My children will live in a decent neighborhood and go to nice schools.*'

Rosie was seated next to Sally on the bus; and she was starting to vomit again into the bag that Luigi had secured on the rest stop. Soon she seemed to recover a little and was lulled to sleep by the humming of the bus. Rosie had slept for several hours when Sally decided he was hungry. Luigi had made breaded veal cutlet sandwiches to eat for their trip, along with some fruit that was carefully packed in a paper bag. When Sally reached into the bag to pull out a sandwich, Rosie started waking up. Sally bit into his sandwich, when suddenly the bus lurched to the right, making a turn. The sudden motion affected Rosie's stomach again, and the turn had forced Rosie to fall against Sally. Suddenly she started vomiting again, trying to reach for the paper bag. Sally was about to take another bite of his sandwich when he noticed that some of her vomit had somehow landed on it.

"Yuh little bitch, look what yuh did to my sandwich! If yuh was a guy I'd pop yuh one. Yuh disgusting, and I ain't sitting next to yuh no more!" Sally yelled. Then he took his sandwich and flung it at her, screaming, "Yuh eat yuh own puke!"

"Stop yelling at Rosie—she'sa sick, ana she can't help it!" Luigi yelled, causing the people sitting around them to notice the screaming family. Sally then got up and sat in another seat, still grumbling. Rosie was oblivious to his insults, but she was too sick to care.

The bus ride lasted twenty-four hours, stopping at various terminals along the way. Each time the bus stopped Luigi would get more paper bags for Rosie. At the last stop he brought her back a Coke. "You drinka this maybe you willa feel better," he said tenderly.

After Rosie fell back asleep, Luigi started thinking about Carmellia again. He already knew that she had a good heart. She had written about how nice it would be to be a mother to his four children. She had never had any children of her own and this would make her life complete. After a few letters she did make a confession that she had married once, but the guy ran off.

'Well now we are even,' thought Luigi. *'We both have one marriage behind us.'* Luigi was very ecstatic about the good life they were going to have together. *'Finally, I'm going to be with Camellia, the first woman I loved,'* he thought. Luigi suddenly wondered what time it was, so he reached inside his pocket and checked his pocket-watch: six twenty-five. He was getting excited as he thought, *'The sign over the ticket office in the bus terminal read 'Arrival Detroit: Seven-Fifteen,' so in less than an hour we will be there'.*

Luigi finally drifted off to sleep, lulled by the constant humming of the bus as it made its way to his destiny. He dreamed of the beautiful vision of Carmellia. She was calling to him, standing near the ocean with the sun behind her, reflecting her golden highlights of her wavy hair. Then he was holding her with his arms around her tiny waist. Luigi was awakened from his dream by the sudden hissing noises of the bus slowing down to stop.

"We're here!" shouted the kids excitedly, except for poor Rosie. She was too busy vomiting again. The bus had come to a full stop, and Luigi looked out of the window, seeing a sign that read *Detroit Bus Terminal.* Everyone stood up ready to leave, except Rosie. Her feet couldn't seem to hold her up, and everything was spinning. Luigi had to carry her off the bus. When they entered the terminal, Luigi was anxiously searching for Carmellia. He set Rosie down gently on the bench. She was a sight. Her pretty hat sat lopsided on her head and her stringy hair had fallen from the new hairdo that she painstakingly arranged for the trip.

"You resta here for a few minutes and I'll have Sally geta you some water." She nodded, trying to force a smile. She felt guilty for having to worry him at a time like this.

Luigi was looking in all directions, trying to spot Carmellia, then suddenly he noticed a fat woman looking in his direction. Suddenly the fat woman was yelling, "Luigi, it's me, Carmellia!" Luigi stood frozen to the spot, and dizziness overcame him, his stomach knotting up as if in empathy with Rosie's illness. The fat woman was coming toward him, smiling. He desperately tried to conceal the revulsion and shock he felt at the sight of her. He hoped that his huge disappointment wasn't too obvious as he reluctantly gave her the hug and a kiss that his custom expected of him.

After the short ride in Carmellia's car, they were at her double-flat house on the corner of Mack Avenue and Fields. When they entered, the dining room table was set, and Carmellia then introduced them to a small lady who stood pouring fresh coffee into all the china cups set on the table.

"This here isa my cousin and my dearest friend Tavita; she lives upstairs with her husband ana her two children," Carmellia proudly announced.

"This isa my family," Luigi proudly announced. "Sally, who isa fifteen, Rosie, who isa fourteen, and my youngest one, Fannie, who isa twelve."

After all the proper pleasantries were said, the whole group of people were all seated around the decorated dining room table, where there was a generous assortment of Italian cookies and little pastries piled onto two large platters. Luigi kept up the facade of politeness that was expected of him. As Carmellia was talking she easily lapsed into the familiar ancient Sicilian language, mixed with broken English. While she nervously rattled on, Luigi was surveying the disastrous situation he found himself in. It had taken most of his money to make this move. He probably had enough money to take the first bus back to New York, but then what, ridicule from his relatives? They had all expressed their misgivings already. He had too much pride for that. He did promise this woman matrimony and he was a man of his word. Luigi found himself studying this strange woman who proclaimed to be Carmellia. He was looking for any kind of resemblance, a hint of recognition, or a flicker of emotion—something, some small shred of evidence that would remind him of his dainty Carmellia. She had no waist, and her body looked about as wide as it was short. Her delicate features were hidden beneath a doughy, puffy surface that was supposed to be a face. Her chin was hidden in folds of fat that seemed to cover where her neck should be. He finally came to the conclusion that the golden highlights of her wavy hair were all that was left of his Carmellia.

Once again he felt that life had dealt him a raw deal. Here was the very woman that he was dreaming about all these years, but now he wished he was in a nightmare and could wake up. *'How could I be so stupid as to not ask for a picture before committing myself?'* He wondered.

Luigi looked at Carmellia again, suddenly feeling guilty for his thoughts, as her cheeks were flushed and her eyes were shining. He suddenly knew he couldn't hurt her for the world. No matter what she looked like on the outside, she was still Carmellia. Luigi also had to examine himself; he had to be realistic and acknowledge the fact that he was no prize either. He couldn't offer a woman any security because, in actuality, he was a poor man. Besides, he had the responsibility of four children to raise. Luigi was actually very shy about meeting women, and it was hard for him to play the suave Romeo when it came to romance. At least with this woman, they had a lot in common, and they would have a wonderful companionship, he reasoned. She was his childhood friend and she was willing to accept him with all these kids. With her, his children would have all the advantages of life in a nice city and live in a nice house; he would earn a decent income at the job he was promised, and his children could have a mother, so maybe life wouldn't be so bad. Luigi had to forget his dream.

Rosie was finally beginning to recover from her dizziness, but her stomach was in knots for a very different reason. Rosie had a sixth sense about people, and she sensed that this woman was evil, from the moment she laid eyes on her. She had come to accept her first impressions, hunches, impulses, dreams and psychic ability. She then remembered hearing stories about this woman being a witch who could perform many psychic deeds. Only Rosie could sense that this woman was using her powers for evil, and she had to warn Papa before it was too late. She found her opportunity when Carmellia, along with Travita, left the dining room in preparation of the late meal she was serving them.

"Papa, I don't like this woman I have bad feelings about her" Rosie whispered.

"Husha up, or she will hear you; I promise we willa talk tomorrow when we are alone," he replied.

Soon Carmellia returned to the dining room carrying a large bowl of pasta. After dinner the conversation turned to Luigi's promised job at Ford Motor Company. "The way it works is you will have to pay thirty-five dollars for the job. I already talked to my cousin who has the connections, so you will get the job," Carmellia explained.

"I am anxious to start work, so I willa go there tomorrow," Luigi said enthusiastically.

Rosie yawned. The long bus ride, her being sick and the late dinner had taken its toll on her.

Carmellia, realizing it was getting late, said, "Oh, dear, I didn't realize how tired you all must be. Letta me show you to your beds." Carmellia graciously showed the girls to their bedroom and where the bathroom was, and then showed Sally a bedroom he could sleep in. When she got everyone settled into bed, she came out to make up the sofa for Luigi. Travita yawned and excused herself, going upstairs to her part of the house.

"This is justa temporary," she added, blushing.

Luigi, taking the hint, asked, "When do you wanna us to get married?"

"I already talked to my priest and ifa we apply for our license tomorrow we cana get married by Sunday."

"That willa be just fine," said Luigi, feeling awkward, then, feeling like he should add something nice, said, "We will hava a wonderful life, justa like we planned so many years ago." Carmellia eyes sparkled as she laughed lightly, filled with happiness. Luigi smiled back at her, and there was something in her laugh that reminded him of a trace of his old Carmellia.

"Well, I'm tired I better getta some sleep," he added. "Tomorrow I have mucha to do, ana thank you for the nica dinner ana for making my children feel so welcome."

"I am the one who should be thanking you for still thinking of me after all these years," Carmellia gushed.

"Gooda night, Carmellia. I know you musta be tired, cooking that delicious food for us. We will talka more in the morning."

"Good night, Luigi," Carmellia giggled as she shut off the dining room light.

The next morning Rosie woke up with a start. She could smell fresh coffee brewing and the delicious aroma of bacon frying, so she nudged Fannie, who was still fast asleep. *'I must try to find a way to talk to Papa to stop this marriage,'* she worried.

When Rosie came into the dining room, she was surprised to see Luigi already up and dressed in his suit. He was laughing with Carmellia. *'He really seems to be enjoying himself,'* Rosie thought.

"Rosie, I'm glad you are uppa so soon. Tell Sally and Fannie that I willa be gone on some business. Me and Carmellia are going to Ford Motor Company so I can puta in an application for a job. Then we are going to apply at city hall for a marriage license," Luigi announced.

"Don't forget, we hava to go to the doctor's for our blood tests," Carmellia added sweetly.

'She acts like the cat that just swallowed a canary,' thought Rosie. Now how will I be able to talk

to Pa alone before he marries this woman? she pondered.

"You kids behave and don't getta into any trouble," Luigi warned.

"If you kids getta hungry, just help yourself," Carmellia added sweetly.

Soon they were gone, laughing and acting like teenagers as they left the house. Rosie had just fixed herself some coffee and freshly made biscuits when she saw Sally coming into the kitchen. A few minutes later Fannie also showed up.

"Where is everybody?" asked Sally, breaking the silence.

"Oh, Pa left with that fat tub of lard," Rosie said sarcastically, "And he's going ta get the marriage license today, so we havta do something quick ta stop him," she added.

"Why should we try ta stop him? That's what he came here for, ta marry Carmellia," Sally reminded.

"Can't yuh see that she's an evil witch?" replied Rosie.

"I can't see anything, except she seems like a nice lady ta me. Anyway she cooks better than yuh do," Sally joked.

"Yuh just too ignorant ta understand that our lives will be hell if Pa marries that witch," Rosie replied angrily, throwing a biscuit at him.

Sally threw up his hand, catching the biscuit. "Yum, tanks for buttering it for me," he said as he took a large bite of the biscuit. "Yuh got marbles in yuh head; I say she's a nice lady."

"I say yuh a pig; look at yuh talking with biscuit crumbs flying out of yuh mouth," Rosie snapped.

Fannie, who sat listening while she ate started giggling, finding the whole conversation funny.

"What in heck are yuh giggling about, funny-face?" teased Sally.

"Anyway," said Rosie, changing the subject, "what should try to do today? We got the whole day alone."

"I say we go outside and meet the neighborhood kids. We might as well get acquainted with them; after all, we'll be living here from now on."

Soon Rosie, Sally and Fannie were outside walking around the block. Rosie was surprised to see that the neat houses with porches were so close to each other.

"I'll bet yuh, Sally, yuh could almost touch your neighbor's house if yuh stretched out yuh arm," Rosie commented.

"Look how clean everything is here and the nice neat lawns with the pretty yards and picket fences," Fannie mentioned.

"Yuh, it looks real nice here, but where's all the kids?" asked Sally.

"Stupid, they don't play in the streets like they do back in Brooklyn; they play in their back yards," Rosie reminded.

"Hey, look, here comes a kid now!" said Sally. A red-headed kid was approaching on a bicycle, when Sally yelled out, "Hey, kid, what does everyone do around here for fun?"

The kid stopped his bicycle, looking at the new kids on the block. "I dunno; sometimes we go roller skating or to the movies. Hey, you talk funny; where are you kids from?" asked the kid.

Sally looking at the kid in mock amazement, said, "Rosie, did yuh hear what that kid just said ta us? He was making fun of us. I guess we hafta show him who's gonna be boss in dis neighborhood."

The kid started looking scared as he mumbled, "No, I didn't mean it the way you took it."

"Dats okay, but we gotta show yuh how we make friends in Brooklyn; Rosie, do yuh want ta take him or should I?" Sally asked.

"Naw, I can handle dis one; yuh can take the next one," Rosie said, putting up her fists. Pretty soon she was dancing around the frightened kid, and before he knew what hit him she landed a punch right in his eye. The kid took off running, leaving his bicycle on the ground, and Rosie laughed, "Well, we made our foist new friend today." Fannie giggled, enjoying the ridiculous scene.

Soon Sally saw another victim walking down the street. "Dis one's mine," he said. Sally attacked the kid before he had a chance to respond. The kid was too astonished to put up a fight, and before he knew what hit him Sally sent him flying to the ground with just one punch. Before the kid could recover, he was offering him a hand helping him up.

"Hi, I'm Sally, and we just moved here from Brooklyn, New York," he introduced himself. The kid just looked at him like he was crazy and took off running, and he didn't stop until he was a safe distance away, thinking that he was going to stay away from these weird kids.

After standing on the street corner and beating up a few more neighborhood kids, Sally and Rosie couldn't understand why they all ran away instead of staying around to get acquainted.

"I don't get it," said Sally. "Dese Detroit kids must be a real bunch of sissies. Dey don't even try ta fight back. They all run away instead of staying around ta be our friends."

Rosie agreed, shaking her head. In Brooklyn, it was the code of the streets that this was the way friends were made. First you beat them up, and the tougher you were, the more popular you were.

"Tomarra, Rosie, we will try again. We'll stand on the corner and take turns beating up da kids. Maybe we just didn't meet da right kids today," Sally reasoned.

That evening Luigi and Carmellia came home and they seemed to be in good spirits.

"Well, I hava job now, and tomorrow I start worka at the Ford Motor Company. Sally, tomorrow I wanna you to looka for a job ana you girls musta start school. Now I hava something important to tella everybody...Sunday, I will maka matrimony with Carmellia," Luigi finished, smiling.

Rosie's heart fell. I must talk to Pa; I must find a way to stop this, she thought.

After supper, she finally got her opportunity when Carmellia went upstairs to talk to Tavita for a minute. "Pa,..... please I must speak to yuh about Carmellia...please don't marry hah; I think it would be a big mistake. I sense that she is evil and we will live in hell," Rosie rushed on.

Luigi stared at her in astonishment before he spoke. "Carmellia isa nica woman. I knew her back in Sicily when I wasa boy. I don't understand where you getta this crazy idea. You shoulda be happy you are getting a mother and be grateful that she willa have us. Anyway it'sa too late, I already gava her my word. So be happy, a wedding isa about to taka place." As an afterthought he added, "I wanta all of you kids to be very respectful towards her, *capisei* (understand)!"

"I will be respectful, but please don't expect hah to be my mother," said Rosie, sobbing as she ran out of the room.

The rain was falling hard as they all rushed from the car to the house. As they neared the door, a sudden flash of lightning and a frightening crash of thunder followed them. The church sermon that had united Luigi and Carmellia had been short and simple. After the family entered the house, shivering from the cold rain that seemed to drown them all, they were greeted by a handful of friends and relatives. Luigi stood shaking his hat, but other then that he seemed unaffected by the thunderstorm.

Carmellia, on the other hand, looked like she had been dumped in the Detroit River. Her little hat, which had a small veil, was plastered to her head and her wavy hair was soaked, turning her waves into short, matted masses of dripping curls. Her make-up was smeared all over her face like melting wax. The dining room table was set with Carmellia's best china, complimenting the delicious meal Tavita had prepared for the guests. After everyone was seated, Carmellia's cousin Enzo held up his glass of wine.

"*Salute*, to your marriage. May you both find happiness and have a very long life together," he announced.

Then he took another long sip and attempted to awkwardly set the glass down. The glass tipped over, spilling out the wine on the expensive white lace tablecloth. Rosie glanced at Carmellia and saw her give him a dirty look before she caught herself. Rosie took the thunderstorm and the spilling of the wine as a sign that this marriage was doomed. *'I don't need to worry anymore; this marriage won't last long.'* thought Rosie, relieved.

Chapter 15—THE STEPMOTHER

It didn't take long before Rosie's premonitions about Carmellia started coming true. Carmellia kept up the facade of being nice for a couple of days, but it wasn't long before she managed to get everything under her control. Rosie was her first victim. Since Carmellia decided to keep her job, she expected the girls to do all the housework, so she handed Rosie a rag and told her to dust all of the furniture. Later, when she came home, she slowly ran her fingers across all the furniture, walking around and checking every piece until she came to a small end table that had been overlooked. "Rosie, comea here," she ordered, pointing her finger at the table. "Do you call thisa clean?"

"I'm sorry...I must have missed that one," Rosie apologized.

"Around here I like everything nica and clean, not likea you dirty people must have lived," Carmellia snapped.

"We are not dirty," Rosie defended.

"You, Rosie, area a very dirty girl; I saw your grey underclothes. Don't you know thata you're supposed to bleach your clothes? Now I guess I'ma supposed to be a mother to you and teach you cleanliness; it looks likea your mother never did."

"My mother was clean! How dare yuh say anything bad about her, and you're not my mother! You will never take her place." The next thing Rosie knew, WHAM! Carmellia smacked her across the face.

"Don't you ever speaka to me like that again, you ungrateful little snot. You shoulda be thankful that I took you in my house, instead of making your father takea you to an orphanage. Everyday whena I come home from work I will expect thisa house to be spotlessly clean. After dinner I will expect you ana Fannie to do the dishes. Also you both will wash ana iron all the clothes, ana I expect you to use bleach ona the white clothes. Now, getta out of my sight!" Rosie ran outside with tears streaming down her face.

That night at supper Carmellia was sickeningly sweet as she proudly served a delicious dinner of roast chicken. After Luigi was full and content, she served a fine desert of apple pie. Luigi looked at her smiling face and then at Rosie's solemn face, which on closer inspection had a red mark on her cheek.

"What'sa de matter with you, with the *guladeeza* (sour face)?" he asked Rosie.
"She smacked me across the face!" Rosie replied, then started crying.

Luigi was in shock. It was all right for him to hit his children, but he was like 'Papa Bear' when it came to anyone else doing that.

"I had to correct her. She didn't want to help me with the housework and started sassing me. You know, Luigi, if I am to be a mother to these children, then they have got to respect me. Now I know you did your best after your wife died, but these kids are unruly and wild. I work every day and it's not too much to ask them to help me with the house work," replied Carmellia in Sicilian.

"You're a liar! You talked bad about my mama! You said we were dirty people!" Rosie sobbed as she ran out of the room crying. Luigi was tempted to side with her, as he knew that part of what Rosie had said was true. Yet he also rationalized that Carmellia was right about the kids being wild. He finally decided that he should support Carmellia in this matter, for the sake of their marriage.

"Rosie, you getta back here and apologize to Carmellia!" he yelled.

A few days later, after another delicious supper, Carmellia smiled at him sweetly and said, "Luigi dear, I wasa thinking…with both of us working we shoulda be able to afford some new furniture."

"What'sa the matter with thisa furniture?" he asked.

"Oh, you men don't notice anything. I've had this furniture for over ten years. It belonged to my parents before me. Everything is falling apart. Look at the sofa, it is ripped and the material is so old it's starting to shred. Today, on my way home from work, I walked past a furniture store and they were having a sale, everything one-half off. I saw a beautiful living room set, and the salesman said we could buy it on time," said Carmellia, lapsing into Sicilian.

Luigi walked over to the living room set and inspected it, but he couldn't find anything wrong with it, so he thought, '*I just received my first paycheck and she took half of it for groceries; now she expects me to pay the house payment, even though she collects half of it from Tavita. And she wants us to go in debt over furniture.*' He then looked at Carmellia's pleading eyes.

"Just take a walk with me and promise you'll look at it," she pleaded.

"All right, I guess it won't hurt to look," Luigi reluctantly replied.

Later, at the furniture store, the fast-talking salesman had him sign for a new sofa with two matching chairs and new cherry wood end tables, plus a new cherry wood bedroom set. Luigi felt sick when he saw the bill—over seven hundred dollars! Then he looked at Carmellia, and her eyes were shining. She deserves it, he reasoned. After all she has done for us, how can *I say no. She is right; I've been poor so long that I don't know how to spend money; besides, she said that we both are making money now, so we can afford it.*

A few days later the new furniture was delivered, and it seemed, after she got the new furniture, that he began to see the changes in Carmellia. First he noticed that she wasn't happy about having sex with him. She started making excuses every time he got near her. Then the big dinners started getting skimpy. He came home to either some soup or plain pasta. *'Where was all the money going that I gave her for food?'* he wondered.

One day Rosie and Fannie started getting hungry and decided to make something to eat. When Rosie opened the cupboard, she was surprised to discover that it was practically bare.

"Now where the heck is all the food? I see her bringing groceries home every day," said Fannie.

"I bet that big fat slob eats it all herself," then, feeling adventurous Rosie added, "Let's go searching around the house."

After searching all the doors in the dining room buffet, Rosie continued, "I bet she hides the food in her bedroom."

Rosie and Fannie then went into Carmellia's bedroom and they began looking around. Fannie opened a dresser drawer and pulled out a huge pair of underpants. As she held them up, they burst into hysterical laughing. Rosie, wanting to add to the fun, grabbed the underpants and put them on over her clothes, then stuffed the two bed pillows into the underpants, and started strutting around the room. Fannie flew into hysterics. Rosie looked so funny with this huge belly and her little stick legs. After awhile they settled down from their giggling, and Rosie said, "Come on, let's keep looking for the food." After having no luck in the dresser drawers and closet, Rosie looked under the bed.

"Wow, look at this!" Fannie exclaimed. Under the bed they discovered mounds of goodies, packages of cookies and candies, packages of donuts and other baked goods, even crackers, rolls cheese and jars of peanut butter and jelly.

"No wonder she's so fat; she eats all this stuff by herself!" Fannie gasped.

"Well, let's start eating some of this delicious food," laughed Rosie, as she opened a package of chocolate cupcakes. Fannie's answer was a giggle as she eyed all the delicious treats. Rosie and Fannie stuffed themselves until their stomachs hurt, then lay back on the floor, too full to move. Fannie stared at Rosie and started giggling.

"What's so funny, funny-face?" she joked.

"Yuh better look in the mirror and see who's got the funny-face," said Fannie, bursting out in a fit of giggles. Rosie jumped up and looked in the mirror. She soon discovered what was so funny. She had a glob of white icing stuck on the tip of her nose. They both broke out in a bad case of hysterics.

Suddenly they heard the front door open and they quickly sobered up. "We better get out of here," Rosie whispered. They tip-toed out of the bedroom, down the hall and, hearing Carmellia heavy foot steps as she entered the kitchen, they hid under the dining room table. In a few minutes Carmellia came out of the kitchen carrying a big bag of groceries. She was smiling, humming a little happy tune as she entered her bedroom. In a few minutes she came out of the bedroom and walked past them, going back into the kitchen by the stairs that led to the upper part of the house. Then they heard her calling, "Tavita, I'm coming up."

After the coast was clear they ran into the kitchen to discover that she had brought home a package of noodles and some vegetables.

"That must be what we're having for supper," Rosie said. "The rest of the food that she brought home, which is under her bed, is her food," Rosie added. Then Rosie made a gesture, holding her finger to her mouth, for them to be quiet, as they snuck up the stairs to listen to Carmellia's conversation with Tavita. Rosie pressed her ear to the door, knowing that behind that door was the kitchen and that was where most of their conversations were held. The voices were muffled at first, but she eventually could make out a few words, then the conversation became clearer as she heard Carmellia mention, "Dirty little brats...Luigi is a stupid man...I like his paycheck...I have my own savings account." Then to Rosie's disappointment all she could hear was some giggling.

Rosie motioned for them to go back down the stairs. When they were back in their section of the house. Rosie angrily said, "See I told yuh she was evil!"

Soon they heard loud footsteps as Carmellia's heavy body shifted her enormous weight from each leg onto the sagging steps as she made her way down the stairs. When she entered the dining room her heavy breathing didn't alter the happy tune she was singing under her breath. She stopped for a second, sensing Rosie and Fannie's presence, but decided to ignore their innocent faces as she continued walking into her bedroom.

After a few minutes the silence of the house was suddenly broken as they heard the loud angry scream. "You little bitches! How dare you pry ina my room and get ina my private things! I'lla beat you both within ana inch of your lives!" she screamed as she came charging out of the bedroom. Fannie and Rosie took off running, but poor Fannie wasn't fast enough. Carmellia grabbed her by the hair and was smacking her in the face. After a hard push Fannie fell flat on her back and Carmellia jumped on top of her. Fannie felt the wind being knocked out of her as Carmellia's heavy body was suffocating her. Rosie immediately jumped on top of Carmellia's heavy back and started pulling her hair and scratching her eyes.

Suddenly the door opened and Luigi stood in disbelief as he stared at the ugly scene. After a few minutes of silence, he sprang to life.

"What'sa going on here!" he yelled, as he started to separate them by grabbing Rosie's small form off Carmellia's huge back.

Carmellia lay on the floor, her face flushed and red, her breathing heavy as she rasped, "They were snooping in my room!"

Rosie started screaming, "She's a food-gobbling fat liar! She's been hoarding all the food under her bed."

Luigi, without a word, marched directly into the bedroom. After a few silent minutes he returned with his arms full of packages. He looked at Carmellia long and hard, his expression full of disgust. Then he threw the packages at Carmellia, who was still lying on the floor. Suddenly his attention turned to poor Fannie, who was still lying on the floor whimpering. He helped her up, shocked at her bruised and battered condition. Luigi's red face was fighting for control as he hugged Fannie, then he said through clenched teeth, "Here's a dollar. You girls go freshen uppa ana go to the picture show. This shoulda be enough money to getta something to eat while you're gone. I willa come to the show later to pick you up, ana don't worry, I willa take care of this matter ofa what happened here today."

A few months later Frankie was feeling very depressed. He missed Luigi and his younger brother and sisters. Even though Louie had tried to make him at home in his apartment, Frankie felt that being with Luigi and the younger kids was where he really belonged. One day Frankie was so overcome with loneliness for them that he knew somehow he had to go to them. He then spied ten dollars that Ceila had left on the kitchen table for a bill to be paid. Frankie quickly grabbed the money and made up his mind to go to Detroit. In his haste he forgot to pack his clothes or any food.

Soon he arrived at the Greyhound bus terminal. *'I'll pay Louie back later when I find a job, he thought. Louie won't be mad; he'll understand.'* Frankie handed the ten dollars to the lady at the ticket window.

"I'm sorry, but this is not enough money to go to Detroit," she said. Frankie had walked all the way to the bus terminal in order to save the small amount of change, hoping that he would have enough money. He was determined he was not going to turn back, so he desperately asked, "How far can I go with this money?"

The lady looked at the bus schedule. "Nine dollars and fifty cents can get you to Akron, Ohio."

Frankie remembered that an old cousin of his mother's lived there. He didn't know her address but felt confident that once there he would be able to find her.' *Maybe she'll put me up for a few days until I can earn some money somehow get a bus to Detroit,*' he thought.

"I'll take the bus ticket," he replied.

The long bus ride left Frankie exhausted and hungry. In his haste to leave he hadn't eaten anything. Now his stomach was grumbling, and he was weak and light-headed. The two candy bars that he ate at the stop over hadn't satisfied his appetite. After he got off the bus, the cool night air made him shiver, and the strange town looked dark and deserted. Swallowing his sudden fear, he walked until he came to a phone booth. He quickly scanned the phone book that was hanging from a chain.

"Now, I hope I can remember how to spell her last name. Let's see...Colombo, that's it," he mumbled aloud. Instead of paying his last five cents for the call, he decided to walk to the address instead. "Fifty Tree- Ninety-Eight, Hickory lane," he repeated to himself aloud. "Now I havta get some directions." Frankie walked down several blocks until he came to a diner. Upon entering, the warmth of the dinner and the aroma of hamburgers sizzling on the grill made him dizzy with hunger. He sat down at the counter and ordered a cup of coffee with his last five cents. Soon an old man sat down next to him. After some friendly conversation, he asked the old man directions to Hickory Lane, and after getting the directions he thanked the old man and hurried out, anxious to leave. After following the old man's directions, he found the little white frame house.

Frankie rapped on the door, shivering with cold and anxious to get inside. Pretty soon some lights came on, and an old lady in a bathrobe opened the door. She was shocked to see Frankie standing there looking so tired and lost.

"Francesco, what'sa de matter, why you coma here?" she asked in broken English. "*Venica casa* (come in)," she welcomed. At her kitchen table Frankie explained his long forlorn tale as he hungrily gulped down the delicious bowl of pasta and side dish of breaded veal chops set before him.

"You poor boy, ofa course you can stay with me. Giroloma wasa my favorite cousin," said Mama Colombo. "Anything I can do for you, I willa do. Righta now you look tired. You go to sleep ona the sofa ana tomorrow we figure out what to do," she added. Frankie stayed with her for a couple of days and at her insistence, he finally called Luigi.

"Where you at?" Luigi asked, his voice filled with concern. "Mama Colombo's ina Ohio. You stay right there ana don't go no place until I go to the telegram office and send you the money fora the bus ride."

The next day Frankie was at the house wearing the new shirt Mama Colombo insisted on giving him. The minute he walked into the house he sensed the tension. Luigi, who was still sleeping on the sofa, woke up, startled.

"Pa, something is wrong here; what are you doing on the sofa?" Then Frankie gave him a wise look: You should still be on your honeymoon; you think I'm too young to know about such things.

Luigi at first tried to deny any problems, but at the sight of Frankie looking so concerned he broke down. "She doesn't like to do her wifely duty. Things aren't so good between us. That'sa why I never sent for you yet. I justa don't know what to do witha this woman."

A little while later, right after Luigi left for work, Frankie got to meet Carmellia again. She entered the room with a small woman, smiling brightly at Frankie, and said, "Frankie, this is my first cousin and close friend Tavita Palitto." Tavita smiled at Frankie, instantly liking him.

"My, what a handsome man you turned out to be; with your wavy black hair and features you look just like Luigi when he was younger," said Carmellia, "except when Luigi was much younger, he was almost blond.......until, I think, he turned twenty-one...then his hair turned pitch black almost overnight. I remember when your mother brought you to me that time, when you were just a boy. I cured you of your problem, remember?"

Frankie smiled, showing his beautiful white teeth, then laughed, embarrassed to be made to remember when he was young and couldn't control his bowels.

"I always liked you, Frankie; you are my favorite of the kids," Carmellia continued. "Now you sit down and *manga*. I've got a nice meal cooked for you."

Frankie wondered why she was so nice to him, buttering him up. He heard all the terrible things Rosie and Fannie had to say about her, so Frankie's sixth sense told him to beware of her, as she was up to something.

The conversation was interrupted when Sally suddenly entered the kitchen.

"Hey, Frankie, how about you and me going out, and I'll show yuh Detroit?"

314

Frankie, eager to get away from these gossiping old women, jumped at the chance.

'Detroit is so clean, with such nice neighborhoods,' Frankie thought as they walked to the corner of Gratiot Avenue and Harper.

"Dis is what they call this town *'Calalooboo,'* which is what is to referred to as the Italian section of the city."

Frankie, looking straight ahead, could see in the distance the faded shadow of the high buildings of the downtown section of Detroit. "That area reminds me of New York," Frankie commented.

"Yah, sometimes I get very homesick when I go downtown," Sally agreed, then he quickly changed the subject by saying, "Here we are at Bill's pool room, so let's shoot some pool."

Sally, being a pro at the pool table, soon started making money as bets were made each time a new game was started. In a couple of hours Sally and Frankie had a roll full of dollar bills.

"Dis is how I make my money, so why should I work? Come on now, I'll show yuh the real sights." Soon they were downtown, having taken the street car, and then they were at a dance hall. When they walked in, the line of pretty girls all turned their heads to see the two handsome young men who had just entered the room.

"I don't know which one is cuter, the dark one or the blond one," said the pretty girl as she smiled at them, trying to get their attention.

Luigi had come home from work and noticed that Sally and Frankie were not at the table, but this wasn't like New York where he could stick his head out of the window and whistle.

It was late at night when Sally and Frankie finally arrived, and when they opened the door they were suddenly attacked with flying shoes. "You sons of a bitchies! You no good bums!" Each time Luigi swore, another shoe came flying at them.

"Pa, we only went out ta have a little fun. I was showing Frankie Detroit," Sally explained.

"Bull-a-shit, you were ina the pool room!" yelled Luigi, as another shoe came flying. "You both are supposed to be working, not playing ina the pool room ana seeing the *puttonas*!"

Frankie tried to explain that he was going to start looking for work right away, but Luigi in his anger cut him off: "You are the one to blame fara taking Sally out! You are the oldest, so I holda you responsible. You can go right back to New York tomorrow—I am kicking you outa this house!" Luigi yelled.

The next day Tavita came downstairs as soon as Luigi left for work. She couldn't help overhearing the argument and felt sympathy for Frankie.

"You can stay upstairs with me and my family," she said, "and Luigi cannot say anything because I pay my share of the rent."

Frankie stayed upstairs with Tavita and soon landed a job at a small factory. Life went on with no further incidence. Luigi soon came to realize that Frankie was not to blame for their night out, but figured Frankie was probably better off staying upstairs since there was so much tension between him and Carmellia. Luigi was soon on speaking terms with Frankie, and Frankie understood full well the troubled relationship between Luigi and Carmellia.

A few days later, just before Luigi was finished working his shift, he was handed a pink slip from the office. After reading the paper, he discovered that it was a notice that he was laid off. '*They can't do this to me,*' he thought. '*I already paid my fee of thirty-five dollars.*' On the way home Luigi paid a visit to the relative who got him the job, and after the long visit he left reassured that he would be able to keep his job. It was explained that they usually laid off the men who paid for their jobs before their ninety days were up. But this cousin's son knew the important people higher up who were affiliated with the Mafia.

When Luigi finally got home he was feeling tired and upset; even though the problem would be solved. He had had a trying day. Parked along the curb was a new Oldsmobile Sedan Touring car. '*I wonder who is visiting us,*' he thought. "Who isa here?" Luigi asked the minute he came into the door.

"Nobody," Carmellia answered.

"Then who's car isa parked outside?"

"It's my new car, Luigi; I needed a new car."

Luigi just stood there dumbfounded. "Are you *potzo* (crazy)? I lost my job today ana you go buy a new car lika bigga shot! I don't even own an old car. I taka the bus to work."

"I bought this new car with *my* money, so don't worry," Carmellia answered sarcastically. She had stopped the pretense of being pleasant to Luigi or the kids for quite some time now.

"It's lika you say, your car, so I don't care, but don't cry to me whena you can't pay the bill," Luigi cautioned. "Now, do I get something to eat tonight?" he added.

"You're late...we already ate, so I'll heat you some leftovers," Carmellia mumbled.

"I had to see my cousin today, to getta my job back," Luigi answered tiredly.

As time went on, Luigi was determined to make this disastrous marriage work, as he was a religious man and he took the sanctimonious vows of marriage very seriously. It was a tremendous challenge for him because aside from the fact that she was repulsive to look at, she was also ugly on the inside. Every day there was some sort of adversity between her and the children. It had been almost two years since he had been married to her and his patience was at the point of exhaustion.

One day, after Luigi left for work and the kids were in school, Tavita and Carmellia were sitting with Frankie at the kitchen table when Tavita said, "Do you know the true story about your father getting killed? My husband and your father were very good friends back in Sicily. Your father was writing to his brother Salvatore about the family war between the Bizzocchis and the Valantis. He was getting someone in the family to write those letters because he was illiterate. Salvatore wrote him back and your father Francesco had the letter read mistakenly by a member of the opposing family. They discovered that both your father and my husband were informers. They had contact with members of the Valanti family over here. Your father was shot first, then three months later my poor husband was killed, leaving me a widow with two small children to support. Now I'm married again, but this husband, Felice, he is no good. I think he cheats on me," she whispered. After she went upstairs to her section of the house Frankie sat and thought about the bizarre situation.

The next morning Frankie came down the stairs and said to Carmellia, "Tavita said you wanted ta see me."

Carmellia smiled and said in Sicilian, "Frankie, I hear you lost your job, so I thought you might like to make some money. And I just want you to know that I didn't agree with Luigi when he blamed you for staying out late with Sally that time. I think you are the best one. Sally, all he does is go to pool rooms while you at least tried to have a job," she added. "Please sit down and have some cookies," she offered. "I have a favor to ask of you. I will pay you fifty cents every time that you drive my car and follow Tavita's husband, Felice, around. Now I want you to mark down everywhere he goes, every step he takes, and who he talks to and the exact times of everything. Will you do this for me?" Carmellia asked.

"Yah, sure, but I don't understand," Frankie mumbled.

"It's best for now that you don't understand, but you will later, and also, this must be kept secret."

Frankie followed Felice around for the next couple of days, reporting in full detail all of his daily activities to Carmellia, and she seemed satisfied with the report.

"Now I must confide in you; you are to tell no one, not even Tavita. I know now that Felice is the person who killed your father and Tavita's husband. This is very important, so I'm giving you fifteen dollars to take a bus to New York and talk to your brothers. Revenge from your father must be taken on him immediately. You must come back here with one of your brothers to assassinate him!" Carmellia ordered, speaking in Sicilian.

Frankie was astonished. He sat in shock at her table, almost choking on the hard cookie he was trying to swallow as she handed him fifteen dollars for the bus fare. *'She is asking me to do murder, so I must talk to Louie right away; Pa will never believe me if I told him,*' he frantically thought.

"Remember, you don't tella anybody until you see your brothers ina New York," Carmellia warned again as he got up to leave.

"I won't," he said, trying to hide his uneasiness.

Once Frankie was in New York, he anxiously ran to Louie's tenement house as soon as he departed the bus. After explaining to story to him, Louie, who was always a cool-headed person, started cussing. "That woman is an evil witch, and I had misgivings about Pa marrying her," Louie raged. "Who does she think she is, asking you and one of us to do murder? We must go see Uncle John at once," he added.

After explaining the story to John Coppola, he just shook his head and said in Italian, "That crazy woman was insanely jealous of my sister, Giroloma. I can't believe that Felice was the one who murdered your father. She's got some kind of outrageous motive for trying to set this up. You stay put and don't make a move; I'm going out right now to make some contacts with the Mafia in Detroit. I'll find out if there is any truth to this."

An hour later Uncle John came back to the house and said, "It isn't true. Felice had nothing to do with killing your father, so I must call Luigi at once." Uncle John then called Luigi on the phone, and said in Italian, "Luigi, Frankie is here in New York; Carmellia sent him here to bring back one of his brothers to help him kill Felice. She says that Felice killed your brother Francesco! I just checked the story with the Mafia in Detroit and it is not true."

Luigi first started to say it couldn't be so, that Carmellia could never do anything like this, but as he

320

listened to John Coppala, reality sank in. Frankie would never devise a story like this; in fact, he had never known Frankie to lie, and how would he get the money for the bus ticket to go to New York? He knew he wasn't working for some time now. This crazy woman that he was married to wanted Frankie and another one of his sons to commit murder! Luigi knew at that moment that the marriage was over.

"You better get away from that crazy woman, as there is no telling what she might cook up next," warned John.

"Frankie, here's twenty bucks…now I want you to go back to Detroit and keep your mouth shut and watch out for the younger kids," Louie ordered.

Luigi hung up the phone, defeated. *'I tried everything I could to make this marriage work, but she has gone too far this time, he thought. Where is she?'* he wondered, looking around the house. *'Upstairs with Tavita. It's where she always goes. She never even tries to stay down here to keep me company anymore. Well, this time I'm going up the stairs to tell her off.'* Luigi angrily started up the steps, and when he reached the top he could hear a faint laugh, so he threw open the door and looked around, but no one was in sight. He walked around the apartment, then he heard faint sounds coming from the bedroom. He angrily flung open the door, staring in frozen shock at the scene before his eyes.

There on the bed were the naked bodies of Carmellia and Tavita, twisted in a vulgar position. Carmellia was moaning in ecstasy as they were making love. The hideous sight of Carmellia's obese fat body in such a vulgar position nauseated Luigi beyond anything he ever had experienced in his life. The expression of ecstasy on Carmellia's flabby face suddenly turned into fear when she realized Luigi was watching her.

"That's it! I'm taking my kids and leaving you as soon as I get paid, you *emporko vistazo* (dirty pig)! You fat *puttona*! It makes me sick to even look at you. To thinka I spent most ofa my life dreaming about you, and now you are the devil from hell!"

The next day Carmellia stayed upstairs; she was too ashamed and scared to face him.

When Luigi came home from work, he looked around the house, asking Rosie where Carmellia was.

"She is upstairs with Tavita," Rosie answered.

"Call Sally and Fannie in," Luigi ordered. Rosie, sensing by the tone of his voice that it was serious, ran to get them. Pretty soon all the kids were sitting at the dining room table.

"Now I'ma calling an important family meeting here tonight," said Luigi, clearing his voice. "Things here are not working out, ana I never aska your opinion before, but I realize now thata you kids are growing up, so I'm asking you now. We hava three choices to make, so think careful before you speak. Either we stay with Carmellia and puta up with her ways, or we can go back to New York ana face the ridicule. The last choice isa that we go on our own here and rent a house. Ifa we do that, it won't be easy. We willa have nothing, not even a bed to sleep in. So, what do you wanna to do? I'm letting all of you maka the decision."

After a few moments of shocked silence, they all began speaking at once. "Let's go on our own!" he heard them all shout, then he heard Sally's voice above everyone else's.

"Let's stay in Detroit, but get our own place. We can make it, Pa," said Sally, with a serious expression on his face, "I promise to get a job and help out."

"Yah, we're siding with Sally," joined Rosie and Fannie.

"I wasa hoping you would all say the sama thing. Now I saw a house for rent today a couple of streets away, ana I already talka to the landlord, so if it's all right with you kids, tomorrow when I getta paid, I will rent it. An other thing, we musta decide is if we should taka all the furniture I bought or leava it here."

"Leave it here with her, and make her pay it off," said Rosie. "If we took it, every time I look at it, I will think of her."

"You're right, and I justa want to forget that crazy woman," said Luigi, "so I would rather sleep ona the floor than ina bed where she slept."

Luigi then looked at his children and realized that this was the first time he had seen them so happy since he brought them here, especially Rosie, who was glowing. "Tomorrow night be ready. Whena I come home from my job we will leave."

The next night when Luigi got home, Carmellia was still upstairs, and he was not surprised to see that the kids were all packed and waiting. Their suitcases including Luigi's were right beside them and Sally was holding the cardboard box that contained all the possessions they had in this world.

"Let's getta out of this crazy house," said Luigi, smiling, and all the kids smiled back as they walked out of the door and out of Carmellia's life forever.

Chapter 16—A NEW BEGINNING

**Nor fate, nor chance, nor any star commands,
success and failure—naught by your own hands.**

**-Samuel Valentine
Cole, *Works and Days***

The short walk was very invigorating as Luigi marched with his kids to their new home. They came to a street corner where the sign read "Armor" and the sign that crossed it read "Edgewood." Luigi stopped his march-like walk and pointed to a house on the corner. "This is it!" he said, smiling. It was a frame house that was called a four-family flat. They walked up to the door and on the right side of the house was their apartment. Luigi took his key out and opened the door. The apartment was cool and musty from being shut up. Rosie and Fannie walked through the apartment which consisted of a living room, kitchen, two bedrooms and a bathroom.

"Well, kids this isa now our new home," Luigi happily announced.

"Let's unpack our things," said Fannie, as she ran to the cardboard box, taking out the large cross and some religious pictures. "Let's find some nails in the walls and hang these up." Soon Fannie and Rosie had the pictures up in odd places on the walls. "Now I feel better," said Rosie. "No evil can reach us now." Then after searching in the cardboard box, she discovered a religious picture with Italian writing on the back, so Rosie took it over to Luigi.

"Pa, what does this writing on this picture say?"

Luigi studied the picture for a few minutes and his eyes misted up as he took out his handkerchief and gruffly said, "It isa poem sent to your mother ina gratitude fora helping someone's child ina need a longa time ago."

"Please read it for us, Pa," Rosie asked.

"I willa read it in Italian ana you can understand it mucha better ana translate it in English," Luigi remarked as he started to read the poem.

> He who gives a child a treat,
> Makes joy-bells ring in heaven's street.
> And he who gives a child a home,
> Builds palaces in kingdom come.
> And she who gives a baby's birth,
> Brings Savior Christ again to earth.
> For life is joy, and mind is fruit,
> And body's precious earth and root.
> (John Masefield, The Everlasting Mercy)

"That was beautiful," said Rosie.

"Your mama helped a lot of people. She wasa never too busy to taka time out to try to be a true friend. She wasa a tough woman ana sometimes she hada bad temper, but she had a golden heart," Luigi reminisced.

Sally interrupted the solemn mood by suddenly saying, "Hey look, I found our old Philco radio while I was fishing around in the cardboard box!"

Luigi, grateful for the opportunity to change the depressing subject of their mother and get everyone in a brighter mood, exclaimed, "Sally, play the radio box!"

Soon the house was filled with music, and Rosie and Fannie were singing along to the catchy tunes. Then the news came on the radio. "Tomorrow starts the Labor Day weekend, Nineteen Thirty-nine, so have a happy holiday," said the announcer.

"Since tomorrow is a holiday, we willa take the bus ana go to the little island called Belle Isle," Luigi said. "Besides, we needa to celebrate! Now we must go to the store ana buy some groceries ana pots an dishes so we can eat tonight."

The long walk to the five and dime, at Gratiot and Harper, didn't alter their elated mood as the kids happily followed Luigi's unique march. Once in the store, Luigi said, "We can't getta everything we need ina one day, but we willa at least worry about getting somea kitchen things so we can eat supper tonight." Soon they were out of the store with a bag which consisted of two pots a few towels, toilet paper, a few utensils and four bowls.

Next they walked to the little grocery store that they conveniently found around the corner from their house. They stopped there and bought a can of tomato paste, then picked out a pasta that contained a certain type of noodle in the display case. They then bought a bottle of milk, a loaf of bread, a pound of butter, a can of coffee and a dozen eggs. When they finally got home, Rosie and Fannie cooked up a very plain pasta sauce, but everyone was too hungry to care how it tasted.

That night Luigi told the kids, "Unpack all your clothes ana lay upon them; we don't have any beds, but thisa will help, and save your coats to cover uppa with if it gets cold."

Even though it seemed like it was one of the most uncomfortable nights that they ever had to endure, no one complained. The adventure of moving had taken its toll; it was not the physical work, but the mental relief of finally being free that made them fall into a restful sleep. It didn't matter that they had no beds; what they had was much better—they were free of an evil person and they had each other.

The next day the sun was shining through the bare windows, and Rosie woke up squinting her eyes as a beam of light blinded her vision. She sat up and looked around, disoriented at first, but quickly remembering that they had finally moved and they were in their own house. Then she remembered the promise of going to the picnic today at Bell Isle, so she nudged Fannie, who was fast asleep. "Wake up! Today is a big day, we're going to Bell Isle!"

Soon everyone was awake, and Luigi went into the kitchen to scramble some eggs. "Rosie, go to the corner store ana buy some more food," he said. "We need another pound of coffee, some donuts, another loaf of bread, and buy somea lunch meat and some soda pop for our picnic today, and don't forget somea paper bags."

On the way to the store Rosie met her first neighbor, a tall thin boy with strange deep-set bright green eyes and pointy eyebrows. He said his name was Mike Lonchar and he helped her carry the groceries back to her house. Rosie, being psychic, felt something strange about this boy. She knew that somehow, sometime in the future, she would be involved with this boy somewhere in her life.

The trip to Bell Isle was fun, as they rode the street car to the park. They spent the rest of the day lying out by the river having a picnic and walking around the beautiful Isle.

They even discovered that there was a zoo in the park, which they enjoyed as they walked around admiring all the different animals. After this respite, they now could face the first week of living in the new house, which was rough, but things gradually got easier. People started hearing about their hardship and pretty soon boxes of clothes and household items were donated to them. They slowly acquired some furnishings and it wasn't long before they had a more comfortable existence.

Soon it was fall and time to begin school again. Rosie was now in high school and wanted to make a good impression. She was worried because she had nothing decent to wear, so she took and old dress and tore it apart by the seams, then cut up a pair of her cotton pajamas. She carefully sewed the pajamas, by hand, seam-by-seam, using the pattern of the old dress. When she was finally finished, the new dress looked presentable.

The first day of school Rosie was nervous as she entered her class at Eastern High School. The class was in session as she hurriedly sat down in the nearest seat. The teacher, a huge burly woman with a stern face, wrote her name on the blackboard, Mrs. Hudson. She then told all the students to stand up and introduce themselves.

When it came Rosie's turn to talk, she stood up and nervously said, "My name is Rose Finazzo and I moved here from Brooklyn, New York about two years ago."

"We have another Rose Finazzo in our school. Are you related?" commented Mrs. Hudson.

"No, not another girl with my name, I have never heard of hah," Rosie answered, noticing some snickering behind her. Then she heard the comment,

"She talks funny, teacher." Rosie was annoyed that Mrs. Hudson made no attempt to correct him.

After awhile Mrs. Hudson handed each student a reading book. "Now want each of you to read from the first chapter when I call on you." Rosie was not surprised when she was called first. As she started to read out loud, the snickering continued, getting louder, and Rosie felt that she was being made an object of ridicule by her classmates, so she looked at the Mrs. Hudson for support, but noticed, to her humiliation, that the teacher was encouraging her embarrassment by the slight smile she had on her face.

"You may stop trying to reading now; I see that you will need to work hard speaking proper English with your New York accent," the teacher chided.

Rosie was embarrassed and infuriated as she said, "Mrs. Hudson, believe me, I do speak proper English; remember, I am the one from an eastern state; it's you Michiganders who have an accent and don't speak proper English!" In her rage she threw the book at Mrs. Hudson, hitting her smack in the forehead, and afterward ran out of the classroom, crying all the way home. *'I'm never going back to school again. This is the last time I'm going to be laughed at and ridiculed by teachers!'* she angrily thought.

Later, when Sally and Fannie came home, they noticed that Rosie had been crying. She sobbed, "I hate Detroit! Everyone here acts so hoity toity! They made fun of the way I talked in school today! And I worked so hard sewing this stupid dress so I could make a good impression. I'm gonna quit school and get a job. I'm tired of never having anything!"

Sally, feeling sorry, said, "I got some money from shooting pool, so let me treat yuh both to the show; there's a movie playing about the East Side Kids in New York."

Just as they were about to leave, Frankie came in. He had moved in with Pa and the kids after arriving from New York. Tavita wanted him to stay with her, but he wanted no part of Tavita and Carmillia's evilness. He felt his place was with his family, so he packed his suitcase and left. Soon afterward he got a job in a factory.

"We're goin' to the show...yuh wanna come?" asked Sally.

Frankie, who loved shows and spent every dime seeing all the latest pictures, answered, "You know I can't refuse and I have some money, so we can get some popcorn, sodas and candy."

Much later at the movie theater they all cried from homesickness, as watching the movie about the mischievous gang of kids from New York brought back memories of their hometown, Brooklyn.

As time went on, things started to gradually improve. The kids started making friends and lost some of their homesickness of New York. They made friends with the Slavic family across the street. They were a large family who had just recently migrated from Pennsylvania. The eldest sister Anna taught the girls how to cook some Slavic dishes and acted as a surrogate mother to them.

Luigi later bought a little Ford car, and every Sunday they all got dressed up to go visiting, usually to see their relatives in Canada. Rosie enjoyed the adventure, especially the ride through the dark underground tunnel. Sally had found a convenient place to practice his boxing and between playing pool and working odd jobs, it kept him occupied.

One day he was shadow-boxing around Rosie, while she was trying to wipe the dishes, and he kept aggravating her until she finally said, "Yuh think yuh pretty smart, don't yuh, Sally, winning all those fights." Then she climbed up on a chair to put the dishes in the high cupboard. Before Sally knew what happened, WHAM! she socked him right in the eye.

Sally ran out of the house, yelling, "Not again! I'll get yuh, yuh little bitch!" Sally had a black eye, only the second one in his whole boxing career, both from Rosie!

Fannie was adjusting fairly well, except for all the interfering from Rosie. She was getting fed up with Rosie's bossiness lately. Rosie acted like the little mother, telling her what to do, who to be friends with all the time and beating her up if it wasn't her way.

One day Fannie was lying in bed watching Rosie sleep when an idea hit her. She quickly threw the blankets over Rosie's head and started to punch her. After that Rosie wasn't so bossy anymore and they got along better.

It wasn't long before they got acquainted with all their neighbors. The Imbrunones lived in the back of the flat on the right side, and Frankie noticed a pretty girl in that family. He waited by the door and every time she came outside he just happened to appear. It wasn't long before he knew he was in love with the pretty girl who said her name was Grace. She had long black curly hair and laughing big brown eyes. He soon discovered that the tall boy from Pennsylvania who lived across the street also liked her. He hoped that Steve Thomas would find another attraction because he knew this girl was special to him. Rosie was becoming fast friends with Steve's younger brother, Mike Lonchar. When he had come from Pennsylvania along with his younger brother, Johnney, to visit his sister Anna, even Fannie, who had met Johnney, had been smitten with the love bug and had developed a crush on him. It was ironic because their destiny was formed on this street. Years later their lives would all be intertwined, because they would all be married to these people who only lived a few steps away from each other.

One day Luigi came home from work to find a neat clean house that had been decorated nicely and four smiling young people. The table had been set just so, and the aroma from a delicious meal filled the house. He looked closely at all his children and saw happiness in their eyes, so Luigi said, "Let's say a prayer ofa thankfulness before we eat this delicious supper." Everyone bowed their heads, crossing themselves and said their prayers.

Afterwards Luigi smiled and said, "We made it, kids! It wasn't easy making thisa new life, but we all pulled together ina troubles and pain. We couldn't have done it without each other—that's what life isa all about, being a family."
* * *